CW00959985

# Shamati

## (I Heard)

# Shamati

## (I Heard)

LAITMAN
KABBALAH PUBLISHERS

Rav Yehuda Ashlag (Baal HaSulam)

SHAMATI (I Heard)

Copyright © 2007 by MICHAEL LAITMAN

All rights reserved

Published by Laitman Kabbalah Publishers
www.kabbalah.info info@kabbalah.info
1057 Steeles Avenue West, Suite 532, Toronto, ON, M2R 3X1, Canada
Bnei Baruch USA, 2009 85th Street #51, Brooklyn, New York, 11214, USA

Printed in Canada

No part of this book may be used or reproduced in any manner without written permission of the publisher, except in the case of brief quotations embodied in critical articles or reviews.

Library of Congress Cataloging-in-Publication Data

Ashlag, Yehudah.

Shamati = (I heard) / Yehuda Ashlag ; compiled by Michael Laitman. --

1st ed.

p. cm.

ISBN 978-1-897448-10-6

1. Cabala. I. Laitman, Michael. II. Title. III. Title: I heard.

BM525.A824 2008

296.1>6--dc22

2008005841

Compilation: Rav Michael Laitman, PhD
Copy Editors: Michael R. Kellogg, Natasha Sigmund
Proofreading: Mark Berelekhis, Sarah Talal
Layout: Luba Visotzki
Cover Design: Bat Sheva Brosh
Printing: Doron Goldin
Post Production: Uri Laitman
Executive Editor and Translator: Chaim Ratz

FIRST EDITION: FEBRUARY 2009
Second printing

## TABLE OF CONTENTS


1. There Is None Else Besides Him ........ 15
2. Divinity in Exile ........ 20
3. The Matter of Spiritual Attainment ........ 21
4. What Is the Reason for the Heaviness One Feels when Annulling before the Creator in the Work? ........ 26
5. Lishma Is an Awakening from Above, and Why Do We Need an Awakening from Below? ........ 28
6. What Is Support in the Torah, in the Work ........ 33
7. What Is the Habit Becomes a Second Nature, in the Work ........ 38
8. What Is the Difference between a Shade of Kedusha and a Shade of Sitra Achra ........ 39
9. What Are Three Things that Broaden One's Mind in the Work.... 42
10. What Is Make Haste My Beloved, in the Work ........ 43
11. Joy WIth a Quiver ........ 44
12. The Essence of One's Work ........ 44
13. A Pomegranate ........ 45
14. What Is the Greatness of the Creator? ........ 46
15. What Is Other Gods in the Work ........ 47
16. What Is the Day of the Lord and the Night of the Lord in the Work ........ 50
17. What Does It Mean that the Sitra Achra Is Called "Malchut without a Crown" ........ 55
18. What Is, My Soul shall Weep in Secret in the Work ........ 58
19. What Is, the Creator Hates the Bodies, in the Work ........ 59
20. Lishma (For Her Name) ........ 72
21. When One Feels Oneself in a State of Ascent ........ 74
22. Torah Lishma (for Her Name) ........ 76
23. You that Love the Lord, Hate Evil ........ 77
24. Out of the Hand of the Wicked ........ 79

25. Things that Come from the Heart ........................................ 80
26. One's Future Depends and Is Tied to Gratitude for the Past ....... 82
27. What Is "The Lord Is High and the Low Will See" ...................... 83
28. I shall Not Die but Live ........................................................ 84
29. When Thoughts Come to a Person ........................................... 85
30. The Most Important Is to Want Only to Bestow ......................... 85
31. All that Pleases the Spirit of the People .................................. 86
32. A Lot Is an Awakening from Above .......................................... 87
33. The Lots on Yom Kippurim and with Haman ............................. 88
34. The Profit of a Land ............................................................. 98
35. Concerning the Vitality of Kedusha ........................................ 105
36. What Are the Three Bodies in a Man ....................................... 110
37. An Article for Purim ............................................................ 112
38. The Fear of God Is His Treasure ............................................ 123
39. And they Sewed Fig-Leaves .................................................. 127
40. Faith in the Rav, What is the Measure ..................................... 129
41. What Is Greatness and Smallness in Faith ............................... 132
42. What Is the Acronym ELUL in the Work ................................... 133
43. The Matter of Truth and Faith ................................................ 141
44. Mind and Heart .................................................................. 143
45. Two Discernments in the Torah and in the Work ........................ 143
46. The Domination of Israel over the Klipot ................................. 145
47. In the Place where You Find His Greatness .............................. 146
48. The Primary Basis ............................................................... 147
49. The Most Important Is the Mindand the Heart ........................... 148
50. Two States ........................................................................ 149
51. If You Encounter This Villain ................................................ 152
52. A Transgression Does Not Put Out a Mitzva ............................. 152
53. The Matter of Limitation ....................................................... 156
54. The Purpose of the Work ...................................................... 157
55. Haman from the Torah, from Where ........................................ 159

56. Torah Is Called Indication .......... 160
57. Will Bring Him as a Burned Offering to His Will .......... 163
58. Joy Is a "Reflection" of Good Deeds .......... 165
59. About the Rod and the Serpent .......... 166
60. A Mitzva that Comes through Transgression .......... 171
61. Round About Him It Stormeth Mightily .......... 172
62. Descends and Incites, Ascends and Complains .......... 174
63. I was Borrowed on, and I Repay .......... 175
64. From Lo Lishma to Lishma .......... 176
65. About the Revealed and the Concealed .......... 178
66. The Giving of the Torah .......... 180
67. Depart from Evil .......... 182
68. Man's Connection to the Sefirot .......... 185
69. First Will Be the Correction of the World .......... 188
70. With a Mighty Hand and with Fury Poured Out .......... 189
71. My Soul Shall Weep in Secret .......... 191
72. Confidence Is the Clothing for the Light .......... 192
73. After the Tzimtzum .......... 193
74. World, Year, Soul .......... 195
75. There Is a Discernment of the Next World, and There Is a Discernment of This World .......... 195
76. With All Thy Offerings Thou ShaltOffer Salt .......... 196
77. One Learns from One's Soul .......... 197
78. The Torah, the Creator,and Israel Are One .......... 197
79. Atzilut and BYA .......... 198
80. Concerning Back to Back .......... 199
81. Concerning Raising MAN .......... 199
82. The Prayer One Should Always Pray .......... 201
83. Concerning the Right Vav, the Left Vav .......... 201
84. What Is "So He Drove the Man Outof the Garden of Eden Lest He Would Take of the Tree of Life" .......... 204

85. What Is the Fruit of Goodly Trees, in the Work ...................... 205
86. And They Built Store-Cities ...................... 207
87. Shabbat Shekalim ...................... 216
88. All the Work Is Only Where There Are Two Ways ...................... 220
89. To Understand the Words of the Holy Zohar ...................... 220
90. In The Zohar, Beresheet ...................... 221
91. Concerning the Replaceable ...................... 221
92. Explaining the Discernment of "Luck" ...................... 222
93. Concerning Fins and Scales ...................... 223
94. And You Shall Keep Your Souls ...................... 224
95. Concerning Removing the Foreskin ...................... 225
96. What Is Waste of Barn and Winery, in the Work ...................... 226
97. Waste of Barn and Winery ...................... 230
98. Spirituality Is Called That Which Will Never Be Lost ...................... 232
99. He Did Not Say Wicked or Righteous ...................... 233
100. The Written Torah and the Oral Torah ...................... 240
101. A Commentary on the Psalm, "For the Leader Upon Roses" ...................... 240
102. And You Shall Take You the Fruit of Goodly Trees ...................... 242
103. Whose Heart Maketh Him Willing ...................... 244
104. And the Saboteur Was Sitting ...................... 245
105. A Wise Disciple Bastard Precedes a High Priest Commoner... 246
106. What Do the Twelve Challahs on Shabbat Imply ...................... 249
107. Concerning the Two Angels ...................... 250
108. If You Leave Me One Day, I Will Leave You Two ...................... 251
109. Two Kinds of Meat ...................... 255
110. A Field which the Lord Has Blessed ...................... 257
111. Breath, Sound, and Speech ...................... 259
112. The Three Angels ...................... 260
113. The Eighteen Prayer ...................... 269
114. Prayer ...................... 272

115. Still, Vegetative, Animate, and Speaking ........ 272
116. Why Did He Say that Mitzvot Do Not Require Intention ........ 274
117. You Labored and Did Not Find, Do Not Believe ........ 274
118. To Understand the Matter of the Knees which Have Bowed unto Baal ........ 276
119. That Disciple who Learned in Secret ........ 277
120. The Reason for Not Eating Nuts on Rosh Hashanah ........ 278
121. She Is Like Merchant-Ships ........ 279
122. Understanding What Is Written in Shulchan Aruch ........ 281
123. His Divorce and His Hand Come as One ........ 282
124. A Shabbat of Genesis and of the Six Thousand Years ........ 283
125. Who Delights the Shabbat ........ 284
126. A Sage Comes to Town ........ 286
127. The Difference between Kernel, Essence, and Added Abundance ........ 288
128. Dew Drips from That Galgalta to Zeir Anpin ........ 290
129. Divinity in the Dust ........ 292
130. Tiberias of Our Sages, Good Is Thy Sight ........ 293
131. Who Comes to Be Purified ........ 293
132. In the Sweat of Thy Face Shalt Thou Eat Bread ........ 294
133. The Lights of Shabbat ........ 294
134. Intoxicating Wine ........ 294
135. Clean and Righteous Slay Thou Not ........ 295
136. The Difference between the First Letters and the Last Letters .. 295
137. Zelophehad Was Gathering Wood ........ 296
138. About Fear that Sometimes Comes upon a Person ........ 297
139. The Difference between the Six Days of Action and the Shabbat ........ 297
140. How I Love Thy Law ........ 298
141. The Holiday of Passover ........ 298
142. The Essence of the War ........ 299

143. Only Good to Israel....299
144. There Is a Certain People....300
145. What Is Will Give Wisdom Specifically to the Wise....301
146. A Commentary on The Zohar....303
147. The Work of Reception and Bestowal....303
148. The Scrutiny of Bitter and Sweet, True and False....304
149. Why We Need to Extend Hochma....304
150. Prune unto the Lord, for He Hath Done Pride....305
151. And Israel Saw the Egyptians....306
152. For a Bribe Doth Blind the Eyes of the Wise....307
153. A Thought Is an Upshot of the Desire....308
154. There Cannot Be an Empty Space in the World....309
155. The Cleanness of the Body....309
156. Lest He Take of the Tree of Life....310
157. I Am Asleep But My Heart Is Awake....311
158. The Reason for Not Eating at Each Other's Home on Passover....313
159. And It Came To Pass in the Course of Those Many Days....314
160. The Reason for Concealing the Matzot....315
161. The Matter of the Giving of the Torah....315
162. Concerning the Hazak We Say After Completing the Series....317
163. What the Authors of The Zohar Said....318
164. There Is a Difference between Corporeality and Spirituality....319
165. An Explanation to Elisha's Request of Elijah....319
166. Two Discernments in Attainment....320
167. The Reason Why It Is Called Shabbat Teshuvah....321
168. The Customs of Israel....322
169. Concerning a Complete Righteous....322
170. Thou Shalt Not Have in Thy Pocket a Large Stone....323

171. Zohar, Amor ........ 324
172. The Matter of Preventions and Delays ........ 326
173. Why Do We Say L'Chaim ........ 327
174. Concealment ........ 328
175. And If the Way Be Too Long for Thee ........ 329
176. When Drinking Brandy After the Havdala ........ 331
177. Atonements ........ 331
178. Three Partners in Man ........ 332
179. Three Lines ........ 332
180. In The Zohar, Amor ........ 335
181. Honor ........ 336
182. Moses and Solomon ........ 337
183. The Discernment of the Messiah ........ 337
184. The Difference between Faith and Mind ........ 337
185. The Uneducated, the Fear of Shabbat Is upon Him ........ 338
186. Make Your Shabbat a Weekday, and Do Not Need People ........ 339
187. Choosing Labor ........ 339
188. All the Work Is Only Where there Are Two Ways ........ 340
189. The Act Affects the Thought ........ 340
190. Every Act Leaves an Imprint ........ 341
191. The Time of Descent ........ 344
192. The Lots ........ 345
193. One Wall Serves Both ........ 347
194. The Complete Seven ........ 348
195. Rewarded–I Will Hasten It ........ 350
196. A Grip for the Externals ........ 351
197. Book, Author, Story ........ 352
198. Freedom ........ 352
199. To Every Man of Israel ........ 353
200. The Purification of the Masach ........ 353
201. Spirituality and Corporeality ........ 354

202. In the Sweat of Thy Face Shalt Thou Eat Bread ..................... 355
203. Man's Pride shall Bring Him Low ..................... 355
204. The Purpose of the Work ..................... 356
205. Wisdom Crieth Aloud in the Streets ..................... 357
206. Faith and Pleasure ..................... 358
207. Receiving In Order to Bestow ..................... 359
208. Labor ..................... 360
209. Three Conditions in Prayer ..................... 360
210. A Handsome Flaw in You ..................... 361
211. As Though Standing before a King ..................... 362
212. Embrace of the Right, Embrace of the Left ..................... 363
213. Acknowledging the Desire ..................... 363
214. Known in the Gates ..................... 365
215. Faith ..................... 367
216. Right and Left ..................... 368
217. If I Am Not for Me, Who Is for Me ..................... 368
218. The Torah and the Creator Are One ..................... 369
219. Devotion ..................... 370
220. Suffering ..................... 371
221. Multiple Authorities ..................... 371
222. The Part Given to the Sitra Achra to separate It from the Kedusha ..................... 372
223. Clothing, Bag, Lie, Almond ..................... 373
224. Yesod de Nukva and Yesod de Dechura ..................... 374
225. Raising Oneself ..................... 375
226. Written Torah and Oral Torah ..................... 375
227. The Reward for a Mitzva—a Mitzva ..................... 375
228. Fish Before Meat ..................... 376
229. Haman Pockets ..................... 377
230. The Lord Is High and the Low Will See ..................... 378
231. The Purity of the Vessels of Reception ..................... 378

232. Completing the Labor ........ 379
233. Pardon, Forgiveness, and Atonement ........ 380
234. Who Ceases Words of Torah
and Engages in Conversation ........ 382
235. Looking in the Book Again ........ 383
236. Mine Adversaries Taunt Me All the Day ........ 383
237. For Man Shall Not See Me and Live ........ 384
238. Happy Is the Man who Does Not Forget Thee
and the Son of Man who Exerts in Thee ........ 384
239. The Difference between Mochin of Shavuot
and that of Shabbat Minchah ........ 385
240. Inquire Your Inquirers when They Inquire Your Face ........ 386
241. Call Upon Him while He Is Near ........ 388
242. What Is the Matter of Delighting the Poor
on a Good Day, in the Work ........ 390
243. Examining the Shade on the Night of Hoshana Rabbah ........ 391

Appendix One: Further Reading ........ 393
Appendix Two: About Bnei Baruch ........ 403

## 1. THERE IS NONE ELSE BESIDES HIM

I heard on *Parashat Yitro*, 1, February 6, 1944

It is written, "there is none else besides Him." This means that there is no other force in the world that has the ability to do anything against Him. And what man sees, that there are things in the world that deny the Higher Household, the reason is that this is His will.

And it is deemed a correction, called "the left rejects and the right adducts," meaning that which the left rejects is considered correction. This means that there are things in the world, which, to begin with, aim to divert a person from the right way, and by which he is rejected from Sanctity.

And the benefit from the rejections is that through them a person receives a need and a complete desire for the Creator to help him, since he sees that otherwise he is lost. Not only does he not progress in his work, but he sees that he regresses, that is, he lacks the strength to observe Torah and *Mitzvot* even in *Lo Lishma* (not for Her Name). That only by genuinely overcoming all the obstacles, above reason, can he observe the Torah and *Mitzvot*. But he does not always have the strength to overcome above reason; otherwise, he is forced to deviate, God forbid, from the way of the Creator, even from *Lo Lishma*.

And he, who always feels that the shattered is greater than the whole, meaning that there are many more descents than ascents, and he does not see an end to these states, and he will forever remain outside of holiness, for he sees that it is difficult for him to observe even as little as a jot, unless by overcoming above reason. But he is not always able to overcome. And what shall be the end?

Then he comes to the decision that no one can help him but the Creator Himself. This causes him to make a heartfelt demand that the Creator will open his eyes and heart, and truly bring him nearer to eternal adhesion with God. It thus follows, that all the rejections he had experienced had come from the Creator.

This means that it was not because he was at fault, that he did not have the ability to overcome. Rather, for those people who truly want to draw near the Creator, and so they will not settle for little, meaning remain as senseless children, he is therefore given help from Above, so he will not be able to say that thank God, I have Torah and *Mitzvot* and good deeds, and what else do I need?

And only if that person has a true desire will he receive help from Above. And he is constantly shown how he is at fault in his present state. Namely, he is sent thoughts and views, which are against the work. This is in order for him to see that he is not one with the Lord. And as much as he overcomes, he always sees how he is farther from holiness than others, who feel that they are one with the Creator.

But he, on the other hand, always has complaints and demands, and he cannot justify the Creator's behavior, and how He behaves toward him. This pains him. Why is he not one with the Creator? Finally, he comes to feel that he has no part in holiness whatsoever.

Although he occasionally receives awakening from Above, which momentarily revives him, but soon after he falls into the place of baseness. However, this is what causes him to come to realize that only God can help and really bring him closer.

A man must always try and cleave to the Creator; namely, that all his thoughts will be about Him. That is to say, that even if he is in the worst state, from which there cannot be a greater decline, he should not leave His domain, namely, that there is another authority which prevents him from entering holiness, and which can bring benefit or harm.

That is, he must not think that there is the force of the *Sitra Achra* (Other Side), which does not allow a person to do good deeds and follow God's ways. Rather, all is done by the Creator.

The Baal Shem Tov said that he who says that there is another force in the world, namely *Klipot* (shells), that person is in a state of "serving other gods." It is not necessarily the thought of heresy that is the transgression, but if he thinks that there is another authority and force apart from the Creator, by that he is committing a sin.

Furthermore, he who says that man has his own authority, that is, he says that yesterday he himself did not want to follow God's ways, that too is considered committing the sin of heresy, meaning that he does not believe that only the Creator is the leader of the world.

But when he has committed a sin, he must certainly regret it and be sorry for having committed it. But here too we should place the pain and sorrow in the right order: where does he place the cause of the sin, for that is the point that should be regretted.

Then, one should be remorseful and say: "I committed that sin because the Creator hurled me down from holiness to a place of filth, to the lavatory, the place of filth." That is to say that the Creator gave him a desire and craving to amuse himself and breathe air in a place of stench.

(And you might say that it is written in books, that sometimes one comes incarnated as a pig. We should interpret that, as he says, one receives a desire and craving to take liveliness from things he had already determined were litter, but now he wants to receive nourishment from them).

Also, when one feels that now he is in a state of ascent, and feels some good flavor in the work, he must not say: "Now I am in a state that I understand that it is worthwhile to worship the

Creator." Rather he should know that now he was favored by the Creator, hence the Creator brought him closer, and for this reason he now feels good flavor in the work. And he should be careful never to leave the domain of Sanctity, and say that there is another who operates besides the Creator.

(But this means that the matter of being favored by the Creator, or the opposite, does not depend on the person himself, but only on the Creator. And man, with his external mind, cannot comprehend why now the Lord has favored him and afterwards did not.)

Likewise, when he regrets that the Creator does not draw him near, he should also be careful that it would not be concerning himself, meaning that he is remote from the Creator. This is because thus he becomes a receiver for his own benefit, and one who receives is separated. Rather, he should regret the exile of the *Shechina* (Divinity), meaning that he is causing the sorrow of Divinity.

One should imagine that it is as though a small organ of the person is sore. The pain is nonetheless felt primarily in the mind and in the heart. The heart and the mind, which are the whole of man. And certainly, the sensation of a single organ cannot resemble the sensation of a person's full stature, where most of the pain is felt.

Likewise is the pain that a person feels when he is remote from the Creator. Since man is but a single organ of the Holy *Shechina*, for the Holy *Shechina* is the common soul of Israel, hence, the sensation of a single organ does not resemble the sensation of the pain in general. That is to say that there is sorrow in the *Shechina* when the organs are detached from her, and she cannot nurture her organs.

(And we should say that this is what our sages said: "When a man regrets, what does *Shechina* say? 'It is lighter than my head.'"). By not relating the sorrow of remoteness to oneself, one is spared falling into the trap of the desire to receive for oneself, which is considered separation from holiness.

The same applies when one feels some closeness to holiness, when he feels joy at having been favored by the Creator. Then, too, one must say that one's joy is primarily because now there is joy Above, within the Holy *Shechina*, at being able to bring her private organ near her, and that she did not have to send her private organ away.

And one derives joy from being rewarded with pleasing the *Shechina*. This is in accord with the above calculation that when there is joy for the part, it is only a part of the joy of the whole. Through these calculations he loses his individuality and avoids being trapped by the *Sitra Achra*, which is the will to receive for his own benefit.

Although, the will to receive is necessary, since this is the whole of man, since anything that exists in a person apart from the will to receive does not belong to the creature, but is attributed to the Creator, but the will to receive pleasure should be corrected to being in order to bestow.

That is to say, the pleasure and joy, which the will to receive takes, should be with the intention that there is contentment Above when the creatures feel pleasure, for this was the purpose of creation–to benefit His creations. And this is called the joy of the *Shechina* Above.

For this reason, one must seek advice as to how he can bring contentment Above. And certainly, if he receives pleasure, contentment shall be felt Above. Therefore, he yearns to always be in the King's palace, and to have the ability to play with the King's treasures. And that will certainly cause contentment Above. It follows that his entire longing should be only for the sake of the Creator.

## 2. DIVINITY IN EXILE

I heard in 1942

The Holy *Zohar* says: "He is *Shochen* (Dweller), and She is *Shechina* (Divinity)." We should interpret its words: It is known with regard to the Upper Light, that they say that there is no change, as it is written, "I the Lord change not." All the names and appellations are only with respect to the *Kelim* (vessels), which is the will to receive included in *Malchut*–the root of creation. From there it hangs down to this world, to the creatures.

All these discernments, beginning with *Malchut*, being the root of the creation of the worlds, through the creatures, is named ***Shechina***. The general *Tikkun* (correction) is that the Upper Light will shine in them in utter completeness.

The Light that shines in the *Kelim* is named ***Shochen***, and the *Kelim* are generally named, ***Shechina***. In other words, **the Light dwells inside the *Shechina***. This means that the Light is called *Shochen* because it dwells within the *Kelim*, that is, the whole of the *Kelim* are named *Shechina*.

Before the Light shines in them in utter completeness, we name that time, **"A Time of Corrections."** This means that we make corrections so that the Light will shine in them in completeness. Until then, that state is called **"Divinity in Exile."**

It means that there is still no perfection in the Upper Worlds. Below, in this world, there should be a state where the Upper Light is within the will to receive. **This *Tikkun* is deemed receiving in order to bestow.**

Meanwhile, the will to receive is filled with ignoble and foolish things that do not make a place where the glory of Heaven can be revealed. This means that where the heart should be a Tabernacle for the Light of God, the heart becomes a place of waste and filth. In other words, ignobility captures the whole of the heart.

This is called "Divinity in the dust." It means that it is lowered to the ground, and each and every one loathes matters of Sanctity, and there is no desire whatsoever to raise it from the dust. Instead, they choose ignoble things, and this brings on the sorrow of the *Shechina*, when one does not make a place in the heart that will become a Tabernacle for the Light of God.

## 3. THE MATTER OF SPIRITUAL ATTAINMENT

I heard

We discern many degrees and discernments in the worlds. We must know that everything that relates to discernments and degrees speaks of the attainment of the souls with regard to what they receive from the worlds. This adheres to the rule, **"What we do not attain we do not know by name."** This is so because the word "name" indicates attainment, like a person who names some object after having attained something about it according to one's attainment.

Hence, reality in general is divided into three discernments, with respect to spiritual attainment:

**1. *Atzmuto* (His Essence)**

**2. *Ein Sof* (Infinity)**

**3. The Souls**

1) We do not speak of ***Atzmuto*** at all. This is because the root and the place of the creatures begin in the thought of creation, where they are incorporated, as it is written, "The end of an act is in the preliminary thought."

2) ***Ein Sof*** pertains to the Thought of Creation, which is "His desire to do good to His creations." This is considered *Ein Sof*, and it is the connection existing between *Atzmuto* and the souls. We perceive this connection in the form of "desire to delight the creatures."

*Ein Sof* is the beginning. It is called "a Light without a *Kli* (vessel)," yet there is the root of the creatures, meaning the connection between the Creator and the creatures, called "His desire to do good to His creations." This desire begins in the world of *Ein Sof* and extends through the world of *Assiya*.

3) The **Souls**, which are the receivers of the good that He wishes to do.

He is called *Ein Sof* because this is the connection between *Atzmuto* and the souls, which we perceive as "His desire to do good to His creations." We have no utterance except for that connection of desire to enjoy and this is the beginning of the engagement, and it is called "Light without a *Kli*."

Yet, there begins the root of the creatures, meaning the connection between the Creator and the creatures, called "His desire to do good to His creations." This desire begins in the world of *Ein Sof* and extends through the world of *Assiya*.

All the worlds are in themselves considered Light without a *Kli*, where there is no utterance. They are discerned as *Atzmuto*, and there is no attainment in them.

Do not wonder that we discern many discernments there. This is because these discernments are there in potential. Afterwards, when the souls come, these discernments will appear in the souls that receive the Upper Lights according to what they have corrected and arranged. Thus, the souls will be able to receive them, each according to its ability and qualification. And then these discernments appear in actual fact. However, while the souls do not attain the Upper Light they, in themselves, are considered *Atzmuto*.

With respect to the souls that receive from the worlds, the worlds are considered *Ein Sof*. This is because this connection between the worlds and the souls, meaning what the worlds give to the souls, extends from the Thought of Creation, which is a correlation between the souls and *Atzmuto*.

This connection is called *Ein Sof*. When we pray to the Creator and ask of Him to help us and to give us what we want, we relate to the discernment of *Ein Sof*. There is the root of the creatures, which wants to impart them delight and pleasure, called "His desire to do good to His creations."

The prayer is to the Creator who created us, and His Name is **"His desire to do good to His creations."** He is called *Ein Sof* because this speaks of prior to the restriction. And even after the restriction, no change occurs in Him as there is no change in the Light and He always remains with this name.

The proliferation of the names is only with respect to the receivers. Hence, the first name that appeared, that is, the root for the creatures, is called *Ein Sof*. And this name remains unchanged. All the restrictions and the changes are made only with regard to the receivers, and He always shines in the first name, "His desire to do good to His creations," endlessly.

This is why we pray to the Creator, called *Ein Sof*, who shines without restriction or end. The end, which appears subsequently, is corrections for the receivers so that they may receive His Light.

The Upper Light is made of two discernments: attaining and attained. Everything we say regarding the Upper Light concerns only how the attaining is impressed by the attained. However, in themselves, meaning only the attaining, or only the attained, they are not called *Ein Sof*. Rather, the attained is called *Atzmuto* and the attaining is called "souls," being a new discernment, which is a part of the whole. It is new in the sense that the will to receive is imprinted in it. And in that sense, creation is called "existence from absence."

For themselves, all the worlds are regarded as simple unity and there is no change in Godliness. This is the meaning of "I the Lord do not change." There are no *Sefirot* and *Behinot* (discernments) in Godliness.

Even the most subtle appellations do not refer to the Light itself, as this is a discernment of *Atzmuto* where there is no attainment. Rather, all the *Sefirot* and the discernments speak only of what a person attains in them. This is because the Creator wanted us to attain and understand the abundance as "His desire to do good to His creations."

In order for us to attain what He had wanted us to attain and understand as "His desire to do good to His creations," He created and imparted us with these senses, and these senses attain their impressions of the Upper Light.

Accordingly, we have been given many discernments, since the general sense is called "the will to receive," and is divided into many details, according to the measure that the receivers are able to receive. Thus, we find many divisions and details, called ascents and descents, expansion and departure etc.

Since the will to receive is called "creature" and a "new discernment," the utterance begins precisely from the place where the will to receive begins to receive impressions. The speech is discernments, parts of impressions. For here there is already a correlation between the Light and the will to receive.

This is called "Light and *Kli*." However, there is no utterance in the Light without a *Kli*, since a Light that is not attained by the receiver is considered *Atzmuto*, where the utterance is forbidden since it is unattainable, and how can we name what we do not attain?

From this we learn that when we pray for the Creator to send us salvation, cure, and so on, there are two things we should distinguish: 1 – The Creator; 2 – That which extends from Him.

In the first discernment, considered *Atzmuto*, the utterance is forbidden, as we have said above. In the second discernment, that which extends from Him, which is considered the Light that expands into our *Kelim*, meaning into our will to receive, that is what we call *Ein Sof*. This is the connection of the Creator with the creatures, being "His desire to do good to His creations." The will to receive is regarded as the expanding Light that finally reaches the will to receive.

When the will to receive receives the expanding Light, the expanding Light is then called *Ein Sof*. It comes to the receivers through many covers so that the lower one will be able to receive them.

It turns out that all the discernments and the changes are made specifically in the receiver, with relation to how the receiver is impressed by them. However, we must discern the matter we are speaking of. When we speak of discernments in the worlds, these are potential discernments. And when the receiver attains these discernments, they are called "actual."

Spiritual attainment is when the attaining and the attained come together, as without an attaining there is no form to the attained, since there is no one to obtain the form of the attained. Hence, this discernment is considered *Atzmuto*, where there is no room for any utterance. Therefore, how can we say that the attained has its own form?

We can only speak from where our senses are impressed by the expanding Light, which is "His desire to do good to His creations," which comes into the hands of the receivers in actual fact.

Similarly, when we examine a table our sense of touch feels it as something hard. We also discern its length and width, all according to our senses. However, that does not necessitate that the table will appear so to one who has other senses. For example, in the eyes of an angel, when it examines the table, it will see it according to *its* senses. Hence, we cannot determine any form with regard to an angel, since we do not know its senses.

Thus, since we have no attainment in the Creator, we cannot say which form the worlds have from His perspective. We only attain the worlds according to our senses and sensations, as it was His will for us to attain Him so.

This is the meaning of "There is no change in the Light." Rather, all the changes are in the *Kelim*, meaning in our senses. We measure everything according to our imagination. From this it follows that if many people examine one spiritual thing, each will attain according to his imagination and senses, thereby seeing a different form.

In addition, the form itself will change in a person according to his ups and downs, as we have said above that the Light is Simple Light and all the changes are only in the receivers.

May we be granted with His Light and follow in the ways of the Creator and serve Him not in order to be rewarded, but to give contentment to the Creator and raise Divinity from the dust. May we be granted adhesion with the Creator and the revelation of His Godliness to His creatures.

## 4. WHAT IS THE REASON FOR THE HEAVINESS ONE FEELS WHEN ANNULLING BEFORE THE CREATOR IN THE WORK?

I heard on *Shevat* 12, February 6, 1944

We must know the reason for the heaviness felt when one wishes to work in annulling one's "self" before the Creator, and to not care for one's own interest. One comes to a state as if the entire world stands still, and he alone is now seemingly absent from this world, and leaves his family and friends for the sake of annulling before the Creator.

There is but a simple reason for this, called "lack of faith." It means that one does not see before whom one nullifies, meaning he does not feel the existence of the Creator. This causes him heaviness.

However, when one begins to feel the existence of the Creator, one's soul immediately yearns to be annulled and connected to the root, to be contained in it like a candle in a torch, without any mind and reason. However, this comes to one naturally, as a candle is annulled before a torch.

It therefore follows that the essence of one's work is only to come to the sensation of the existence of the Creator, meaning to feel the existence of the Creator, that "the whole earth is full of His glory." This will be one's entire work, meaning all the vigor that he puts into the work will be only to achieve that, and not for any other things.

One should not be misled into having to acquire anything. Rather, there is only one thing a person needs, namely **faith** in the Creator. He should not think of anything, meaning that the only reward that he wants for his work should be to be rewarded with faith in the Creator.

We must know that there is no difference between a small illumination and a great one, which a person attains. This is because there are no changes in the Light. Rather, all the changes are in the vessels that receive the abundance, as it is written, "I the Lord change not." Hence, if one can magnify one's vessels, to that extent he magnifies the luminescence.

Yet, the question is, with what can one magnify one's vessels? The answer is, in the extent to which he praises and gives thanks to the Creator for having brought one closer to

Him, so one would feel Him a little and think of the importance of the thing, meaning that he was awarded some connection with the Creator.

As is the measure of the importance that one pictures for oneself, so the measure of the luminescence grows in him. One must know that he will never come to know the true measure of the importance of the connection between man and the Creator because one cannot assess its true value. Instead, as much as one appreciates it, so he attains its merit and importance. There is a power in that, since thus one can be permanently imparted this luminescence.

## 5. *LISHMA* IS AN AWAKENING FROM ABOVE, AND WHY DO WE NEED AN AWAKENING FROM BELOW?

I heard in 1945

In order to attain *Lishma*, it is not in one's hands to understand, as it is not for the human mind to grasp how such a thing can be in the world. This is because one is only permitted to grasp, that if one engages in Torah and *Mitzvot*, he will attain something. There must be self-gratification there; otherwise, one is unable to do anything.

Instead, this is an illumination that comes from Above, and only one who tastes it can know and understand. It is written about that, "Taste and see that the Lord is good."

Thus, we must understand why one should seek advice and counsels regarding how to achieve *Lishma*. After all, no counsels will help him, and if God does not give him the other nature, called "the Will to Bestow," no labor will help one to attain the matter of *Lishma*.

The answer is, as our sages said (*Avot*, 2:21), "It is not for you to complete the work, and you are not free to idle away from it." This means that one must give the awakening from below, since this is discerned as a prayer.

A prayer is considered a deficiency, and without deficiency there is no fulfillment. Hence, when one has a need for *Lishma*, the fulfillment comes from Above, and the answer to the prayer comes from Above, meaning one receives fulfillment for one's need. It follows, that one's work is needed to receive the *Lishma* from the Creator only in the form of a lack and a *Kli* (Vessel). Yet, one can never attain the fulfillment alone; it is rather a gift from God.

However, the prayer must be a *whole* prayer, that is, from the bottom of the heart. It means that one knows one hundred percent that there is no one in the world who can help him but the Creator Himself.

Yet, how does one know that, that there is no one to help him but the Creator Himself? One can acquire that awareness precisely if he has exerted all the powers at his disposal and it did not help him. Thus, one must do every possible thing in the world to attain "for the Creator." Then one can pray from the bottom of one's heart, and then the Creator hears his prayer.

However, one must know, when exerting to attain the *Lishma*, to take upon himself to want to work entirely to bestow, completely, meaning only to bestow and to not receive anything. Only then does one begin to see that the organs do not agree to this idea.

From that one can come to clear awareness that he has no other counsel but to pour out his complaint before the Lord to help him so that the body will agree to enslave itself to the Creator unconditionally, as one sees that he cannot persuade his body to annul his self entirely. It turns out that precisely when one sees that there is no reason to hope that his body will agree to work for the Creator by itself, one's prayer can be from the bottom of the heart, and then his prayer is accepted.

We must know that by attaining *Lishma*, one puts the evil inclination to death. The evil inclination is the will to receive, and acquiring the will to bestow cancels the will to receive from being able to do anything. This is considered putting it to death. Since it has been removed from its office, and it has nothing more to do since it is no longer in use, when it is revoked from its function, this is considered putting it to death.

When one contemplates "What profit hath man of all his labor wherein he labors under the sun," one sees that it is not so difficult to enslave oneself to His Name, for two reasons:

1. Anyhow, meaning, whether willingly or unwillingly, one must exert in this world, and what has one left of all the efforts he has made?
2. However, if one works *Lishma*, one receives pleasure during the work itself too.

According to the proverb of the Sayer of Dubna, who spoke about the verse, "thou hast not called upon Me, O Jacob, neither hast thou wearied thyself about Me, O Israel." He said that it is like some rich man who departed the train and had a small bag. He placed it where all the merchants place their baggage and the porters take the packages and bring them to the hotel where the merchants stay. The porter had thought that the merchant would certainly have taken a small bag by himself and there is no need for a porter for that, so he took a big package.

The merchant wanted to pay him a small fee, as he usually pays, but the porter did not want to take it. He said: "I put in the depositary of the hotel a big bag; it exhausted me and I barely carried your bag, and you want to pay me so little for it?"

The lesson is that when one comes and says that he has exerted extensively in keeping Torah and *Mitzvot*, the Creator tells him, "thou hast not called upon Me, O Jacob." In other words, it is not my baggage that you took, but this bag belongs to someone else. Since you say that you had much effort in Torah and *Mitzvot*, you must have had a different landlord for whom you were working; so go to him and he will pay you.

This is the meaning of, **"neither hast thou wearied thyself about Me, O Israel."** This means that he who works for the Creator has no labor, but on the contrary, pleasure and elated spirit.

However, one who works for other purposes cannot come to the Creator with complaints that the Creator does not give him vitality in the work, since he did not work for the Creator, for the Lord to pay for his work. Instead, one can complain to those people that he had worked for to administer him pleasure and vitality.

And since there are many purposes in *Lo Lishma*, one should demand of the goal for which he had worked to give him the reward, namely pleasure and vitality. It is said about them, "They that make them shall be like unto them; yea, every one that trusts in them."

However, according to that, it is perplexing. After all, we see that even when one takes upon oneself the burden of the Kingdom of Heaven without any other intention, he still does not feel any liveliness, to say that this liveliness compels him to take upon himself the burden of the Kingdom of Heaven. And the reason one does take upon oneself that burden is only because of faith above reason.

In other words, one does it by way of coercive overcoming, unwillingly. Thus, we might ask: Why does one feel exertion in this work, with the body constantly seeking for a time when it can be rid of this work, as one does not feel any liveliness in the work? According to the above, when one works in humbleness, and has only the purpose of working in order to bestow, why does the Creator not impart him taste and vitality in the work?

The answer is that we must know that this matter is a great correction. Were it not for that, meaning if Light and liveliness had illuminated instantaneously when one began to take upon himself the burden of the Kingdom of Heaven, one would have had liveliness in the work. In other words, the will to receive, too, would have consented to this work.

In that state he would certainly agree because he wants to satiate his desire, meaning he would work for its own benefit. Had that been the case, it would never have been possible to achieve *Lishma*.

This is so because one would be compelled to work for one's own benefit, as one would feel greater pleasure in the work of God than in corporeal desires. Thus, one would have to remain in *Lo Lishma*, since thus he would have had satisfaction in the work. Where there is satisfaction, one cannot do anything, as without profit, one cannot work. It follows that if one received satisfaction in this work of *Lo Lishma*, one would have to remain in that state.

This would be similar to what people say, that when there are people chasing a thief to catch him, the thief, too, runs and yells, "Catch the thief." Then, it is impossible to recognize who is the real thief so as to catch him and take the theft out of his hand.

However, when the thief, meaning the will to receive, does not feel any flavor and liveliness in the work of accepting the burden of the Kingdom of Heaven, if in that state one works with faith above reason, coercively, and the body becomes accustomed to this work against the desire of one's will to receive, then one has the means by which to come to a work that will be with the purpose of bringing contentment to one's Maker.

This is so because the primary requirement from a person is to come to *Dvekut* (Adhesion) with the Creator through one's work, which is discerned as equivalence of form, where all of one's deeds are in order to bestow.

It is as the verse says, "Then shalt thou delight thyself in the Lord." The meaning of "Then" is that first, in the beginning of one's work, he did not have pleasure. Instead, one's work was coercive.

However, afterwards, when one has already accustomed oneself to work in order to bestow, and not examine oneself–if he is feeling a good taste in the work–but believes that he is working to bring contentment to his Maker through his work, one should believe that the Creator accepts the labor of the lower ones regardless of how and how much is the form of their work. In everything, the Creator examines the intention, and that brings contentment to the Creator. Then one is imparted, "Then shalt thou delight thyself in the Lord."

Even during the work of God he will feel delight and pleasure, as now one really does work for the Creator because the effort he made during the coercive work qualifies one to be able to work for the Creator in earnest. You find that, then too, the pleasure that one receives relates to the Creator, meaning specifically for the Creator.

## 6. WHAT IS SUPPORT IN THE TORAH IN THE WORK

I heard in 1944

When one studies Torah and wants all his actions to be in order to bestow, one needs to try to always have support in the Torah. Support is considered nourishment, which is love, fear, elation, and freshness and so on. And one should extract all that from the Torah. In other words, the Torah should give one these results.

However, when one studies Torah and does not have these results, it is not considered Torah. This is because Torah refers to the Light *clothed* in the Torah, meaning, as our sages said, "I have created the evil inclination, I have created the Torah as a spice." This refers to the Light in it, since the Light in it reforms it.

We should also know that the Torah is divided into two discernments: 1-Torah, 2-*Mitzva.* In fact, it is impossible to understand these two discernments before one is awarded walking in the path of God by way of "The counsel of the Lord is with them that fear Him." This is so because when one is in a state of preparation to enter the Lord's Palace, it is impossible to understand the Path of Truth.

However, it is possible to give an example that even a person in the preparation period may somewhat understand. It is as our sages said (*Sutah* 21): "Rabbi Yosef said, 'A *Mitzva* protects and saves while practiced, etc.. The Torah protects and saves both when practiced and when not practiced.'"

The thing is that "when practiced" refers to when one has some Light. One can use this Light that he had obtained only while the Light is still with him, as now he is in gladness because of the Light that shines for him. This is discerned as a *Mitzva*, meaning that he has not yet been rewarded with the Torah, but elicits a life of *Kedusha* (Sanctity) only from the Light.

This is not so with the Torah: when one attains some way in the work, one can use the way that one has attained even when one is not practicing it, that is, even while one does not have the Light. This is because only the luminescence has departed from him, whereas one can use the way that one attained in the work even when the luminescence leaves him.

Still, one must also know that while practiced, a *Mitzva* is greater than the **Torah when not practiced**. When practiced means that now one receives the Light; this is called "practiced," when one receives the Light in it.

Hence, while one has the Light, a *Mitzva* is more important than the Torah when one has no Light, meaning when there is no liveliness of the Torah. On the one hand, the Torah is important because one can use the way one has acquired in the Torah. On the other hand, it is without vitality, called "Light." In a time of *Mitzva* one does receive vitality, called "Light." Therefore, in this respect, a *Mitzva* is more important.

**Thus, when one is without sustenance, one is considered "evil."** This is because now one cannot say that the Creator leads the world in a conduct of "Good that Doeth Good." This is called that he is called "evil," since he condemns his Maker, as now he feels that he has no vitality, and **has nothing to be glad about so that he may say** that now he offers gratitude to the Creator for giving him delight and pleasure.

One cannot say that he believes that the Creator leads His Providence with others benevolently, since we understand the path of Torah as a sensation in the organs. If one does not feel the delight and pleasure, what does it give him that another person has delight and pleasure?

If one had really believed that Providence is revealed as benevolence to his friend, that belief should have brought one delight and pleasure from believing that the Creator leads the world in a guidance of delight and pleasure. If it does not bring one liveliness and joy, what is the benefit in saying that the Creator does watch over one's friend with a guidance of benevolence?

The most important is what one feels in one's own body—whether one feels good or bad. One enjoys one's friend's pleasure only if he enjoys his friend's benefit. In other words, we learn that with the sensation of the body, the reasons aren't important. It is only important if one feels good.

In that state one says that the Creator is "Good that Doeth Good." If one feels bad, one cannot say that the Creator behaves with him in a benevolent way. Thus, precisely if one enjoys one's friend's happiness, and receives high spirits from that, and feels gladness because his friend feels good, then he can say that the Creator is a good leader.

If one has no joy, he feels bad. Thus, how can he say that the Creator is benevolent? Therefore, a state where one has no liveliness and gladness is already a state where he has no love for the Creator and ability to justify his Maker and be happy, as is appropriate with one who is granted with serving a great and important king.

We must know that the Upper Light is in a state of complete rest. And any expansion of the Holy Names occurs by the lower ones. In other words, all the names that the Upper Light has, come from the attainment of the lower ones. This means that the Upper Light is named according to their attainments. Put differently, one names the Upper Light according to the way in which one attains it, meaning according to one's sensation.

If one does not feel that the Creator gives him anything, what name can he give the Creator if he does not receive anything from Him? Rather, when one believes in the Creator, every single state that one feels, he says that it comes from the Creator. In that state one names the Creator according to one's feeling.

If one feels happy in the state he is in, he says that the Creator is called "Benevolent," since that is what he feels, that he receives good from Him. In that state one is called *Tzadik* (Righteous), since he *Matzdik* (justifies) his Maker (who is the Creator).

If one feels bad in the state he is in, one cannot say that the Creator sends him good. Therefore, in that state one is called *Rasha* (Evil), since he *Marshia* (Condemns) his Maker.

However, there is no such thing as in-between, when one says that he feels both good and bad in his state. Instead, either one is happy, or one is unhappy.

Our sages wrote (*Berachot* 61): "The world was not created etc. but either for the complete evil, or for the complete righteous." This is because there is no such reality where one feels good and bad together.

When our sages say that there is in-between, it is that with the creatures, who have a discernment of time, you can say in-between, in two times, one after the other, as we learn that there is a matter of ascents and descents. These are two times: once he is evil, and once he is righteous. But in a single moment, that one should feel good and bad simultaneously, this does not exist.

It follows that when they said that Torah is more important than a *Mitzva*, it is precisely at **a time when it is not practiced**, meaning when one has no vitality. Then the Torah is more important than a *Mitzva*, which has no vitality.

This is so because one cannot receive anything from a *Mitzva*, which has no vitality. But with the Torah, one still has a way in the work from what he had received while he was practicing the Torah. Although the vitality has departed, the way remains in him, and he can use it. There is a time when a *Mitzva* is more important than Torah, meaning when there is vitality in the *Mitzva* and no vitality in the Torah.

Thus, when not practiced, meaning when one has no vitality and gladness in the work, one has no other counsel but **prayer**. However, **during the prayer one must know that he is evil** because he does not feel the delight and pleasure in the world, although he makes calculations that he can believe that the Creator gives only good.

Despite that, not all of one's thoughts, which one has, are true in the way of the work. In the work, if the thought leads to action, meaning a sensation in the organs, so that the organs feel that the Creator is benevolent, the organs should receive vitality and gladness from it. If one has no vitality, what good are all the calculations if now the organs do not love the Creator because He imparts them abundance?

Thus, one should know that if one has no vitality and gladness in the work, it is a sign that he is evil, because he is unhappy. All the calculations are untrue if they do not yield an act, meaning to a sensation in the organs that one loves the Creator because He imparts delight and pleasure to the creatures.

## 7. WHAT IS HABIT BECOMES A SECOND NATURE IN THE WORK

I heard in 1943

Through accustoming oneself to some thing, that thing becomes second nature for that person. Hence, there is nothing that one cannot feel its reality. This means that although one has no sensation of the thing, he still comes to feel it by accustoming to that thing.

We must know that there is a difference between the Creator and the creatures regarding sensations. For the creatures there is the feeler and the felt, the attaining and the attained. This means that we have a feeler who is connected to some reality.

However, a reality without a feeler is only the Creator Himself. In Him, "there is no thought and perception whatsoever." This is not so with a person; his whole existence is only through the sensation of reality. Even the validity of reality is evaluated as valid only with regard to the one who senses the reality.

In other words, what the feeler tastes is what he considers truth. If one tastes a bitter taste in reality, meaning he feels bad in the situation he is in, and suffers because of that state, that person is considered wicked in the work. This is because he condemns the Creator, since He is called "Benevolent," because He only bestows goodness to the world. Yet, with respect to that person's sensation, the person feels that he has received the opposite from the Creator, meaning the situation he is in is bad.

We should therefore understand what our sages wrote (*Berachot* 61), "The world was not created but either for complete wicked, or for complete righteous." It means the following: Either one tastes and feels a good taste in the world and then one justifies the Creator and says that God gives only goodness to the world, or if one feels and tastes a bitter taste in the world then one is wicked. This is so because one condemns the Creator.

It turns out that everything is measured according to one's sensation. However, all these sensations have no relation to the Creator, as it says in the "Poem of Unification," "As she, so you will always be, shortage and surplus in you will not be." Hence, all the worlds and all the changes are only with respect to the receivers, as one attains them.

## 8. WHAT IS THE DIFFERENCE BETWEEN A SHADE OF *KEDUSHA* AND A SHADE OF *SITRA ACHRA*

I heard on *Tamuz*, July 1944

It is written (Song of Songs, 2), "Until the day breathes, and the shadows flee away." We must understand what are shadows in the work and what are two shadows. The thing is that when one does not feel His Providence, that He leads the world in a manner of “Good that doeth good,” it is regarded as a shadow that hides the sun.

In other words, as the corporeal shadow that hides the sun does not change the sun in any way, and the sun shines in its fullest power, so one who does not feel the existence of His Providence does not induce any change Above. Rather, there is no change Above, as it is written, “I the Lord do not change.”

Instead, all the changes are in the receivers. We must observe two discernments in this shade, meaning in this concealment:

1. When one still has the ability to overcome the darkness and the concealments that one feels, justify the Creator, and pray to the Creator, that the Creator will open his eyes to see that all the concealments that one feels come from the Creator, meaning that the Creator does all that to a person so that one may find one’s prayer and yearn to cleave unto Him.

   This is so because only through the suffering that one receives from Him, wishing to break free from the trouble and flee from the torments, then one does everything he can. Hence, when receiving the concealments and the affliction, one is certain to make the known cure, to do much praying that the Creator will help him and deliver him from the state he is in. In that state, one still believes in His Providence.

2. When one comes to a state where he can no longer prevail and say that all the suffering and pains one feels are because the Creator had sent them to him so as to have a reason to ascend in degree, one comes to a state of heresy. This is because one cannot believe in His Providence, and naturally, one cannot pray.

It follows that there are two kinds of shadows, and this is the meaning of, "and the shadows flee away," meaning that **the shadows will flee from the world**.

The shade of *Klipa* (Shell) is called "Another god is sterile and does not bear fruit." In *Kedusha* (Sanctity), however, it is called, "Under its shadow I delighted to sit, and its fruit was sweet to my palate." In other words, one says that all the concealments and the afflictions one feels are because the Creator has sent him these situations so that one would have a place to work above reason.

When one has the strength to say that, that is, that the Creator causes him all that, it is to one's benefit. This means that through that one can come to work in order to bestow and not for oneself. At that time one comes to realize, meaning believes that the Creator enjoys specifically this work, which is built entirely on above reason.

It follows that one does not pray to the Creator that the shadows will flee from the world. Rather, one says, "I see that the Creator wants me to serve Him in this manner, entirely above reason." Thus, in everything that one does, one says, "Of course the Creator enjoys this work, so why should I care if I work in a state of concealment of the face?"

Because one wants to work in order to bestow, meaning that the Creator will enjoy, he has no abasement from this work, meaning a sensation that he is in a state of concealment of the Face, that the Creator does not enjoy this work. Instead, one agrees to the leadership of the Creator, meaning however the Creator wants one to feel the existence of the Creator during the work, one agrees wholeheartedly. This is so because one does not consider what can please him, but considers what can please the Creator. Thus, this shade brings him life.

This is called, "Under its shadow I delighted," meaning one covets such a state where one can make some overcoming above reason. Thus, if one does not exert in a state of concealment, when there is still room to pray that the Creator will bring him closer, and he is negligent in that, hence one is sent a second concealment in which one cannot even pray. This is because of the sin of not exerting with all one's might to pray to the Creator. For this reason one comes to a state of such lowliness.

However, after one comes to that state, one is then pitied from Above, and again one is given an awakening from Above. The same order begins anew until finally one strengthens in prayer, and the Creator hears his prayer, and brings one near, and reforms it.

## 9. WHAT ARE THREE THINGS THAT BROADEN ONE'S MIND IN THE WORK

I heard on *Elul*, August 1942

The Holy *Zohar* interprets what our sages had written: "Three things broaden one's mind. These are, a handsome woman, a handsome abode, and handsome *Kelim* (Vessels)." It says, "A handsome woman, this is the Holy *Shechina* (Divinity). A handsome abode, this is one's heart; and handsome *Kelim*, these are one's organs."

We must explain that the Holy *Shechina* cannot appear in its true form, which is a state of grace and beauty, except when one has handsome *Kelim*, which are the organs, elicited from the heart. This means that one must first purify one's heart to be a handsome abode by annulling the will to receive for oneself and accustoming oneself to work where all one's actions will be only in order to bestow.

From this extend handsome *Kelim*, meaning one's desires, called *Kelim*, will be clean from reception for oneself. Rather, they will be pure, discerned as bestowal.

However, if the abode is not handsome, the Creator says, "he and I cannot dwell in the same abode." This is because there must be equivalence of form between the Light and the *Kli* (Vessel). Hence, when one takes upon oneself faith in purity, both in mind and in heart, one is imparted with a handsome woman, meaning the Holy *Shechina* appears to him in a form of grace and beauty, and this broadens one's mind.

In other words, through the pleasure and gladness that one feels, the Holy *Shechina* appears within the organs, filling the outer and inner *Kelim*. This is called "broadening the mind."

Obtaining that is through envy, lust, and honor, which bring one out of the world. **Envy** means through envy in the Holy *Shechina*, regarded as zeal in "The zeal of the Lord of hosts." **Honor** means that one wants to increase the glory of heaven, and **lust** is by way of "Thou hast heard the desire of the humble."

## 10. WHAT IS MAKE HASTE MY BELOVED IN THE WORK

I heard on *Tamuz*, July 1944

Bear in mind, that when one begins to walk on a path of wanting to come to do everything for the Creator, one comes to states of ascents and descents. Sometimes one comes to such a great decline that one has thoughts of escaping Torah and *Mitzvot*, meaning thoughts come to a person that he has no desire to be in the domain of *Kedusha* (Sanctity).

In that state one should believe that it is the opposite, meaning that it is *Kedusha* that runs away from him. The reason is that when one wants to blemish *Kedusha*, *Kedusha* moves forward and runs away from him first. If one believes it and overcomes during the escape, then the *Brach* (Escape) is turned into *Barech* (bless), as it is written, "Bless, Lord, his substance, and accept the work of his hands."

## 11. JOY WITH A QUIVER

I heard in 1948

Joy is considered love, which is existence. This is similar to one who builds a house for oneself without making any holes in the walls. You find that he cannot enter the house, as there is no hollow place in the walls of the house by which to enter the house. Therefore, a hollow space must be made through which one will enter the house.

Hence, where there is love, there should be fear as well, as fear is the hollow. In other words, one must awaken the fear that one will not be able to aim to bestow.

It follows that when there are both, there is wholeness. Otherwise, each wants to revoke the other, and for this reason one must try to have both of them in the same place.

This is the meaning of the need for love and fear. Love is called existence, whereas fear is called dearth and hollow. Only with the two of them together is there wholeness. And this is called "two legs," and precisely when one has two legs can one walk.

## 12. THE ESSENCE OF ONE'S WORK

I heard during a meal on the 2nd day of Rosh HaShanah, October 5, 1948

The essence of one's work should be how to come to feel taste in bestowing contentment to one's Maker, since all that one does for oneself distances him from the Creator, due to the disparity of form. However, if one performs an act to benefit the Creator, even the smallest act, it is still considered a *Mitzva* (commandment/precept).

Hence, one's primary exertion should be to acquire a force that feels taste in bestowing, which is through lessening the force that feels taste in self-reception. In that state one slowly acquires the taste in bestowing.

## 13. A POMEGRANATE

I heard during a meal on the 2nd night of Rosh HaShanah, October 5, 1948

A Pomegranate, he said, implies to what our sages said, "Even the vain ones amongst you are as filled with *Mitzvot* as a pomegranate" (*Iruvin* 19). He said, *Rimon* (Pomegranate) comes from the word *Romemut* (Loftiness), which is above reason. And the meaning will be that the "The vain amongst you are filled with *Mitzvot*." The measure of the filling is as much as one can go above reason, and this is called *Romemut*.

There is only emptiness in a place where there is no existence, as it is written, "hangeth the earth over nothing." You find that **what is the measure of the filling**, of the empty place? The answer is, **according to one's elevation of oneself above reason.**

This means that the emptiness should be filled with **loftiness**, meaning with above reason, and to ask of the Creator to give one that strength. It will mean that all the emptiness was created, meaning it comes to a person **to feel thus, that he is empty**, only in order to fill it with the *Romemut* of the Creator. In other words, one is to take everything above reason.

And this is the meaning of, "and God hath so made it, that men should fear before Him." It means that these thoughts of emptiness come to a person in order for one to have a need to take upon himself faith above reason. And for that we need the help of God. It follows that at that time one must ask of the Creator to give him the power to believe above reason.

It turns out that it is precisely then that one needs the Creator to help him, since the exterior mind lets him understand the opposite. Hence, one has no other counsel but to ask of the Creator to help him.

It is said about that, "One's desire overcomes one everyday; and were it not for the Creator, one would not prevail." Thus, only then is the state when one understands that there is no one to help him but the Creator. And this is "and God hath so made it, that men should fear before Him." The matter of fear is discerned as faith, and only then is one in need of God's salvation.

## 14. WHAT IS THE GREATNESS OF THE CREATOR?

I heard in 1948

The *Romemut* (greatness/sublimity) of the Creator means that one should ask of the Creator for the strength to go above reason. It means that there are two interpretations to the greatness of Creator:

A. To not be filled with knowledge, which is intellect, with which one can answer one's questions. Rather, one wants the Creator to answer one's questions. It is called *Romemut* because all the wisdom comes from Above and not from man, meaning that one can answer one's own questions.

Anything that one can answer is regarded as answering everything with the external mind. This means that the will to receive understands that it is worthwhile to keep Torah and *Mitzvot*. However, if above reason compels one to work, it is called "against the opinion of the will to receive."

B. The greatness of the Creator means that one becomes needy of the Creator to grant one's wishes. Therefore:

    1. One should go above reason. Thus one sees that he is empty, and consequently becomes needy of the Creator.
    2. Only the Creator can give one the strength to be able to go above reason. In other words, what the Creator gives is called, "The *Romemut* of the Creator."

## 15. WHAT IS OTHER GODS IN THE WORK

I heard on *Av* 24, August 3, 1945

It is written, "Thou shalt have no other gods before Me." The Holy *Zohar* interprets that there should be stones to weigh with. It asks about it, how is the work weighed in stones, by which one knows one's state in the ways of God? It replies that it is known that when one begins to work more than one is used to, the body begins to kick and reject this work with all its might.

This is because, regarding bestowal, it is a load and a burden for the body. It cannot tolerate this work, and the resistance of the body appears in one in the form of alien thoughts. It comes and asks the questions of "who" and "what," and through these questions one says that all these questions are certainly sent to him by the *Sitra Achra* (other side), to obstruct him in the work.

It says that if at that time one says that they come from the *Sitra Achra*, one breaches what is written, **"Thou shalt have no other gods before Me."** The reason is that one should believe that it comes to him from the Holy *Shechina*, since **"There is none else besides Him."** Instead, the Holy *Shechina* shows one his true state, how one is walking in the ways of God.

This means that by sending him these questions, called "alien thoughts," that is, through these alien thoughts she sees how he answers the questions regarded as "alien thoughts." And all this, one should know one's true state in the work so he will know what to do.

It is like a parable: A friend wanted to know how much his friend loved him. Certainly, when face-to-face, his friend hides himself because of the shame. Thus, one sends a person to speak badly about his friend. Then he sees his friend's reaction while he is away from his friend, and then one can know the true measure of his friend's love.

The lesson is that when the Holy *Shechina* shows her face to a person, meaning when the Creator gives one liveliness and joy, in that state one is ashamed to say what he thinks about the work of bestowal and of not receiving anything for oneself. However, when not facing it, meaning when the liveliness and gladness cool down, which is considered not facing it, then one can see one's true state regarding in order to bestow.

If one believes that it is written that there is none else besides Him, and that the Creator sends all the alien thoughts, meaning that He is the operator, one certainly knows what to do, and how to answer all the questions. It seems as though she sends him messengers to see how he speaks slander of her, of his Kingdom of Heaven, and this is how we can interpret the above matter.

One can understand that, that everything comes from the Creator. This is because it is known that the beatings that the body beats a person with its alien thoughts, since they do not come to a person when he does not engage in the work, but these beatings that come to a person in a complete sensation, to the point that these thoughts smash his mind, they come specifically after preceding Torah and work more than the usual. **This is called stones to weigh with**.

It means that these stones fall in one's mind when one wants to understand these questions. Afterwards, when one goes to weigh the purpose of one's work, if it is really worthwhile to work in order to bestow, work with all his might and soul, and that all his desires will be only to hope that what there is to acquire in this world is only in the purpose of his work to bring contentment to his Maker, and not in any corporal matter.

At that time there begins a bitter argument, since one sees that there are arguments both ways. The writings warn about that, **"Thou shalt have no other gods before Me."** Do not say that another god gave you the stones to weigh your work with, but **"before Me."**

Instead, one should know that this is considered **"before Me."** This is so that one will see the true form of the basis and the foundation upon which the structure of the work is built.

The heaviness in the work is primarily because they are two texts that deny one another. On the one had, one should try that all his work will be to reach *Dvekut* (Adhesion) with the Creator, that all his desire will be only to bestow contentment to his Maker, and not at all to himself.

On the other hand, we see that this is not the primary goal, since the purpose of creation was not that the creatures would give to the Creator, since He has no deficiency in Him that the creatures will give Him anything. On the contrary, the purpose of creation was due to His desire to do good to His creatures, meaning that the creatures would receive delight and pleasure from Him.

These two matters contradict one another from one end to the other. On the one hand one should bestow, and on the other hand, one should receive. In other words, there is the discernment of the correction of creation, being to achieve *Dvekut*, discerned as equivalence of form, being that all his actions will be only to bestow. Afterwards it is possible to achieve the purpose of creation, which is to receive delight and pleasure from the Creator.

Hence, when one has accustomed oneself to walk in ways of bestowal, one has no vessels of reception anyhow. When one walks in ways of reception, he has no vessels of bestowal.

Thus, through the **"stones to weigh with"** one acquires both. This is because after the negotiation he had during the work, when he overcomes and assumes the burden of the Kingdom of Heaven in the form of bestowal in mind and heart, it causes that when one is about to draw the Sublime Abundance, since he already has a solid foundation that everything should be in the form of bestowal, hence, even when one receives some luminescence, one already receives in order to bestow. This is because the whole foundation of his work is built solely on bestowal. This is considered that he "receives in order to bestow."

## 16. WHAT IS THE DAY OF THE LORD AND THE NIGHT OF THE LORD IN THE WORK

I heard in 1941, Jerusalem

Our sages said this about the verse, "Woe unto you that desire the day of the Lord! Wherefore would ye have the day of the Lord? It is darkness, and not light" (*Amos* 5): "There is a parable about a rooster and a bat that were awaiting the light. The rooster said to the bat: 'I await the light for the light is mine; but you, what need have you for light?'" (*Sanhedrin* 98,2). The interpretation is that since the bat has no eyes to see, what does it gain from the sunlight? On the contrary, for one who has no eyes, the sunlight only darkens more.

We must understand that parable, meaning how the eyes are connected to looking in the Light of God, which the text names "the day of the Lord." They gave a parable in that regard about a bat, that one with no eyes remains in the dark.

We must also understand what is the day of the Lord and what is the night of the Lord, and what is the difference between them. We discern the day of people by the sunrise, but with the day of the Lord, in what do we discern it?

The answer is, as the appearance of the sun. In other words, when the sun shines on the ground, we call it "day." And when the sun does not shine, it is called "darkness." It is the same with the Creator. A day is called "revelation" and darkness is called "concealment of the face."

This means that when there is revelation of the face, when it is as clear as day for a person, this is called "a day." It is as our sages said (*Psachim* 2) about the verse, "The murderer riseth with the light, to kill the poor and needy; and in the night he is as a thief." Since he said, "and in the night he is as a thief," it follows that light is day. He says there, that if the matter is as clear to you as light that comes over the souls, he is a murderer, and it is possible to save him in his soul. Thus we see that regarding day, the *Gemarah* says that it is a matter as clear as day.

It follows that the day of the Lord will mean that Providence–how the Creator leads the world–will be clearly in the form of benevolence. For example, when one prays, his prayer is immediately answered and he receives what he has prayed for, and one succeeds wherever one turns. This is called "the day of the Lord."

Conversely, darkness, which is night, will mean concealment of the face. This brings one doubts in the benevolent guidance and alien thoughts. In other words, the concealment of the guidance brings one all these alien views and thoughts. This is called "night" and "darkness." Namely, one experiences a state where one feels that the world has turned dark on him.

Now we can interpret what is written, "Woe unto you that desire the day of the Lord! Wherefore would ye have the day of the Lord? It is darkness, and not light." The thing is that those who await the day of the Lord, it means that they are waiting to be imparted faith above reason, that faith will be as strong as if they see with their eyes, with certainty, that it is so, meaning that the Creator guides the world in benevolence.

In other words, they do not want to see how the Creator leads the world in benevolence, because seeing is contradictory to faith. In other words, faith is precisely where it is against reason. And when one does what is against one's reason, this is called "faith above reason."

This means that they believe that the guidance of the Creator over the creatures is benevolent. And while they do not see it with absolute certainty, they do not say to the Creator, "We want to see the benevolence as seeing within reason." Rather, they want it to remain in them as faith above reason.

But they ask of the Creator **to impart them with such strength that this faith will be so strong, as if they see it within reason**. It means that there will not be a difference between faith and knowledge in the mind. This is what they, meaning those who want to cleave to the Creator, refer to as **"the day of the Lord."**

In other words, if they feel it as knowledge, then the Light of God, called "the Upper Abundance," will go to the vessels of reception, called "separated vessels." And they do not want this, since it would go to the will to receive, which is the opposite of *Kedusha* (Sanctity), which is against the will to receive for self-gratification. Instead, they want to be adhered to the Creator, and this can only be through equivalence of form.

However, to achieve that, meaning in order for one to have a desire and a craving to cleave to the Creator, since one is born with a nature of a will to receive only for one's own benefit, how is it possible to achieve something that is completely against nature? For this reason one must make great efforts until he acquires a second nature, which is the will to bestow.

When one is imparted the will to bestow, he is qualified to receive the Upper Abundance with it, and not blemish, since all the flaws come only through the will to receive for oneself. In other words, even when doing something in order to bestow, deep inside there is a thought that he will receive something for this act of bestowal that he is now performing.

In a word, one is unable to do anything if he does not receive something in return for the act. One must enjoy, and any pleasure that one receives for oneself, that pleasure must cause him separation from the life of lives, by reason of the separation.

This stops one from being adhesive with the Creator, since the matter of *Dvekut* (Adhesion) is measured by equivalence of form. It is thus impossible to have pure bestowal without a mixture of reception from one's own powers. Therefore, for one to have the powers of bestowal, we need a second nature, so one will have the strength to achieve equivalence of form.

In other words, the Creator is the giver and does not receive anything, for He lacks nothing. This means that what He gives is also not because of a want, meaning that if He had no one to give to, He would feel it as a want.

Instead, we must perceive it as **a game**. That is, it is not that when He wants to give, it is something that He needs; but this is all like **a game**. It is as our sages said regarding the mistress: She asked, "What does the Creator do after He has created the world?" The answer was, "He sits and plays with a whale," as it is written, "There go the ships of the sea, and Leviathan (the sea monster), which You have formed to sport in it" (*Avoda Zarah (Idol Worshiping)*, p. 3).

The matter of the Leviathan refers to *Dvekut* and connection (as it is written, "according to the space of each, with wreaths"). It means that the purpose, which is the connection of the Creator with the creatures, is only in sport; it is not a matter of a desire and a need.

The difference between a game and a desire is that everything that comes in the desire is a necessity. If one does not obtain one's wish, one is deficient. However, in sport, even if one does not obtain the thing, it is not considered a lack, as they say, "it is not so bad that I did not obtain what I thought, because it is not so important." This is so because the desire that one had for it was only playful, and not serious.

It follows, that the whole purpose is that one's work will be entirely in bestowal, and he will not have a desire and craving to receive pleasure for his work.

This is a high degree, as it is implemented in the Creator. And this is called "the day of the Lord."

The day of the Lord is called "wholeness," as it is written, "Let the stars of the morning thereof be dark; let it look for light, but have none." Light is considered wholeness.

When one acquires the second nature, the will to bestow, which the Creator gives one after the first nature, being the will to receive, and now receives the will to bestow, then one is qualified to serve the Creator in completeness, and this is considered "the day of the Lord."

Thus, one who has not acquired the second nature and can serve the Creator in the form of bestowal, and waits to be awarded that, meaning bestowal, meaning when one has already exerted and did what he could to obtain that force, he is considered to be awaiting the day of the Lord, meaning to have equivalence of form with the Creator.

When the day of the Lord comes, he is elated. He is happy that he has come out of the power of the will to receive for himself, which separated him from the Creator. Now one cleaves to the Creator, and considers it as having risen to the top.

However, it is the opposite with one whose work is only in self-reception. One is happy as long as one thinks that he will have any reward from his work. When one sees that the will to receive will not receive any reward for its work, one becomes sad and idle. Sometimes one comes to ponder about the beginning, and says, "I did not swear on this."

Thus, moreover, the day of the Lord is attaining the power to bestow. If one were to be told that this will be his profit from engaging in Torah and *Mitzvot*, one would say, "I consider it darkness, not light," since this knowledge brings one to darkness.

## 17. WHAT DOES IT MEAN THAT THE *SITRA ACHRA* IS CALLED "*MALCHUT* WITHOUT A CROWN"

I heard in 1941, Jerusalem

**Crown** means *Keter*, and *Keter* is the Emanator and the Root. *Kedusha* (Sanctity) is connected to the root, meaning *Kedusha* is considered being in equivalence of form with its root. It means that as our root, namely the Creator, wants only to bestow, as it is written, "His desire to do good to the creatures," so *Kedusha* is only to bestow upon the Creator.

*Sitra Achra*, however, is not so. She aims only to receive for herself. For this reason she is not in adhesion with the root, being *Keter*. Hence the *Sitra Achra* is referred to as having no *Keter* (crown). In other words, she has no *Keter* because she is separated from the *Keter*.

Now we can understand what our sages said (*Sanhedrin* 29), "All who add, subtract." This means that if you add to the count, it subtracts. It is written (*Zohar*, *Pekudei* item 249), "It is the same here, relating to what is inside, it writes, 'Moreover thou shalt make the tabernacle with ten curtains.' Relating to what is outside, it writes, 'eleven curtains,' adding letters, meaning adding the *Ayin* (the added Hebrew letter) to the twelve, and subtracting from the count. It subtracts one from the number twelve because of the addition of the *Ayin* to the twelve."

It is known that calculation is implemented only in *Malchut*, who calculates the height of the degree (through the *Ohr Hozer* in her). Also, it is known that *Malchut* is called "the will to receive for itself."

When she annuls her will to receive before the root, and does not want to receive, but only to give to the root, like the root, which is a will to bestow, then *Malchut*, called ***Ani*** (I), becomes ***Ein*** (naught). Only then does she extend the Light of *Keter* to build her *Partzuf* and becomes **twelve** *Partzufim* of *Kedusha*.

However, when she wants to receive for herself, she becomes the **evil *Ayin*** (Eye). In other words, where there was a combination of ***Ein***, meaning annulment before the root, which is *Keter*, it has become ***Ayin*** (meaning seeing and knowing within reason).

This is called adding. It means that one wants to add knowing to the faith, and work within reason. In other words, she says that it is more worthwhile to work within reason, and then the will to receive will not object to the work.

This causes a **deficit**, meaning that they were separated from the *Keter*, called "the will to bestow," which is the root. There is no longer the matter of equivalence of form with the root, called *Keter*. For this reason, *Sitra Achra* is called "*Malchut* without a Crown." It means that *Malchut* of the *Sitra Achra* does not have *Dvekut* (adhesion) with the *Keter*. For this reason, they have only eleven *Partzufim*, without *Partzuf Keter*.

This is the meaning of what our sages wrote, "ninety nine die of **evil eye**," meaning because they have no discernment of a *Keter*. It means that the *Malchut* in them, being the will to receive, does not want to annul before the root, called *Keter*. This means that they do not want to make of the *Ani* (I), called " the will to receive," a discernment of an ***Ein*** (naught), which is the annulment of the will to receive.

Instead, they want to add. And this is called **"the evil *Ayin*"** (Eye). That is, where there should be an *Ein* with *Aleph* (the first letter in the word *Ein*), they insert the evil *Ayin* (Eye, the first letter in the word). Thus, they fall from their degree due to a lack of *Dvekut* with the root.

This is the meaning of what our sages said, "Anyone who is proud, the Creator says, 'He and I cannot dwell in the same abode,'" as he makes two authorities. However, when one is a state of *Ein*, and one annuls oneself before the root, meaning that one's sole intention is only to bestow, like the root, you find only one authority here–the authority of the Creator. Then, all that one receives in the world is only to bestow upon the Creator.

This is the meaning of what he had said, "The whole world was created for me, and I, to serve my Maker." For this reason

I must receive all the degrees in the world so that I can give everything to the Creator, called "to serve my Maker."

## 18. WHAT IS MY SOUL SHALL WEEP IN SECRET, IN THE WORK

I heard in 1940, Jerusalem

When concealment overpowers one and he comes to a state where the work becomes tasteless, and he cannot picture and feel any love and fear, and he cannot do anything in holiness, then his only counsel is to cry to the Creator to take pity on him and remove the screen from his eyes and heart.

The issue of crying is a very important one. It is as our sages write: "all the gates were locked except for the gates of tears." The world asks about that: If the gates of tears are not locked, what is the need for the gates at all? He said that it is like a person who asks his friend for some necessary object. This object touches his heart, and he asks and begs of him in every manner of prayer and plea. Yet, his friend pays no heed to all that. And when one sees that there is no longer reason for prayers and pleas, he then raises his voice in weeping.

It is said about that: "All the gates were locked except for the gates of tears." Thus, when were the gates of tears not locked? Precisely when all the gates were locked. It is then that there is room for the gates of tears and then one sees that they were not locked.

However, when the gates of prayer are open, the gates of tears and weeping are irrelevant. This is the meaning of the gates of tears being locked. Thus, when are the gates of tears not locked? Precisely when all the gates are locked, the gates of tears are open. This is because one still has the counsel of prayer and plea.

This is the meaning of **"My soul shall weep in secret,"** meaning when one comes to a state of concealment, then "My soul shall weep," because one has no other option. This is the meaning of "Whatsoever thy hand attaineth to do by thy strength, that do."

## 19. WHAT IS THE CREATOR HATES THE BODIES, IN THE WORK

I heard in 1943, Jerusalem

The Holy *Zohar* says that the Creator hates the bodies. He said that we should interpret it as referring to the will to receive, called *Guf* (Body). The Creator created His world in His glory, as it is written, "Every one that is called by My Name, and whom I have created for My glory, I have formed him, yea, I have made him."

Therefore, this contradicts the body's argument that everything is for it, meaning only for its own benefit, while the Creator says the opposite, that everything should be for the Creator. Hence, our sages said that the Creator said, "he and I can not dwell in the same abode."

It follows that the primary separator from being in adhesion with the Creator is the will to receive. It is apparent when the evil comes; meaning, the will to receive comes and asks, "Why do you want to work for the Creator?" We think that it speaks as humans do, that it wants to understand with its intellect. Yet, this is not the truth, since it does not ask for whom one is working. This is certainly a rational argument, as this argument awakens in one with a reason.

Instead, the argument of the wicked is a physical question. That is, it asks, **"What mean you by this service?"** In other words, which profit will you have for the exertion you are making? It means that it asks, "If you are not working for yourself, what will the body, called 'the will to receive for oneself,' get out of it?"

Since this is a bodily argument, the only reply is a bodily reply, "He blunted its teeth, and had he not been there, he would not have been redeemed." Why? Because the will to receive for itself has no redemption even at the time of redemption. This is because the matter of redemption will be when all the profits enter the vessels of bestowal and not the vessels of reception.

The will to receive for itself must always remain in deficit, since filling the will to receive is actual death. The reason is, as we have said above, that creation was primarily for His glory (and this is an answer to what is written, that His wish is to do good to His creatures, and not for Himself).

The interpretation will be that the essence of creation is to reveal to all that the purpose of creation is to do good to His creatures. This is specifically when one says that he was born to honor the Creator. At that time, in these vessels, the purpose of creation appears, which is to do good to His creatures.

For this reason one must always examine oneself, the purpose of one's work, meaning if the Creator receives contentment in every act that one performs, because he wants equivalence of form. This is called **"All your actions will be for the Creator,"** meaning one wants the Creator to enjoy whatever one does, as it is written, "to bring contentment to his Maker."

Also, one needs to conduct oneself with the will to receive and say to it, "I have already decided that I do not want to receive any pleasure because you want to enjoy. This is because with your desire I am forced to be separated from the Creator, since disparity of form causes separation and distance from the Creator."

One's hope should be that since one cannot break loose from the dominion of the will to receive, he is therefore in perpetual ascents and descents. Hence, one awaits the Creator, to be rewarded with the Creator opening his eyes, and to have the power to overcome and work only to benefit the Creator. It is as it is written, **"One thing have I asked of the Lord, that will I seek after." That**, meaning the Holy *Shechina* (Divinity). And one asks (Psalms 27:4), **"that I may dwell in the house of the Lord all the days of my life."**

The house of the Lord is the Holy *Shechina*. And now we can understand what our sages said about the verse, **"And ye shall take you on the first day,"** the first to count the iniquities. We must understand why is there joy if there is room for an iniquity-count here? He said that we must know that there is a matter of importance **in the labor**, when there is a contact between the individual and the Creator.

It means that one feels that he needs the Creator, since, in the state of labor, one sees that there is no one in the world who can save him from the state he is in but the Creator alone. Then one sees that **"There is none else besides Him,"** who can save him from the state he is in, and from which he cannot escape.

This is called having close contact with the Creator. If one knows how to appreciate that contact, meaning that one should believe that then he is in adhesion with the Creator, meaning that one's entire thought is of the Creator, meaning that He will help him. Otherwise one sees that he is lost.

However, one who is awarded private Providence, and sees that the Creator does everything, as it is written, **"He alone does and will do all the deeds,"** he naturally has nothing to add, and in any case, one has no room for prayer for the Creator's help. This is because one sees that even without one's prayer the Creator still does everything.

Hence, at that time one has no place to be able to do good deeds since one sees that everything is done without him by the Creator anyhow. Thus, in that state one has no need for the Creator to help him do anything. Thus, at that time one has no contact with the Creator, to need him to the extent that he is lost if the Creator does not help him.

It follows that he does not have the contact that he had had with the Creator during the labor. He said that it is like a person who is between life and death, and asks of his friend to save him from death. How does one ask of one's friend? One certainly tries to ask one's friend to have mercy on him and save him from death with every power at one's disposal. He certainly never forgets to pray to one's friend, since one sees that otherwise he will lose his life.

However, one who asks of one's friend for luxuries that are not so necessary, the pleading is not so much in adhesion with his friend to give him what he asks for to the point that his mind will not be distracted from asking. You find that with things that are not related to life-saving, the pleading is not that adhesive with the giver.

Thus, when one feels that he should ask of the Creator to save him from death, meaning from the state of, "The evil in their life are called dead," the contact between the person and the Creator is close contact. For this reason, for the righteous, a place of work is to need the Creator's help; otherwise he is lost. This is what the righteous crave: a place to work so they will have close contact with the Creator.

It follows that if the Creator gives room for work, these righteous are very happy. This is why they said, "first to the iniquity-count." For them it is joyous to now have a place to work, meaning that now they have become needy of the Creator and can now come into close contact with the Creator.

This is because one cannot come to the King's Palace but for some purpose.

This is the meaning of, **"And ye shall take you."** It specifies **you**. This is because everything is in the hands of God except the fear of God. In other words, the Creator can give abundance of Light because this is what He has. But the darkness, the place of dearth, this is not in His domain.

Since there is a rule that **there is fear of God only from a place of dearth**, and a place of dearth is called "the will to receive," it means that **only then is there a place for labor. In what? In that it resists.**

The body comes and asks, "What mean you by this service?" and one has nothing to answer to its question. Then one must assume the burden of the Kingdom of Heaven above reason as an ox to the burden and as a donkey to the load without any arguments. Instead, He said and His will was done. **This is called "you," meaning this work belongs precisely to you**, and not to Me, meaning the work that your will to receive necessitates.

However, if the Creator gives one some luminescence from Above, the will to receive surrenders and annuls like a candle before a torch. Then one has no labor anyhow, since one no longer needs to take upon himself the burden of the Kingdom of Heaven coercively as an ox to the burden and as a donkey to the load, as it is written, **"ye that love the Lord, hate evil."**

It means that the love of God extends only from the place of evil. In other words, to the extent that one has hatred for evil, meaning that one sees how the will to receive obstructs one from achieving the completeness of the goal, to that extent one needs to be imparted the love of God.

However, if one does not feel that one has evil, one cannot be granted the love of God. This is because he has no need for it, as he already has satisfaction in the work.

As we have said, one must not be angry when he has work with the will to receive, that it obstructs him in the work. One would certainly be more satisfied if the will to receive had been absent from the body, **meaning that it would not bring its questions to man**, obstructing him in the work of keeping Torah and *Mitzvot*.

However, one should believe that the obstructions of the will to receive in the work come to him from Above. One is given the force to discover the will to receive from Above because there is room for work precisely when the will to receive awakens.

Then one has close contact with the Creator, to help one turn the will to receive to be in order to bestow. And one should believe that **from that extends contentment to the Creator**, from one's praying to Him, to draw him near by *Dvekut* (Adhesion), called "equivalence of form," discerned as the annulment of the will to receive to be in order to bestow. The Creator says about that, **"My sons defeated Me."** That is, I gave you the will to receive, and you ask of Me to give you a will to bestow instead.

Now we can interpret what is brought in the *Gemarah* (*Hulin* p. 7): "Rabbi Pinehas Ben Yair was going to redeem the captive. He came across the river Ginai (the name of the river was Ginai). He said to Ginai, 'Divide your waters, and I will pass in you.' It told him: 'You are going to do the will of your Maker, and I am going to do the will of my Maker. You, perhaps do, perhaps not do, while I certainly do.'"

He said that the meaning is that he told the river, meaning the will to receive, to let him through it and reach the degree of doing the will of God, meaning to do everything in order to bestow contentment upon his Maker. The river, the will to receive, replied that since the Creator created it with this nature of wanting to receive delight and pleasure, it therefore does not want to change the nature in which the Creator had created it.

Rabbi Pinehas Ben Yair waged war on it, meaning he wanted to invert it to a will to bestow. This is called waging war on the creation, which the Creator had created in nature, called "the will to receive," which the Creator had created, which is the whole of creation, called "existence from absence."

One must know that during the work, when the will to receive comes to a person with its arguments, no arguments and no rationalities help with it. Though one thinks that they are just arguments, it will not help one defeat one's evil.

Instead, as it is written, **"He blunted its teeth."** This means to advance only by actions, and not by arguments. This is called that one has to increment powers coercively. This is the meaning of what our sages wrote, **"He is coerced until he says 'I want.'"** In other words, through persistence, habit becomes a second nature.

One must especially try to have a strong desire to obtain the will to bestow and overcome the will to receive. The meaning of a strong desire is that a strong desire is measured by the proliferation of the in-between rests and the arrests, meaning the cessations between each overcoming.

Sometimes one receives a cessation in the middle, meaning a descent. This descent can be a cessation of a minute, an hour, a day, or a month. Afterwards, one resumes the work of overcoming the will to receive, and the attempts to achieve the will to bestow. A strong desire means that the cessation does not take him a long time and he is immediately reawakened to the work.

It is like a person who wants to break a big rock. He takes a big hammer and hammers many times all day long, but they are weak. In other words, he does not hammer the rock in one swing but brings the big hammer down slowly. After that he complains that this work of breaking the rock is not for him, that it must take a hero to have the ability to break this big rock. He says that he was not born with such great powers to have the ability to break the rock.

However, one who lifts this big hammer and strikes the rock in a big swing, not slowly but with a great effort, the rock immediately surrenders to him and breaks down. This is the meaning of, **"like a hammer that breaketh the rock in pieces."**

Similarly, in the holy work, which is to bring the vessels of reception into *Kedusha* (Sanctity), we have a strong hammer, meaning words of Torah that give us good counsels. However, if it is not consistent, but with long intermissions in-between, one escapes the campaign and says that he was not made for this, but this work requires one who was born with special skills for it. Nevertheless, one should believe that anyone can achieve the goal, though he should try to always increment one's efforts in overcoming. And then one can break the rock in a short time.

We must also know that for the effort to make contact with the Creator, there is a very harsh condition here: the effort must be in the form of **adornment**. Adornment means something that is important to a person. One cannot work gladly if the labor is not of importance, meaning that one has joy at now having contact with the Creator.

This matter is implied in the Citron. It is written about the citron, **a fruit of the citrus tree**,[1] that it should be clean above its nose. It is known that there are three discernments: A) Adornment, B) Scent, and C) Taste.

**Taste** means that the Lights are poured from Above downward, meaning below the *Peh* (Mouth), where there are the palate and the taste. This means that the Lights come in vessels of reception.

**Scent** means that the Lights come from below upward. This means the Lights come in vessels of bestowal, in the

1 In Hebrew, citrus is *Hadar*, from the word *Hidur* (adornment).

form of receiving and not bestowing below the palate and the throat. This is discerned as, **"and he shall smell in the fear of the Lord"** said about the Messiah. It is known that scent is ascribed to the nose.

**Adornment** is beauty, discerned as above one's nose, meaning scentless. It means that there is neither taste nor smell there. Thus, what is there by which one can survive? There is only the adornment in it, and this is what sustains him.

We see about the citron that the adornment is in it precisely before it is suitable for eating. However, when it is suitable for eating, there is no adornment in it anymore.

This comes to tell us about the **work of the first to count the iniquities**. It means that precisely when one works in the form of "And ye shall take you," meaning the work during the acceptance of the burden of the Kingdom of Heaven, when the body resists, then there is room for the joy of **adornment**.

This means that during this work the adornment is apparent. This means that if he has gladness from this work, it is because he considers this work as adornment, and not as disgrace.

In other words, sometimes one despises this work of assuming the burden of the Kingdom of Heaven, which is a time of a sensation of darkness, when one sees that no one can save him from the state he is in but the Creator. Then he takes upon himself the Kingdom of Heaven above reason, as an ox to the burden and as a donkey to the load.

One should be glad that now he has something to give to the Creator, and the Creator enjoys him having something to give to the Creator. But one does not always have the strength to say that this is a **handsome** work, called **"adornment,"** but he despises this work.

This is a harsh condition for one to able to say that he chooses this work over the work of whiteness, meaning that he does not sense a taste of darkness during the work, but then one feels a taste in the work. It means that then he does not have to work with the will to receive to agree to take upon himself the Kingdom of Heaven above reason.

If one does overcome oneself, and can say that this work is pleasant when he now keeps the *Mitzva* (Commandment) of faith above reason, and he accepts this work as adornment, this is called "A joy of *Mitzva*."

This is the meaning of the prayer being more important than the response to the prayer. This is because in prayer one has a place for labor, and he needs the Creator, meaning he awaits heaven's mercy. At that time one has a true contact with the Creator, and then he is in the King's Palace. However, when the prayer is answered, he has already departed the King's Palace since he has already taken what he had asked for and left.

Accordingly, we should understand the verse, "Thine oils have a goodly fragrance; thy name is as oil poured forth." **Oil** is called "The Upper Light" when it flows. **"Poured forth"** means during the cessation of the abundance. At that time the scent remains from the oil. (Scent means that a *Reshimo* (Reminiscence) of what he'd had remains nonetheless. **Adornment**, however, is called so in a place where there is no hold at all, meaning even the *Reshimo* does not shine).

This is the meaning of *Atik* and AA. During the expansion, the abundance is called AA, which is *Hochma* (Wisdom), meaning **open Providence**. *Atik* comes from the (Hebrew) word *VaYe'atek* (Detachment), meaning the departure of the Light. In other words, it does not shine; and this is called **"concealment."**

This is the time of rejection to clothing, which is the time of the reception of the King's crown, which is considered *Malchut* (Kingdom) of Lights, regarded as **The Kingdom of Heaven**.

It is written about it in the Holy *Zohar*, "The Holy *Shechina* said to Rabbi Shimon, 'There is no place to hide from you' (meaning there is no place where I can hide myself from you)." It means that even in the greatest concealment in reality he still takes upon himself the burden of the Kingdom of Heaven with great joy.

The reason for it is that he follows a line of a will to bestow, and thus he gives what is in his hand. If the Creator gives him more, he gives more. And if he has nothing to give, he stands and cries like a crane for the Creator to save him from the evil waters. Hence, in this manner, too, he has contact with the Creator.

The reason that this discernment is called *Atik*, and *Atik* is the highest degree, is that the farther the thing is from clothing, the higher it is. One can feel in the most abstract thing, called "the absolute zero," since there man's hand does not reach.

This means that the will to receive can seize only in a place where there is some expansion of Light. Before one purifies one's vessels so as to not blemish the Light, one is unable for the Light to come to him in a form of expansion in the *Kelim* (Vessels). Only when one marches on the path of bestowal, meaning in a place where the will to receive is not present, whether in mind or in heart, there the Light can come in utter completeness. Then the Light comes to him in a sensation that he can feel the sublimity of the Upper Light.

However, when one has not corrected the vessels to be in order to bestow, when the Light comes to a form of expansion, the Light must restrict and shine only according to the purity of the *Kelim*. Hence, at that time the Light appears to be in utter smallness. Therefore, when the Light is abstracted from clothing in the *Kelim*, the Light can shine in utter completeness and clarity without any restrictions for the lower one.

It follows that the importance of the work is precisely when one comes to a state of naught, meaning when one sees that he annuls his whole existence and being, for then the will to receive has no power. Only then does one enter the *Kedusha*.

We must know that "God hath made even the one as well as the other." It means that as much as there is disclosure in *Kedusha*, to that extent the *Sitra Achra* (Other Side) awakens. In other words, when one claims, "it is all mine," meaning the entire body belongs to *Kedusha*, the *Sitra Achra*, too, argues against him that the whole body should serve the *Sitra Achra*.

Hence, one must know that when one sees that the body claims that it belongs to the *Sitra Achra*, and cries the famous questions of **"Who"** and **"What"** with all its might, it is a sign that one is walking on the path of truth, meaning that one's sole intention is to bestow contentment upon one's Maker. Thus, the primary work is in precisely that state.

One must know that it is a sign that this work hits the target. The sign is that he fights and sends his arrows to the head of the serpent, since it yells and argues the argument of **"What"** and **"Who,"** meaning, "What mean you by this service?" In other words, what will you gain by working only for the Creator and not for yourselves? And the argument of **"Who"** means that this is Pharaoh's argument who said, "Who is the Lord that I should obey His voice?"

It seems as if the **"Who"** argument is a rational argument. It is a common conduct that when one is told to go and work for someone, one asks **for whom**? Hence, when the body claims, "Who is the Lord that I should obey His voice," it is a rational argument.

However, according to the rule that the ratio is not an object in itself, but is rather a **mirror** of what is present in the senses, it appears so in the mind. And this is the meaning of, "And the sons of Dan: Hushim." This means that the mind judges only according to what the senses let it scrutinize and devise some inventions and contrivances to suit the demands of the senses.

In other words, what the senses demand, the mind tries to provide their wish. However, the mind itself has no need for itself, for any demand. Hence, if there is a demand for bestowal in the senses, the mind operates according to a line of bestowal, and the mind does not ask questions, since it is merely serving the senses.

The mind is like a person looking in the mirror to see if he is dirty. And all the places that the mirror shows are dirty, he goes and washes and cleans, since the mirror showed him that there are ugly things in one's face that need to be cleaned.

However, the hardest thing of all is to know what is considered an ugly thing. Is it the will to receive, meaning the body's demand to do everything only for oneself, or is the will to bestow the ugly thing, which the body cannot tolerate? The mind cannot scrutinize it, like the mirror, which cannot say what is ugly and what is beauty, but it all depends on the senses, and only the senses determine that.

Hence, when one accustoms oneself to work coercively, to work in bestowal, then the mind too operates by lines of bestowal. At that time it is impossible that the mind will ask the "Who" question, when the senses have already grown accustomed to work in bestowal.

In other words, the senses no longer ask the question, "What mean you by this service" since they are already working in order to bestow, and, naturally, the mind does not ask the "Who" question.

You find that the essence of the work is in "What mean you by this service?" And what one hears, that the body does ask the "Who" question, it is because the body does not want to degrade itself so. For this reason it asks the "Who" question. It appears to be asking a rational question, but the truth is that, as we have said above, the primary work is in the "What."

## 20. *LISHMA* (FOR HER NAME)

I heard in 1945

Concerning *Lishma* (for Her Name). In order for a person to obtain *Lishma*, one needs an awakening from Above, because it is an illumination from Above, and it is not for the human mind to understand. But he that tastes knows. It is said about that, **"Taste and see that the Lord is good."**

Because of that, upon assuming the burden of the Kingdom of Heaven, one needs it to be in utter completeness, meaning only to bestow and not at all to receive. And if a person sees that his organs do not agree with this view, he has no other counsel except for prayer–to pour his heart out to the Creator, to help him make his body consent to enslaving itself to the Creator.

And do not say that if *Lishma* is a gift from Above, then what good is one's surmounting and efforts and all the remedies and corrections that one performs in order to come to *Lishma*, if it depends on the Creator? Our sages said in that regard, "You are not free to rid yourself of it." Rather, one must offer the awakening from below, and that is considered "prayer." There cannot be a genuine prayer if he does not know in advance that without prayer it cannot be attained.

Therefore, the acts and the remedies that he performs in order to obtain *Lishma* create the corrected vessels to want to receive *Lishma*. Then, after all the deeds and the remedies can he pray in earnest because he saw that all his deeds brought him no benefit. Only then can he pray an honest prayer from the bottom of his heart, and then the Creator hears his prayer and gives him the gift of *Lishma*.

We should also know that by obtaining *Lishma*, one puts the evil inclination to death. This is because the evil inclination is called receiving for one's own benefit. And by attaining the aim to bestow, one cancels the self-gratification. And death means that one no longer uses one's vessels of reception for oneself. And since it is no longer active, it is considered dead.

If one considers what one receives for his work under the sun, one will find that it is not so difficult to subordinate oneself to the Creator, for two reasons:

1. One must strain oneself in this world in any case, whether one wants to or not.
2. Even during the work, if one works *Lishma*, one receives pleasure from the work itself.

It is as the Sayer from Dubna says about the verse, "Though has not called upon me oh Jacob, neither has thou worried thyself about me oh Israel." It means that he who works for the creator has no effort. On the contrary, one has pleasure and elation.

But he who does not work for the Creator, but for other goals, cannot complain to the Creator for not giving him liveliness in the work, since he is working for another goal. One can complain only to the one he works for, and demand to be given vitality and pleasure during his work. It is said about him: "Anyone that trusts them shall be like them that maketh them."

Do not be surprised that when one assumes the burden of the Kingdom of Heaven, when he wants to work in order to bestow upon the Creator, that he still feels no vitality at all, and that this vitality would compel one to assume the burden of the Kingdom of Heaven. Rather, one should accept it coercively, against his better judgment. Meaning, the body does not agree to this enslavement, why the Creator does not shower him with vitality and pleasure.

In fact, this is a great correction. Were it not for that, if the will to receive had agreed to this work, one would never have been able to obtain *Lishma*. Rather, he would always work for his own benefit, to satisfy his own desires. It is as people say, that the thief himself yells, "Catch the thief." And then you cannot tell which is the real thief in order to catch him and reclaim the theft.

But when the thief, meaning the will to receive, does not find the work of accepting the burden of the Kingdom of Heaven tasteful, since the body accustoms itself to work against its own desire, one has the means by which to come to work only in order to bring contentment to one's Maker, since one's sole intention should be only for the Creator, as it says, "Then shalt thou delight thyself in the Lord." Thus, when he served the Creator in the past, he did not sense any pleasure in the work. Rather his work was done by coercion.

However, now that one has accustomed oneself to work in order to bestow, one is rewarded with delighting in the Creator, and the work itself renders one pleasure and vitality. And this is considered that the pleasure, too, is specifically for the Creator.

## 21. WHEN ONE FEELS ONESELF IN A STATE OF ASCENT

I heard on *Heshvan* 23, November 9, 1944

When one feels oneself in a state of ascent, that he is high-spirited, when he feels that he has no desire but only for spirituality, it is then good to delve in the secrets of the Torah, to attain its internality. Even if one sees that although one exerts oneself to understand anything, and still does not know anything, it is still worthwhile to delve in the secrets of the Torah, even a hundred times in a single thing.

One should not despair, meaning say that it is useless since he does not understand anything. This is so for two reasons:

A) When one studies some issue and yearns to understand it, that yearning is called "a prayer." This is because a prayer is a lack, meaning that one is craving what he lacks, that the Creator will satisfy his desire.

The extent of the prayer is measured by the desire, since the thing that one needs most, the desire for it is greater. For according to the measure of the need, so is the measure of the yearning.

There is a rule that in the thing that one makes the most effort, the exertion increases the desire, and one wants to receive fulfillment for one's deficiency. Also, a desire is called "a prayer," "the work in the heart," since "the Merciful One wants the hearts."

It turns out that then one can give a true prayer because when one studies the words of the Torah, the heart must be freed from other desires and give the mind the strength to be able to think and scrutinize. If there is no desire in the heart, the mind cannot scrutinize, as our sages said, "One always learns where one's heart desires."

In order for one's prayer to be accepted, it must be a whole prayer. Hence, when scrutinizing in a whole measure, one educes from it a whole prayer, and then one's prayer can be accepted, because the Creator hears a prayer. But there is a condition: the prayer must be a whole prayer, and not have other things mixed in the middle of the prayer.

B) The second reason is that at that time, since one is separated from corporeality to some extent, and is closer to the attribute of bestowal, the time is better suited to connect with the interior of the Torah, which appears to those who have equivalence with the Creator. This is because the Torah, the Creator, and Israel are one. However, when one is in a state of self-reception he belongs to the externality, and not to the internality.

## 22. TORAH *LISHMA* (FOR HER NAME)

I heard on February 6, 1941

Torah is called *Lishma* primarily when one learns in order to know with utter certainty, within reason, without any doubts of lucidity of the truth, that there is a judge and there is judgment. There is a judgment means that one sees reality as it appears to our eyes. This means that when we work in faith and bestowal, we see that we are growing and climbing daily, since we always see a change for the better.

Conversely, when we work in a form of reception and knowledge, we see that we decline every day down to the ultimate lowness in reality.

When examining these two situations we see that there is a judgment and there is a judge. This is because while we do not follow the laws of the Torah of truth, we are instantly punished. In that state we see that there is a just judgment. In other words, we see that this is precisely the best and most capable way to achieve the truth.

This is considered that the judgment is just, that only in this manner can we come to the ultimate goal, to understand within reason, with complete and absolute understanding of which there is no higher, that only by way of faith and bestowal can we achieve the purpose.

Thus, if one studies for this purpose, to understand that there is a judgment and there is a judge, this is called Torah *Lishma* (for Her Name). This is also the meaning of what our sages said, "Great is the study that leads to an act."

It seems that it should have said, "that brings to actions," meaning to be able to do many deeds, in the plural form, and not in singular form. However, the thing is that, as mentioned above, the study should bring one only faith, and faith is called one *Mitzva* (Commandment), which sentences the whole world to merit.

Faith is called "doing," because it is common conduct that one who does some thing, there must first be a reason that compels one to do within the reason. It is like the correlation between the mind and the action.

However, when some thing is above reason, that the reason does not let one do that thing, but to the contrary, then one must say that there is no reason in this act, but only an act. This is the meaning of, "If one performs one *Mitzva*, he is happy, for he has sentenced himself, etc. to a scale of merit." This is the meaning of "Great is the study that leads to an act," meaning an act without reason, called "above reason."

## 23. YOU THAT LOVE THE LORD, HATE EVIL

I heard on *Sivan* 17, June 2, 1931

In the verse, "O ye that love the Lord, hate evil; He preserveth the souls of His saints; He delivered them out of the hand of the wicked," he interprets that it is not enough to love the Creator, and to want to be awarded adhesion with the Creator. One should also hate evil.

The matter of hatred is expressed by hating the evil, called "the will to receive." And one sees that one has no artifice to be rid of it, and at the same time one does not want to accept the situation. And one feels the losses that the evil causes him, and also sees the truth that one cannot annul the evil by himself, since it is a natural force by the Creator, who has imprinted the will to receive in man.

In that state, the verse tells us what one can do, meaning hate evil. And by that the Creator will keep him from that evil, as it is written, "He preserveth the souls of His saints." What is preservation? "He delivered them out of the hand of the wicked." In that state one is already a successful person, since he has some contact with the Creator, be it the tiniest connection.

In fact, the matter of evil remains and serves as an *Achoraim* (Posterior) to the *Partzuf*. But this is only by one's correction: through sincere hatred of evil, it is corrected into a form of *Achoraim*. The hatred comes because if one wants to obtain adhesion with the Creator, then there is a conduct among friends: if two people come to realize that each hates what one's friend hates, and loves what and whom one's friend loves, then they come into a perpetual bonding, as a stake that will never fall.

Hence, since the Creator loves to bestow, the lower ones should also adapt to want only to bestow. The Creator also hates to be a receiver, as He is completely whole and does not need a thing. Thus, man, too, must hate the matter of reception for oneself.

It follows from all the above, that one must bitterly hate the will to receive, for all the ruins in the world come only from the will to receive. And through the hatred, one corrects it and surrenders under the *Kedusha* (Sanctity).

## 24. OUT OF THE HAND OF THE WICKED

I heard on *Av* 5, July 25, 1944,
at the completion of *The Zohar*

It is written, "O ye that love the Lord, hate evil; He preserveth the souls of His saints; He delivered them out of the hand of the wicked." He asks, what is the connection between "hate evil" and "He delivered them out of the hand of the wicked?"

In order to understand that, we must first bring the words of our sages, "The world was not created, but either for complete righteous, or for complete evil." He asks, is it worthwhile creating the world for complete evil, but not worthwhile for incomplete righteous?

He replies: from the perspective of the Creator, nothing has two meanings in the world. It is only from the perspective of the receivers, meaning according to the sensation of the receivers. This means that either the receivers feel a good taste in the world, or they feel a terribly bitter taste in the world.

This is because with every act that they do, they calculate it in advance when they do it, since no act is done purposelessly. Either they want to better their present state or to harm someone. But small things are not worthy of a purposeful operator.

Hence, those who accept the modes of conduct of the Creator in the world, determine it as good or bad depending on how they feel: whether it is good or bad. **Because of that "you that love the Lord,"** who understand that the purpose of creation was to do good to His creatures, in order for them to come to feel it, they understand that it is received precisely by *Dvekut* (Adhesion) and nearing the Creator.

Thus, if they feel any remoteness from the Creator, they call it "bad." In that state, one considers oneself evil, since an intermediary state is unreal. In other words, either one feels the existence of the Creator and His Providence, or one imagines that “The earth is given into the hand of the wicked.”

Since one feels about oneself that he is a man of truth, meaning that he cannot deceive himself and say that he feels when he does not feel, hence, he immediately begins to cry to the Creator to have mercy on him and deliver him from the net of the *Sitra Achra* and all the alien thoughts. Because one is crying earnestly, the Creator hears his prayer. (And perhaps this is the meaning of “The Lord is nigh unto all them that call upon Him in truth.”) At that time “He delivered them out of the hand of the wicked.”

As long as one does not feel one’s true self, meaning the measure of one’s evil to a sufficient amount to awaken one to cry to the Creator out of the affliction that one feels with one’s recognition of evil, one is still unworthy of redemption. This is because one has not yet found the *Kli* (Vessel) to the hearing of the prayer, called “from the bottom of the heart.”

This is so because one still thinks that there is some good in him, meaning he does not descend to the bottom of the heart. In the bottom of the heart one thinks that he still has some good, and he does not notice with what love and fear he relates to the Torah and the *Mitzvot*, and this is why he does not see the truth.

## 25. THINGS THAT COME FROM THE HEART

I heard on *Av* 5, July 25, 1944 during a festive meal for the completion of part of *The Zohar*

Regarding things that come from the heart, enter the heart. Hence, why do we see that even if things have already entered the heart, one still falls from his degree?

The thing is that when one hears the words of Torah from his teacher, he immediately agrees with his teacher, and resolves to observe the words of his teacher with his heart and soul. But afterwards, when he comes out to the world, he sees, covets, and is infected by the multitude of desires roaming the world, and he and his mind, his heart, and his will are annulled before the majority.

As long as he has no power to judge the world to a scale of merit, they subdue him. He mingles with their desires and he is led like sheep to the slaughter. He has no choice; he is compelled to think, want, crave, and demand everything that the majority demands. He then chooses their alien thoughts and their loathsome lusts and desires, which are alien to the spirit of the Torah. In that state he has no strength to subdue the majority.

Instead, there is only one counsel then, to cling to his teacher and to the books. This is called "From the mouth of books and from the mouth of authors." Only by cleaving to them can he change his mind and will for the better. However, witty arguments will not help him change his mind, but only the remedy of *Dvekut* (adhesion), for this is a wondrous cure, as the *Dvekut* reforms him.

Only while one is inside *Kedusha* (Sanctity) can one argue with oneself and indulge in clever polemics, that the mind necessitates that he should always walk on the path of the Creator. However, one should know that even when he is wise and certain that he can already use this wit to defeat the *Sitra Achra* (other side), one must bear in mind that all this is worthless.

This is not an armament that can defeat the war on desire, for all these concepts are but a consequence he has attained after the aforementioned *Dvekut*. In other words, all the concepts upon which he builds his building, saying one must always follow in the path of the Creator, is founded in the *Dvekut* with his teacher. Thus, if he loses the foundation, then all the concepts are powerless, since they will now be lacking the foundation.

Hence, one must not rely on one's own mind, but cleave once more to books and authors, for only that can help him, and no wit and intellect, as they are lifeless.

## 26. ONE'S FUTURE DEPENDS AND IS TIED TO GRATITUDE FOR THE PAST

I heard in 1943

It is written, **"The Lord is high and the low will see,"** that only the low can see the greatness. The letters *Yakar* (Precious) are the letters *Yakir* (will know). It means that one knows the greatness of a thing to the extent that it is precious to one.

One is impressed according to the importance of the thing. The impression brings one to a sensation in the heart, and according to the measure of one's recognition of the importance, to that extent joy is born in him.

Thus, if one knows one's lowness, that one is not more privileged than one's contemporaries, meaning that one sees that there are many people in the world who were not given the strength to work the holy work even in the simplest of ways, even without the intent and in *Lo Lishma* (not for Her Name), even in *Lo Lishma* of *Lo Lishma*, and even in preparation for the preparation of the clothing of *Kedusha* (Sanctity), while he was imparted the desire and the thought to nevertheless occasionally do holy work, even in the simplest possible way, if one can appreciate the importance of it, according to the importance that one ascribes to the holy work, to that extent one should give praise and be grateful for it.

This is so because it is true that we cannot appreciate the importance of being able to sometimes keep the *Mitzvot* of the Creator, even without any intent. In that state one comes to feel elation and joy of the heart.

The praise and the gratitude that one gives for it expand the feelings, and one is elated by every single point in the holy work, and knows who's worker he is, and thus soars ever higher. This is the meaning of what is written, "I thank Thee for the grace that Thou hast made with me," meaning for the past, and by this one can confidently say, and he does say, "and that Thou will do with me."

## 27. WHAT IS "THE LORD IS HIGH AND THE LOW WILL SEE"

I heard on *Shabbat Terumah*, March 5, 1949, Tel-Aviv

"The Lord is high and the low will see." How can there be equivalence with the Creator when man is the receiver and the Creator is the giver? The verse says to that, "The Lord is high and the low..."

If one annuls oneself, then one has no authority that separates him from the Creator. In that state one "will see," meaning he is imparted *Mochin de Hochma*, "and the haughty He knoweth from afar." However, a proud one, meaning one who has one's own authority, is distanced, since one lacks the equivalence.

Lowness is not considered one's lowering of oneself before others. This is humbleness, and one feels wholeness in this work. Rather, lowness means that the world despises one. Precisely when people despise, it is considered lowness. At that time one does not feel any wholeness, for it is a law that what people think affects a person.

Therefore, if people respect him, he feels whole; and those that people despise, they think of themselves as low.

## 28. I SHALL NOT DIE BUT LIVE

I heard in 1943

In the verse, **"I shall not die but live,"** in order for one to achieve the truth, there must be a sensation that if one does not obtain the truth, one feels oneself as **dead**, because he wants to live. This means that the verse, "I shall not die but live" is said about one who wants to obtain the truth.

This is the meaning of "Jonah *Ben* (son of) Amithai." **Jonah** comes from the Hebrew word *Honaa* (Fraud), and ***Ben*** **(son)** from the Hebrew word *Mevin* (Understands). One understands because one always examines the situation one is in and sees that he has deceived himself, and he is not walking on the path of truth.

This is so because truth means to bestow, meaning *Lishma*. The opposite of that is fraud and deceit, meaning only to receive, which is *Lo Lishma*. By that one is later imparted the "Amithai," meaning ***Emet*** **(Truth)**.

This is the meaning of "thine eyes are as doves." *Eynaim* (Eyes) of *Kedusha* (Sanctity), called *Eynaim* of the Holy *Shechina* (Divinity), are *Yonim* (Doves). They deceive us and we think that she has no *Eynaim*, as it is written in the *Holy Zohar*, "A fair maiden with no eyes."

The truth is that one who is awarded the truth sees that she does have eyes. This is the meaning of "A bride whose eyes are handsome, her whole body needs no scrutiny."

## 29. WHEN THOUGHTS COME TO A PERSON

I heard in 1943

"The Lord is thy shade." If one thinks, the Creator too thinks of him. And when the Creator thinks, it is called "the mountain of the Lord." This is the meaning of "Who shall ascend into the mountain of the Lord, and who shall stand in His holy place?" "He that hath clean hands." This is the meaning of "But Moses' hands were heavy," "and a pure heart," which is the heart.

## 30. THE MOST IMPORTANT IS TO WANT ONLY TO BESTOW

I heard after *Shabbat Vayikra*, March 20, 1943

The most important is to not want anything except to bestow because of His greatness, because any reception is flawed. It is impossible to exit reception, but only to take the other extreme, meaning bestowal.

The moving force, meaning the extending force and the force that compels to work, is only His greatness. One must think that, ultimately, the efforts and the labor must be made, but through these forces one can yield some benefit and pleasure. In other words, one can please a limited body with one's work and effort, which is either a passing guest or an eternal one, meaning that one's energy remains in eternity.

This is similar to a person who has the power to build a whole country, and he builds only a hut that is ruined by a strong wind. You find that all the forces were wasted. However, if one remains in *Kedusha* (Sanctity), then all the forces remain in eternity. It is only from this that one should receive one's basis for the work, and all other bases are disqualified.

The force of faith is sufficient for one to work in the form of bestowal. It means that one can believe that the Creator receives one's work, even though one's work is not so important in one's eyes. Nevertheless, the Creator receives everything. If one attributes the work to Him, He welcomes and wants all the works, however they are.

Thus, if one wants to use faith by way of reception, then faith is not enough for him. This means that at that time he has doubts in the faith. The reason is that reception is not the truth, meaning in fact, one has nothing from the work; only the Creator will have from his work.

Therefore, one's doubts are true. In other words, these alien thoughts that surface in one's mind are true arguments. However, if one wants to use faith to walk in ways of bestowal, he will certainly have no doubts in the faith. If one has doubts, one must know that he probably does not want to walk on a way of bestowal, because for bestowal, faith is enough.

## 31. ALL THAT PLEASES THE SPIRIT OF THE PEOPLE

I heard

All that pleases the spirit of the people. He asked, "But we have found that the greatest and most renowned were in disagreement. Thus, the spirit of the people is not pleased with it."

He answered that they did not say "all the people," but "the spirit of the people." It means that only the bodies are in disagreement, meaning that each is working with the will to receive.

However, "the spirit of the people" is already spirituality. And "pleases"—that the righteous that extends the bounty extends for the whole generation. And only because they have not yet clothed their spirit, they cannot attain and feel the bounty that the righteous extended.

## 32. A LOT IS AN AWAKENING FROM ABOVE

I heard on *Terumah* 4, February 10, 1943

A lot is an awakening from above, when the lower one does not assist in anything. This is the meaning of "cast Pur," "the lot." Haman was complaining and said, "neither keep they the king's laws."

It means that enslavement begins for the worker in a state of *Lo Lishma* (not for Her Name), meaning for self-reception. Hence, why was the Torah given to them, because afterwards they are granted *Lishma* (for Her Name) and they are given the Lights and the attainment of supremacy?

Then comes the complainant and asks, "Why are they given these sublime things for which they did not work and did not hope, but their every thoughts and goals were only things that concern their own needs, called *Lo Lishma*"? This is the meaning of "The wicked may prepare it, but the just will wear it."

It means that he was previously working in a state of wicked, meaning *Lo Lishma*, but for the receiver. Afterwards he was awarded *Lishma*, meaning that all the work enters the domain of *Kedusha* (Sanctity), meaning everything to bestow. This is the meaning of, "the just will wear it."

This is the meaning of *Purim* as *Yom Kippurim* (Day of Atonement). *Purim* is an awakening from Above, and *Yom Kippurim* is an awakening from below, meaning through repentance. However, there is awakening from Above there, too, corresponding to the lots that were there, "one lot for the Lord, and the other lot for Azazel," and the Creator is the scrutinizer.

## 33. THE LOTS ON *YOM KIPPURIM* AND WITH HAMAN

I heard on *Terumah* 6, February 12, 1943

It is written (Leviticus 16:8), "And Aaron shall cast lots upon the two goats: one lot for the Lord, and the other lot for Azazel." With Haman it is written (Esther 3:7), "they cast Pur, that is, the lot."

A lot applies where there cannot be a scrutiny in the mind because the mind does not reach there to be able to sort out which is good and which is evil. In that state a Pur is cast, when they rely not on their mind, but on what the lot tells them. It follows that when using the word "lot," it comes to tell us that now we are going above reason.

Regarding the seventh of *Adar* (sixth day of the Hebrew calendar), on which Moses was born and on which Moses died, we must understand what *Adar* means. It comes from the word *Aderet* (mantle), as it is written about Elijah (Kings 1 19:19) "and cast his mantle upon him." *Aderet* comes from the word *Aderet Se'ar* (hair), which are discerned as *Se'arot* (hair) and *Dinim* (judgments), which are alien thoughts and ideas in the work, distancing one from the Creator.

Here there is a matter of overcoming them. And although one sees many contradictions found in His Providence, one should still overcome them through faith above reason, and say that they are benevolent Providence. This is the meaning of what is written about Moses, "And Moses hid his face." It means that he saw all the contradictions and held them through exertion by the power of faith above reason.

It is as our sages said, "In return for **'And Moses hid his face; for he was afraid to look'** he was rewarded with, **'and the similitude of the Lord doth he behold.'**" This is the meaning of, "Who is blind, but My servant? Or deaf, as My messenger?"

It is known that *Eynaim* (eyes) are called "reason," "mind," meaning the mind's eyes. This is because with something that we perceive in the mind, we say, "but we see that the mind and the reason necessitate that we say so."

Hence, one who goes above reason is as one who has no eyes, and he is called "blind," meaning pretends to be blind. Also, one who does not want to hear what the spies tell him and pretends to be deaf is called "deaf." This is the meaning of "Who is blind, but My servant? Or deaf, as My messenger?"

However, when one says, "that have eyes, and see not, that have ears, and hear not," it means that he does not want to obey what the reason necessitates, and what the ears hear, as it is written about Joshua the son of Nun, that a bad thing never entered his ears. This is the meaning of *Aderet Se'ar*, that he had many contradictions and judgments. Each contradiction is called *Se'ar* (hair), and under each *Se'ar* there is a dent.

It means that one makes **a dent in the head,** meaning **the alien thought fissures and punctures one's head.** When one has many alien thoughts it is considered having many *Se'arot*, and this is called *Aderet Se'ar*.

This is the meaning of what is written about Elisha: "So he departed thence, and found Elisha the son of Shaphat, who was plowing with twelve yoke of oxen before him, and he with the twelfth; and Elijah passed over unto him, and cast his mantle upon him" (Kings 1, 19). (Yoke means a pair of *Bakar* (oxen), since they were plowing with pairs of oxen together that were tightened. This is called a yoke.) *Baker* means *Bikoret* (criticism), and twelve refers to the completeness of the degree (like twelve months and twelve hours).

It means that one already has all the discernments of the *Se'arot* that can be in the world, and then **form the *Se'arot*, the *Aderet Se'ar* is made**. However, with Elisha, it was in the form of the morning of Josef, as it is written, "As soon as the morning was light, the men were sent away, they and their asses."

It means that one has already been awarded the Light that rests over these contradictions, since through the contradictions, called criticism, when wanting to overpower them, it is by drawing Light on them. It is as it is written, "He that comes to purify is aided."

Because one has already drawn the Light on all the criticism, and has nothing more to add, since all the criticism has been completed in him, then the criticism and the contradictions in him end by themselves. This follows the rule that there is no purposeless operation, since there is no purposeless operator.

We must know that what appears to one as things that contradict the guidance of "Good that Doeth Good," is only to compel one to draw the Upper Light on the contradictions, when wanting to prevail over the contradictions. Otherwise one cannot prevail. This is called "the greatness of the Creator," which one extends when having the contradictions, called *Dinim* (judgments).

It means that the contradictions can be annulled if one wants to overcome them, only if one extends the greatness of the Creator. You find that these *Dinim* cause the drawing of the greatness of the Creator. This is the meaning of what is written, **"and cast his mantle upon him."**

It means that afterwards he attributed the whole mantle of hair to Him, **meaning to the Creator**. It means that now one sees that the Creator gave him this mantle deliberately in order to draw the Upper Light on them.

However, one can only see that later, meaning after one has already been granted the Light that rests on these contradictions and *Dinim* that he had had in the beginning. This is so because he sees that without the hair, meaning the descents, there would not be a place for the Upper Light to be there, as there is no Light without a *Kli* (vessel).

Hence, one sees that all the greatness of the Creator that he had obtained was because of the *Se'arot* and the contradictions he had had. This is the meaning of, "the Lord on high is mighty." It means that the greatness of the Creator is awarded through the *Aderet*, and this is the meaning of, **"Let the high praises of God be in their mouth."**

This means that through the faults in the work of God, it causes one to elevate oneself upward, as without a push one is idle to make a movement. One consents to remain in the state one is in, whereas if one descends to a lower degree than one understands, that gives one the power to prevail, for one cannot stay in such a bad situation, since one cannot consent to remain like that, in the state one has descended to.

For this reason one must always prevail and come out of the state of descent. In that state one must draw upon himself the greatness of the Creator. That, in turn, causes one to extend higher forces from Above, or he will remain in utter lowness. It follows that through the *Se'arot* one gradually discovers the greatness of the Creator, until one finds the Names of the Creator, called "the thirteen attributes of Mercy." This is the meaning of **"and the elder shall serve the younger,"** and **"the wicked shall prepare it, but the just shall wear it,"** and also, **"and thou shalt serve thy brother."**

It means that the whole enslavement, meaning the contradictions that were, appeared to be obstructing the Holy Work, and were working against *Kedusha* (Sanctity). Now, when granted the Light of God, which is placed over these contradictions, one sees the opposite, that they were serving *Kedusha*. This means that through them, there was a place for *Kedusha* to clothe in their dresses. And this is called **"the wicked**

**shall prepare it, but the just shall wear it,"** meaning that they gave the *Kelim* (vessels) and the place for the *Kedusha*.

Now we can interpret what our sages wrote (*Hagiga* 15a), "Rewarded–a righteous. He takes his share and his friend's share in heaven. Convicted–a wicked. He takes his share and his friend's share in hell." It means that one takes the *Dinim* and the alien thoughts of one's friend, which we should interpret over the whole world, meaning that this is why the world was created filled with so many people, each with his own thoughts and opinions, and all are present in a single world.

It is so deliberately, so that each and every one will be incorporated in all of one's friend's thoughts. Thus, when one repents, the profit from it will be *Hitkalelut* (mingling/incorporation/integration).

It is so because when one wants to repent, one must sentence oneself and the entire world to a scale of merit, since he himself is incorporated in all the alien notions and thoughts of the entire world. This is the meaning of, **"Convicted–a wicked. He takes his share and his friend's share in hell."**

It follows that when one was still wicked, called "**Convicted,**" one's own share was of *Se'arot*, contradictions, and alien thoughts. One was also mingled with one's friend's share in hell, meaning he was incorporated in all the notions of all the people in the world.

Therefore, later when one becomes **"Rewarded–a righteous"**, meaning after one repents, he sentences himself and the entire world **"to a scale of merit, he takes his share and his friend's share in heaven."** This is because one must draw Upper Light for the alien thoughts of all the people in the world, too, since he is mingled with them, and he must sentence them to a scale of merit.

This is precisely through extending the Upper Light over these *Dinim* of the public. Although they themselves cannot receive this Light that he had drawn on their behalf because they do not have the prepared *Kelim* for that, but he drew it for them as well.

Yet, we must understand according to the famous rule that one who causes extension of Lights in Upper Degrees, they say that to the extent that one induces Light in the Upper One, one receives from these Lights, too, since he was the cause. Accordingly, the wicked, too, should have received a part of the Lights that they induced in the righteous.

To understand that, we must precede with the matter of the lots. There were two lots, as it is written, **"one lot for the Lord, and the other lot for Azazel."** It is known that a lot is a matter of above reason. Hence, when the lot is above reason it causes the other to be for Azazel.

This is the meaning of "it shall whirl upon the head of the wicked." It is so because he extended the Upper Light through these contradictions. You find that in this manner the greatness of the Creator increases, and for the righteous it is a drawback, since their whole desire is only within reason. And when the Light that comes based on above reason increases, they wither away and become annulled.

Hence, **all the wicked have is their help to the righteous to extend the greatness of the Creator**, and afterwards, when they are annulled. This is called "Rewarded–he takes his share and his friend's share in heaven." (This implies that only one who helped make the correction of creating the reality of appearance of the Light through good deeds, hence this act remains in *Kedusha*. One receives what one induces Above, to make a place for the expansion of the Light. In that state the lower one receives what it causes to the Upper One. However, the contradictions and the *Dinim* are cancelled, since they are replaced by the greatness of the Creator, which appears over the above reason, while they want it to appear specifically on *Kelim* of within reason; and this is why they are annulled. This is how it can be interpreted).

However, the alien thoughts, too, which the public caused to draw greatness over them, that Light remains for them. When they are worthy of receiving, they will receive what each causes the drawing of the Upper Light on them, too.

This is the meaning of "A path that runs through the split of the hair," brought in the Holy *Zohar* (Part 15, and in *The Sulam Commentary* item 33 p.56), which distinguishes between right and left. The two lots that were on *Yom Kippurim*, which is repentance out of fear. Also, there was a lot on *Purim*, which is repentance out of love.

This is so because it was then prior to the building of the Temple, and at that time they needed repentance out of love. But first, there had to be a need for them to repent. This need causes *Dinim* and *Se'arot* (plural for hair). And this is the meaning that Haman was given authority from Above, by way of, I place government over you, that he will rule over you.

This is why it was written that Haman **"had cast pur, that is, the lot,"** on the month of *Adar*, which is the **twelfth**, as it is written "twelve oxen," written with regard to Elisha. It is written, "two rows, six in a row," which is the month of *Adar*, meaning **Aderet Se'ar**, which are the greatest *Dinim*.

By that, Haman knew that he would defeat Israel, since Moses had died on the month of *Adar*. However, he did not know that Moses was born on it, by way of "and they saw that it was good." **It is so because when one strengthens in the toughest situation, one is granted the greatest Lights**, called "the greatness of the Creator."

This is the meaning of **"fine twined linen."** In other words, because they have been granted "the path that runs in the split of the hair," "two rows, six in a row," then **twined**, from the words **a stranger removed**. It means that the *Sitra Achra*, meaning the stranger, is annulled and gone because he has already completed his task.

You find that all the *Dinim* and the contradictions came only to show the greatness of the Creator. Hence, with Jacob, who was a smooth man, without *Se'arot*, it was impossible to disclose the greatness of the Creator, since he had no cause and need to extend them. For this reason Jacob was unable to receive the blessings from Issac, as he had no *Kelim* (Vessels), and there is no Light without a *Kli* (Vessel). This is why Rebecca advised him to take Esau's clothes.

And this is the meaning of **"and his hand had hold on Esau's heel."** This means that although he did not have any hair, he took it from Esau. This is what Isaac saw and said, "the hands are the hands of Esau, but the voice was the voice of Jacob." In other words, Isaac liked the correction that Jacob did and by that his *Kelim* for the blessings were made.

This is the reason that we need such a big world with so many people. It is so that each will be incorporated in his friend. It follows that each individual is incorporated in thoughts and desires of an entire world.

This is why a person is called "a small world" in itself, for the above reason. This is also the meaning of "Not rewarded." This means that when one has still not been purified, "He takes his share and his friend's share in hell." It means that he is incorporated with his friend's hell.

Moreover, even when one has already corrected one's own part of hell, if he has not corrected his friend's share, meaning he has not corrected his part that is incorporated with the world, one is still not considered whole.

Now we understand that although Jacob himself was smooth, without *Se'arot*, **he still held the heel of Esau**. It means that he takes the *Se'arot* by being incorporated with Esau.

Hence, when one is rewarded with correcting them, he takes his friend's share in Heaven, referring to the measure of the greatness of the Upper Light that he had extended over the *Se'arot* of the public. He is awarded that, although the public still cannot receive because their qualification for it is missing.

Now we can understand the argument of Jacob and Esau. Esau said, "I have **enough**," and Jacob said, "I have **everything**," meaning "two rows, six in a row," meaning **within reason and above reason**, which is the will to receive and the Light of *Dvekut* (Adhesion).

Esau said, "I have enough," which is a Light that comes in vessels of reception, within reason. Jacob said that he had everything, meaning both discernments. In other words, he was using the vessels of reception, and also had the Light of *Dvekut*.

This is the meaning of the mixed multitude that made the calf and said, "this is thy god oh Israel," meaning ***Ele*** **(These)** without the ***Mi*** **(who)**, meaning that they wanted to connect only to the *Ele*, and not to the *Mi*. It means that they did not want both, which is the ***Mi*** and the ***Ele***, which together make up the Name ***Elokim*** **(God)**, meaning **enough and everything**. This they did not want.

This is the meaning of the *Cherubim*, which are *Kravia* and *Patia*. One *Cherub* on the one end, which is the discernment of **enough**, and one *Cherub* on the other end, which is the discernment of **everything**. This is also the meaning of "the Voice speaking unto him from between the two cherubim."

But how can that be? After all they are ends, opposite from one another. Still, he still had to make a *Patia* (fool) and thus receive. And this is called above reason: one does what one is told although he does not understand anything that he is told.

Regarding the **"everything,"** called above reason, one should try to work with gladness since through gladness the true measure of the **everything** appears. If one has no gladness, then one should afflict oneself at having no gladness, since this is the primary place of the work, to discover the gladness by working above reason.

Hence, when one has no gladness from this work, one should afflict oneself for it. And this is the meaning of the text, **"whose heart maketh him willing,"** which means being sick and tormented at not having gladness from this work.

This is also the meaning of "because thou didst not serve the Lord thy God with gladness by reason of **the abundance of all things**." Instead, you left the **everything** and took only the **enough**. Hence, in the end you will be far below and without anything, meaning you will lose the **enough** too. However, to the extent that one has the **"everything,"** and is in gladness, to that extent one is imparted the **"enough."**

Accordingly, we should interpret "the women weeping for Tammuz" (Ezekiel 8). Rashi interprets that they had idolatry, that he had lead inside his eyes, and they were heating it to melt the lead out of the eyes.

We should interpret the matter of crying, meaning that they have no gladness because there is dust in the eyes. Dust is *Behina Dalet*, meaning the Kingdom of Heaven, which is faith above reason.

This discernment bears the form of dust, meaning it is unimportant. And this work has the taste of dust, that is, it is as unimportant as is dust. The allegory about the women weeping for Tammuz is that they burn this idolatry so that through the heating, the dust will come out from the lead.

It implies that they are crying for the work that they were given to believe in His benevolent guidance above reason, while within reason they see only contradictions in His guidance. This work is the work of *Kedusha*, and they want to remove the dust, meaning the work of above reason, called "dust." However, the eyes, called "sight," imply seeing His guidance, being **within reason.** And this is called **"idolatry."**

This resembles a person whose trade is to make pots and vessels from earth, whose work is to make clay pots. The order is that first of all, he makes round balls of clay, and then cuts and makes holes in the balls. And when the young son sees what his father is doing he cries, "Father, why are you ruining the balls?" The son does not understand that the father's primary goal is the holes, since only the holes can become receptacles, and the son wants to block the holes that the father made in the balls.

So it is here. This dust inside the eyes, which blocks his vision, so wherever he looks he finds contradictions in Providence. Yet, this is the whole *Kli* by which he can discover the sparks of unconditional love, called "a joy of *Mitzva*." It is said about that, "had the Creator not helped him, he would not have prevailed." It means that if the Creator had not given him these thoughts, he would have been unable to receive any ascension.

## 34. THE PROFIT OF A LAND

I heard on *Tevet* 1942

It is known that nothing appears in its true form, only through its opposite, "as far as light excelleth darkness." This means that everything points to another, and by the opposite of some thing, the existence of its opposite can be perceived.

Hence, it is impossible to attain something in complete clarity if its parallel is absent. For example: it is impossible to estimate and say that something is good, if its opposite is missing, pointing to the bad. It is the same with bitterness and sweetness, love and hate, hunger and satiation, thirst and saturation, adhesion and separation. It turns out that it is impossible to come to love adhesion prior to acquiring the hate of separation.

To be rewarded with the degree of hating separation, one must first know what separation is, meaning what he is separated from, and then one may say that he wants to correct that separation. In other words, one should examine from what and from whom he is separated. After that he can try to amend it and connect himself to the one he has become separated from. If, for example, one understands that he will benefit from joining with Him, then he can assume and know what one loses by remaining separated.

Gain and loss are measured according to the pleasure and the suffering. One stays away from something that causes one suffering, and hates it. The measure of the distance depends on the measure of the suffering, since it is human nature to escape from suffering. Hence, one depends on the other, meaning to the extent of the suffering, one exerts and does all kinds of deeds so as to stay away from it. In other words, the torments cause hate for the thing that induces torments, and to that extent one stays far from it.

It follows that one should know what is equivalence of form in order to know what he must do to achieve adhesion, called "equivalence of form." By that he will come to know what are disparity of form and separation.

It is known from books and from authors that the Creator is benevolent. This means that His guidance appears to the lower ones as benevolence; and this is what we must believe.

Therefore, when one examines the conduct of the world, and begins to examine himself or others, how they suffer under Providence instead of delighting, as is fitting for His

Name—Benevolent—it is then hard for him to say that Providence is benevolent and imparts abundance.

However, we must know that in that state, when they cannot say that the Creator imparts only good, they are considered wicked because suffering makes them condemn their Maker. Only when they see that the Creator imparts them pleasure do they justify the Creator. It is as our sages said, "Who is righteous? He who justifies his Maker," meaning he who says that the Creator leads the world in a **righteous** way.

Thus, when one suffers, one draws far from the Creator, since he naturally becomes hateful of Him who imparts him torments. Consequently, where one should have loved the Creator, he now becomes the opposite, for he has come to hate the Creator.

Accordingly, what should one do in order to come to love the Creator? For that purpose we are granted the remedy of engaging in Torah and *Mitzvot*, for the Light in it reforms. There is Light there, which lets one feel the severity of the state of separation. And slowly, as one intends to acquire the Light of Torah, hatred for separation is created in him. He begins to feel the reason that causes him and his soul to be separated and far from the Creator.

Thus, one must believe that His guidance is benevolent, but since one is immersed in self-love, it induces disparity of form in him, since there was a correction called in order to bestow, called "equivalence of form." Only in this manner can we receive this **delight and pleasure**. The **inability to receive the delight and pleasure** that the Creator wants to give evokes in the receiver hatred for separation, and then one can discern the great benefit in equivalence of form and one begins to yearn for adhesion.

In consequence, every form points to another form. Thus, all the descents where one feels that he has come to separation are an opportunity to discern between something and its opposite. In other words, one should learn the benefits of the ascents from the descents. Otherwise, one would be unable to appreciate the importance of being brought near from Above, and the ascents that he is given. He would not be able to extract the importance that he could extract, as when one is given food without ever having felt hunger.

It turns out that the descents, which are the times of separation, produce the importance of adhesion in the ascents, while the ascents make him hate the descents that the separation causes him. In other words, he cannot assess how bad the descents are, when one speaks slander about Providence and does not even feel whom he slanders, to know that he must repent for such a sin. This is called "slandering against the Creator."

Thus, it follows that precisely when one has both forms can he discern the distance between one and the other, "as far as Light excelleth darkness." Only then can one assess and regard the matter of adhesion, by which the delight and pleasure in the **Thought of Creation** can be acquired, being "His desire to do good to His creations." Everything that appears to our eyes is but what the Creator wants us to attain the way we do, since they are ways by which to achieve the complete goal.

Yet, it is not so simple to acquire adhesion with the Creator. It requires great effort and exertion to acquire the sensation and feeling of delight and pleasure. Before that, one must justify Providence, believe above reason that the Creator behaves in goodness with the creatures, and say, "They have eyes and see not."

Our sages say, "Habakkuk came and ascribed them to one," as it is written, **"The righteous shall live by his faith."** It means that one need not engage oneself in details, but concentrate his entire work on a single point, a **rule**, which is faith in the Creator. This is what he should pray for, meaning that the Creator will help him become capable of advancing in the form of faith above reason. There is power in the faith: through it, one comes to hate the separation. This is considered that faith indirectly makes him hate the separation.

We see that there is a great difference between **faith, seeing, and knowing**. Something that can be seen and known, if the mind necessitates that it is good to do that thing and decides on that once, that decision is enough regarding that thing that he decided on. In other words, he executes in the form that he had decided. This is so because the mind accompanies him in every single act so as not to break what the mind had told him, and lets him understand by one hundred percent, to the extent that the mind brought him to the decision he has reached.

However, faith is a matter of potential agreement. In other words, he overpowers the mind and says that it is indeed worthwhile to work as faith necessitates to work–above reason. Hence, faith above reason is useful only during the act, when he believes. Only then is he willing to exert above reason in the work.

Conversely, when he leaves faith for but a moment, meaning when faith weakens for a brief moment, he immediately ceases the Torah and the work. It does not help him that a short while ago he took upon himself the burden of faith above reason.

However, when he perceives in his mind that this is a bad thing for him, that it is something that risks his life, he needs no repetitive explanations and reasoning why it is a dangerous thing. Rather, since he once fully realized in his mind that he should practice these things, of which the mind tells him specifically which is bad and which is good, he now follows that decision.

We see the difference that exists between what the mind necessitates and what only faith necessitates, and what is the reason that when something is based on faith we must constantly remember the form of the faith, otherwise he falls from his degree into a state of wickedness. These states might happen even in a single day; one may fall from his degree many times in one day because it is impossible that faith above reason will not stop even for a moment during one day.

We must know that the reason for forgetting the faith stems from the fact that faith above the reason and the mind is against all the desires of the body. Since the desires of the body come by the nature imprinted in us, called "will to receive," whether in the mind or in the heart, hence, the body always draws to our nature. Only when cleaved to faith does it have the power to bring him out of the bodily desires and go above reason, meaning against the body's reason.

Hence, before one acquires the vessels of bestowal, called adhesion, faith cannot be found in him on a permanent basis. When faith does not shine for him, he sees that he is in the lowest possible state, and it all comes to him because of the disparity of form, which is the will to receive for himself. This separation causes him all the torments, ruins all the buildings and all the efforts he had put into the work.

He sees that the minute he loses faith, he is in a worse state than when he started on the path of work in bestowal. Thus one acquires hatred for the separation, since he immediately begins to feel torments in himself, and in the entire world. It becomes hard for him to justify His Providence over the creatures, regarding it as benevolent, and then he feels that the whole world has grown dark before him, and he has nothing from which to receive gladness.

Hence, every time one begins to correct the flaw of slandering Providence he acquires hate for the separation. And through the hate that he feels in the separation he comes to love adhesion. In other words, to the extent that he suffers during the separation, so he draws nearer to adhesion with the Creator. Similarly, to the extent that he feels the darkness as bad, he comes to feel that adhesion is a good thing. Then he knows how to value it when he receives some adhesion, for the time being, and then knows how to appreciate it.

Now we can see that all the torments that exist in the world are but a preparation for the real torments. These are the torments that one must reach, or he will not be able to acquire anything spiritual, as there is no Light without a vessel. These torments, the real torments, are called "condemnation of Providence and slandering." This is what one prays for, to not slander Providence, and these are the torments that the Creator accepts. This is the meaning of the saying that the Creator hears the prayer of every mouth.

The reason the Creator responds to these torments is that then one does not ask for help for his own vessels of reception, since we can say that if the Creator grants him everything he wishes, it might bring him farther from the Creator due to the disparity of form that he would thus acquire. Rather, it is to the contrary: one asks for faith, for the Creator to give him strength to prevail and be awarded equivalence of form, for he sees that by not having permanent faith, meaning when faith does not shine for him, he comes to thoughts of doubt about Providence.

That, in turn, brings him to a state called "evil," when he condemns his Maker. It turns out that all the suffering he feels is because he slanders Providence. It turns out that what hurts him is that where he should have been praising the Creator, saying "Blessed is He who has created us in His Glory," meaning that the creatures respect the Creator, he sees that the world's conduct is unfitting for His glory, since everyone complains and demands that first it should be open Providence that the Creator leads the world in benevolence. Since it is not open, they say that this Providence does not glorify Him, and that pains him.

Thus, by the torment one feels, he is compelled to slander. Hence, when he asks of the Creator to impart him the power of faith and to be awarded benevolence, it is not because he wants to receive good so as to delight himself. Rather, it is so that he will not slander; this is what pains him. For himself, he wants to believe above reason that the Creator leads the world in benevolence, and he wants his faith to settle in the sensation as though it is within reason.

Therefore, when he practices Torah and *Mitzvot* he wants to extend the Light of God not for his own benefit, but since he cannot bear not being able to justify His Providence, which is in benevolence. It pains him that he desecrates the name of God, whose name is **Benevolent**, and his body claims otherwise.

This is all that pains him since by being in a state of separation, he cannot justify His guidance. This is considered hating the state of separation. And when he feels this suffering, the Creator hears his prayer, brings him near Him, and he is rewarded with adhesion. This is because the pains that he feels due to the separation make him be rewarded with adhesion; and then it is said, "As far as Light excelleth darkness."

This is the meaning of "the profit of a land every way." **Land** is creation; **every way** means that by the benefit, meaning when we see the difference between the state of separation and the state of adhesion, by that we are granted adhesion with the **every**, since the Creator is called "the root of **every thing**."

## 35. CONCERNING THE VITALITY OF *KEDUSHA*

I heard in 1945, Jerusalem

The verse says (Psalms 104): "Yonder sea, great and wide, therein are creeping things innumerable, living creatures, both small and great."

We should interpret:

1. The **sea** as the sea of the *Sitra Achra*.
2. **Great and wide** means that it manifests itself and shouts "Give, give," referring to great vessels of reception.

3. **Living creatures** means that there are Upper Lights there, which one steps and tramples on with one's feet.
4. **Innumerable**, that there are small with large animals, meaning whether one has small vitality, or whether he has great vitality, it is all in that sea.

This is so because there is a rule that from Above they give giving, and take, they do not take (all that is given from Above is not received in return, but stays below). Hence, if one extends something from Above and then blemishes it, it remains below, but not with man. Instead, it falls to the sea of the *Sitra Achra*.

In other words, if one extends some luminescence and cannot sustain it permanently because one's *Kelim* (Vessels) are not yet clean to be fit for the Light, meaning that one will receive it in vessels of bestowal like the Light that comes from the Giver, the luminescence must depart from him.

At that time this luminescence falls into the hands of the *Sitra Achra*. This continues several times, meaning that one extends, and then it departs from him.

Hence, the illuminations increase in the sea of the *Sitra Achra*, until the cup is full. This means that after one finds the full measure of the effort that one can find, the *Sitra Achra* gives him back everything she had taken into her own authority. This is the meaning of **"He hath swallowed down riches, and he shall vomit them up again."** It follows that all that the *Sitra Achra* had taken into her own authority was only as a deposit, meaning as long as she had command over man.

And the whole matter of the dominion that she has is so that there will be room for one to scrutinize one's vessels of reception and admit them into *Kedusha* (Sanctity). In other words, had she not governed a person, one would settle for little and then one's vessels of reception would remain separated. Thus, one would never be able to gather all the *Kelim* that belong to the root of one's soul, admit them into *Kedusha*, and extend the Light that belongs to him.

Hence, it is a correction that each time one extends something and has a descent, he must begin anew, meaning new scrutinies. And what one had from the past has fallen into the *Sitra Achra*, and she holds it in her authority as a deposit. Afterwards one receives everything that she had received from him this whole time.

Yet, we must also know that if one could sustain any luminescence, even a small one, but if it were permanent, one would already be considered whole. In other words, one would have been able to advance with this illumination. Hence, if one loses the luminescence, one should regret it.

This is similar to a person who placed a seed in the ground so that a big tree would grow from it, but took the seed out of the ground right away. Thus, what is the benefit in the work of putting the seed in the ground?

Moreover, we can say that he not only took out the seed from the ground and corrupted it, we can say that he dug out a tree with ripe fruits out of the ground and corrupted them.

It is the same here: if one had not lost this tiny luminescence, a great Light would have grown out of it. It follows that it is not necessarily that he had lost the power of a small luminescence, but it is as though a great Light indeed had been lost from him.

We must know that it is a rule that one cannot live without liveliness and pleasure, since it stems from the root of creation, which is His desire to do good to His creatures. Hence, every creature cannot exist without liveliness and pleasure. Therefore, every creature must go and look for a place from which it can receive delight and pleasure.

But the pleasure is received in three times: in the past, in the present, and in the future. However, the principal reception of pleasure is in the present. Although we see that one receives pleasure from the past and from the future, too, it is because the past and the future shine in the present.

Therefore, if one does not find a sensation of pleasure in the present, one receives liveliness from the past, and he can tell the others how he was happy in past times. One can receive sustenance from that in the present, or picture for oneself that he hopes that in the future he will be happy. But measuring the sensation of the pleasure from the past and the future depends on the extent to which they shine for one in the present. Also, we must know that this occurs both in corporeal pleasures and in spiritual pleasures.

As we see, when one works, even in corporeality, the order is that during the work one is unhappy because he exerts himself. And one can only continue in the work because the future shines for him, when he will receive the payment for his work. This shines for a person in the present, and this is why he can continue the work.

However, if one is unable to picture the reward that he will receive in the future, one must take pleasure from the future, not from the reward that he will receive for his work in the future. In other words, he will not enjoy the reward, but he will not feel suffering from the exertion. This is what he enjoys now, in the present, what he will have in the future.

The future shines for him in the present, **in that soon the work will be over**, meaning the time that he must work, and he will receive rest. Thus, the pleasure of rest that one will ultimately receive still shines for him. In other words, one's profit will be that he will not be afflicted by what he now feels from the work. And this gives him the strength to be able to work now.

If one is unable to picture for oneself that soon he will be rid of the torments that he suffers now, one will come to despair and sadness, and that state can bring one to take one's own life.

This is why our sages said, "One who takes one's life has no part in the next world," because he denies Providence, that the Creator leads the world in a form of "good that doeth good." Instead, one should believe that these states come to him because Above they want it to bring him *Tikkun* (Correction), meaning that one will collect *Reshimot* (reminiscence) from these states so that he will be able to understand the conduct of the world more intensely and more strongly.

These states are called ***Achoraim*** **(Posterior)**. And when one overcomes these states, he will be awarded the discernment of ***Panim*** **(Anterior)**, meaning that the Light shines into these *Achoraim*.

There is a rule that one cannot live if one has no place from which to receive delight and pleasure. Thus, when one is unable to receive from the present, one must still receive sustenance from the past or from the future. In other words, the body seeks sustenance for itself in every means at its disposal.

Then, if one does not agree to receive sustenance from corporeal things, the body has no choice but to agree to receive sustenance from spiritual things because it has no other choice.

Hence, it must agree to receive delight and pleasure from vessels of bestowal, since it is impossible to live without sustenance. It follows that when one is accustomed to keeping Torah and *Mitzvot Lo Lishma* (not for Her Name), meaning to receive reward for one's work, one has an ability to picture receiving some reward later on, and one can already work on the calculation that he will receive delight and pleasure afterwards.

However, if one works not in order to be rewarded, but wants to work without any reward, how can one picture for oneself having anything from which to receive sustenance? After all, one cannot create any picture, because he has nothing to do it on.

Hence, in *Lo Lishma*, there is no necessity to give one sustenance from Above, since one has sustenance from the picture of the future, and **Only necessity is given from Above, not luxury**. Hence, if one wants to work only for the Creator and has no wish whatsoever to take sustenance for other things, there is no other counsel, but he must be given sustenance from Above. This is so because one demands only the bare necessity to go on living, and then one receives sustenance from the structure of the Holy Divinity.

It is as our sages said, "Anyone who is saddened for the public is rewarded and sees the comfort of the public." The public is called "The Holy *Shechina* (Divinity)," since public means a collective, meaning the assembly of Israel, since *Malchut* is the collection of all the souls.

Since one does not want any reward for oneself, but wants to work for the Creator, which is called "raising Divinity from the dust," so it will not be lowered so, meaning that they do not want to work for the Creator, but all that one sees that will produce benefit for oneself, then there is fuel for the work. And what concerns the benefit of the Creator, and one does not see what reward he will receive in return, the body objects to this work because it feels a taste of dust in this work.

Such a person does want to work for the Creator, but the body resists it. And one asks of the Creator to give him power to nonetheless be able to work to raise Divinity from the dust. Hence, one is awarded the *Panim* (face) of the Face of the Creator, which appear to him, and the concealment departs from him.

## 36. WHAT ARE THE THREE BODIES IN A MAN

I heard on *Adar* 24, March 19, 1944

Man is made of three bodies:

A. The inner body, which is a clothing for the soul of *Kedusha* (Sanctity).

B. The *Klipa* of *Noga* (Shell).

C. The serpent's skin.

In order to save one from the two bodies, so that they do not interfere with the *Kedusha*, and in order for one to be able to use only the inner body, the counsel for that is that there is a remedy—to contemplate solely on things that concern the inner body.

That means that one's thought should always remain in the singular authority, meaning "there is none else besides him." Rather, He does and will do all the deeds, and there is no creation in the world that can detach him from the *Kedusha*.

And because one does not think for those two bodies, they die, because they have no nourishment and nothing to sustain them, since the thoughts we think for them are their provision. This is the meaning of "in the sweat of thy face shalt thou eat bread." Prior to the sin of the Tree of Knowledge, sustenance was not dependent on the bread. That is, there was no need to extend Light and sustenance, but it illuminated.

However, after the sin, when *Adam ha Rishon* had been affixed to the serpent's body, then life had been tied in with the bread, meaning with nourishment that must always draw anew. And if they are not given nourishment, they die. And this became a great correction, in order to be saved from those two bodies.

Thus one must try with all one's might not to think thoughts that concern them, and perhaps this is what our sages said, "thoughts of transgression are harder than a transgression," because thoughts are their nourishment. In other words, they receive sustenance from the thoughts one thinks for them.

Hence, one must think only for the inner body, for it is a clothing for the soul of *Kedusha*. That means that one should think thoughts that are after one's skin. This means that after the body's skin is called outside one's body, meaning outside one's own benefit, but only thoughts of benefiting others. And this is called "after one's skin."

This is so because after one's skin, there is no grip for the *Klipot* (plural for *Klipa*), for the *Klipot* hold only that which is within one's skin, meaning that which belongs to one's body, and not outside one's body, called "outside one's skin." That means that they possess anything that comes within the clothing of the body, and they cannot hold anything that is not clothed within the body.

When one persists with thoughts that are after one's skin, one is awarded what is written, **"And when after my skin this is destroyed, then without my flesh shall I see God"** (Job 19, 26). "This" is the Holy Divinity, and she stands after one's skin. "Destroyed" means that it has been corrected to stand "after my skin." At that time one is awarded **"without my flesh shall I see God."**

It means that *Kedusha* comes and clothes the interior of the body, specifically when one agrees to work outside one's skin, meaning without any clothing. The wicked, however, who want to work precisely at a time when there is clothing in the body, called within the skin, then they will die without wisdom. This is because then they have no clothing and they are not awarded anything. However, it is specifically the righteous that are rewarded with clothing within the body.

## 37. AN ARTICLE FOR *PURIM*

I heard in 1948

We must understand several precisions in the *Megilla*[2]:

1. It is written, "After these things did King Ahasuerus promote Haman." We must understand what is "After these things," meaning after Mordecai had saved the king. It seems reasonable that the King should have

2 *Megillat Esther (Scroll of Esther)*, referring to *The Book of Esther*

promoted Mordecai. But what does it say? That He promoted Haman.

2. When Esther told the king, "for we are sold, I and my people," the king asked, "Who is he and where is he?" It means that the king knew nothing of it, although it explicitly says that the king told Haman, "The silver is given to thee, the people also, to do with them as it seemeth good to thee." Thus, we see that the king did know of the sale.
3. About "according to every man's wish," our sages said (*Megilla* 12), "Rabba said, 'to do according to the will of Mordecai and Haman.'" It is known that where it says only "King" it refers to The King of the world. Thus, how can it be that the Creator will do as the will of a wicked one?
4. It is written, "Mordecai knew all that was done." It means that only Mordecai knew, since prior to that, it states, "but the city of Shushan was perplexed." Thus, the whole city of Shushan knew about it.
5. It is written, "for the writing which is written in the king's name, and sealed with the king's ring, may no man reverse." Thus, how did he give the second letters afterwards, which ultimately cancel the first letters?
6. What does it mean that our sages said, "On *Purim*, one must intoxicate until one cannot tell the cursed Haman from the blessed Mordecai"?
7. What does it mean that our sages said about the verse, "And the drinking was according to the law," what is "according to the law?" Rabbi Hanan said on behalf of Rabbi Meir, "according to the law of Torah." What is the law of Torah? More eating than drinking.

To understand the above, we must first understand the matter of Haman and Mordecai. Our sages said about the verse, "according to every man's wish," meaning Haman and Mordecai. We should interpret that Mordecai's wish is called "the rule of Torah," which is more eating than drinking, and Haman's wish is the opposite, more drinking than eating.

We asked, "How can it be that He would make a meal according to the will of a wicked one"? The answer to that is written next to it: "none did compel." It means that the drinking was not coercive, and this is the meaning of, "none did compel."

It is as our sages said about the verse, "And Moses hid his face; for he was afraid to look." They said that in return for "And Moses hid his face," he was rewarded, "and the similitude of the Lord doth he behold." This means that precisely because he did not need that (meaning he could make a *Masach* (Screen) over it), hence he was permitted to receive. It is also written, "I have laid help upon one that is mighty." It means that the Creator gives help to one who is mighty and can walk in the ways of God.

It is written, **"And the drinking was according to the law."** What is "according to the law?" Because "none did compel." It means that he did not need the drinking, but once they started to drink, they were taken after it. This implies that they were tied to the drinking, meaning they needed the drinking, or else they would not be able to move forward.

This is called **"compel,"** and this is considered that they had cancelled the method of Mordecai. This is also the meaning of what our sages said, that that generation was sentenced to perish because they enjoyed the meal of a wicked one.

In other words, had they received the drinking in the form of, "none did compel," they would not have annulled Mordecai's wish, and this is the method of Israel. However, afterwards, when they took the drink in a form of "did compel," it follows that they themselves sentenced **the law of Torah** to perish, which is the discernment of Israel.

This is the meaning of more eating than drinking. The matter of drinking refers to disclosing *Hochma* (Wisdom), called "knowing." Eating, on the other hand, is called *Ohr de Hassadim* (Light of Mercy), which is faith.

This is the meaning of Bigthan and Teresh, who sought to lay hands on the king of the world. "And the thing became known to Mordecai… … inquisition was made of the matter, and it was found to be so." The matter of seeking was not at once, and Mordecai did not obtain it easily, but after great labor **was the matter of this flaw revealed to him**. Once it had become evident to him, **"they were both hanged," meaning after the sensation of the blemish in it,** they were **hanged**, meaning they removed these actions and desires from the world.

"After these things," meaning after all the labor and the exertions Mordecai had made by the scrutiny that he had made, the king wanted to reward him for his effort of working only *Lishma* (for Her Name) and not for himself. Since there is a rule that the lower one cannot receive anything without a need, as there is no Light without a vessel, and a vessel is called a need, since it is not a need for oneself, how can anything be given to him?

Had the king asked Mordecai what he should give him for his labor, and since Mordecai is a righteous one, whose work is only to bestow without any need to ascend in degrees, but he contents himself with little, the king wished to give the Light of Wisdom, which extends from the left line, and Mordecai's work was only from the right line.

What did the king do? He promoted Haman, meaning he made the left line important. This is the meaning of **"and set his seat above all the ministers."** In addition, he gave him the power, meaning all the king's slaves kneeled and bowed before Haman, **"for the king had so commanded,"** that he would receive control, and everyone accepted him.

The matter of kneeling is the acceptance of the ruling, because they liked Haman's way in the work more than Mordecai's way. All the Jews in Shushan accepted Haman's sovereignty until it was hard for them to understand Mordecai's views. After all, everyone understands that the work of walking in the left line, called **knowing**, is easier for walking in the ways of the Creator.

It is written that they asked, **"Why transgressest thou the king's commandment?"** Since they saw that Mordecai persisted with his opinion of walking in the way of **faith, they became perplexed**, and did not know which side was right.

They went and asked Haman who was right, as it is written, "**they told Haman,** to see whether Mordecai's words would stand; for he had told them that he was a **Jew**." It means that the way of the Jew is more eating than drinking, meaning **faith** is the rudiment, and this is the whole basis of Judaism.

This caused Haman a great disturbance; why would Mordecai not agree with his view? Hence, when everyone saw Mordecai's way, who argued that he alone was taking the path of Judaism, and those who take another path are considered to be idol worshipping, it is written, **"Yet all this availeth me nothing, so long as I see Mordecai the Jew sitting at the king's gate."** This is because Mordecai claims that only through him is **the gate to the king**, not that of Haman.

Now we can understand why it is written, "Mordecai knew," meaning that it is specifically Mordecai who knew. **But it is written, "but the city of Shushan was perplexed,"** meaning everybody knew.

We should interpret that the city of Shushan was perplexed and did not know who was right, but **Mordecai knew** that if there would be Haman's dominion, that would be the annihilation of the people of Israel. In other words, he would obliterate the whole of Israel from the world, meaning the people of Israel's way of Judaism, whose basis of the work is faith above reason, called "covered Mercy," to go with the Creator with eyes shut, and to always say about oneself, "they have eyes and see not," since Haman's whole grip is on the left line, called knowing, which is the opposite of faith.

This is the meaning of the lots that Haman cast, as it was on *Yom Kippurim* (Day of Atonement), as it is written, "one lot for the Lord, and the other lot for Azazel." The lot for the Lord means a discernment of "right," which is *Hassadim* (Mercy), called "eating," which is faith. The lot for Azazel is the left line, which is in fact considered "good for nothing," and all the *Sitra Achra* (Other Side) stems from here.

Hence, a blockage on the Lights extends from the left line, as only the left line freezes the Lights. This is the meaning of **"cast pur, that is, the lot,"** meaning it interprets what it casts. It says "*pur*," which concerns ***Pi Ohr*** (a Mouth of Light, pronounced *Pi Ohr*).

All the Lights were blocked through the lot for *Azazel*, and you find that he cast all the Lights down. Haman thought that **"the righteous shall prepare it and the wicked shall wear it."** In other words, Haman thought, concerning all the efforts and the exertions that Mordecai had made along with all who accompanied him, the reward that they deserve, Haman thought that he would take that reward.

It means that Haman thought that he would take the Lights that appear through the corrections of Mordecai into his own dominion. All that was because he saw that the king gave him the power to extend Light of Wisdom below. Hence, when he came to the king saying "to destroy the Jews," meaning revoke Israel's dominion, which is faith and Mercy, and make knowledge disclosed in the world, the king had replied to him: **"The silver is given to thee, the people also, to do with them as it seemeth good to thee,"** meaning as Haman sees fit, according to his dominion, which is **left and knowing.**

The whole difference between the first and the second letters is in the word "**Jews.**" In "The copy of the writing" (the copy refers to the content that came out from before the king. Afterwards, the copy of the writing is interpreted, explaining the intention of the copy) it was said, **"to be given out for a decree in every province, was to be published unto all peoples, that they should be ready against that day."** It does not say who are destined, but Haman interpreted the copy of the writing, as it is written, **"and there was written, according to all that Haman commanded."**

The word **Jews** is written in the second letters, as it is written, "The copy of the writing, to be given out for a decree in every province, was to be published unto all the peoples, and that **the Jews** should be ready against that day to avenge themselves on their enemies."

Hence, when Haman came before the king, the king told him that the silver that had been pre-prepared is given to you, meaning you need not do anything more since "the people also [given to thee], to do with them as it seemeth good to thee."

In other words, the people already wants to do as seemeth good to thee, meaning the people wants to receive your dominion. Yet, the king did not tell him to revoke the dominion of Mordecai and the Jews. Instead, it had been preordained that now, at this time, there will be a disclosure of *Hochma*, which is as finding grace in your eyes.

The copy of the writing, "to be given out for **a decree** in every province, was to be published unto all peoples." It means that the **decree** was that it will be published **that the matter of the disclosure of *Hochma*** (is) **for all the nations.**

However, it did not say that the discernment of Mordecai and the Jews would be revoked, which is faith. Instead, the intention was that there would be disclosure of *Hochma* (Wisdom), but they would still choose *Hassadim* (Mercy).

Haman said that since now is the time of disclosure of *Hochma*, the disclosure of *Hochma* is certainly now given so as to use the *Hochma*, as who is it who does something that is not for use? If it is not used, it follows that the operation was in vain. Hence, it must be the will of God, and the Creator had made that disclosure so as to use the *Hochma*.

Mordecai's argument was that the matter of the disclosure is only to show that what they take for themselves, to walk in the right line, which is concealed *Hassadim*, is not because there is no choice and this is why they take this path.

This seems like coercion, meaning that they have no other choice since presently there is no revealed *Hochma*. Instead, now that there is revealed *Hochma* there is room for choosing of their own free will. In other words, they choose a path of *Hassadim* more than the left, which is the disclosure of *Hochma*.

This means that the disclosure was only so they could reveal the importance of *Hassadim*, that it was more important to them than *Hochma*. It is as our sages said, **"thus far coercively, henceforth willingly."** And this is the meaning of **"the Jews ordained, and took upon them."** It follows that the disclosure of *Hochma* came now only so they would be able to receive the method of the Jew willingly.

And that was the dispute between Mordecai and Haman. Mordecai's argument was that what we now see, that the Creator reveals the dominion of *Hochma*, is only so that they would receive the *Hochma*, but in order to better the *Hassadim*.

It means that now they will have a place to show that their reception of the *Hassadim* is voluntary, meaning they have room to receive *Hochma*, since now is the time of the dominion of the left, which shines *Hochma*, and still they choose *Hassadim*. It follows that they now show—by receiving the *Hassadim*—that the right rules the left.

Thus, the **Jewish decree** is the important one, and Haman claimed the opposite, that the Creator's current disclosure of the left line, which is *Hochma*, is in order to use the *Hochma*. Otherwise, it would mean that the Creator had done something needlessly, meaning that He had done something and there is no one to enjoy it. Hence, we should not regard what Mordecai says, but everyone should listen to his voice, and use the disclosure of *Hochma* that now appeared.

It follows that the second letters did not revoke the first. Rather, they presented an explanation and interpretation to the first copy of the writing, that the matter of the publication to all the peoples, the matter of the disclosure of the *Hochma* that now shines, is **for the Jews**. In other words, it is so that the Jews would be able to choose *Hassadim* of their own free will, and not because there is no other path to choose.

This is why it is written in the second letters, **"and that the Jews should be ready against that day to avenge themselves on their enemies."** It means that the dominion that *Hochma* now has is in order to show that they prefer *Hassadim* to *Hochma*, and this is called "to avenge themselves on their enemies." This is because their enemies want *Hochma* specifically, whereas the Jews reject the *Hochma*.

Now we can understand what we have asked about the question of the king, "Who is he, and where is he, that durst presume in his heart to do so?" And why did He ask? After all, the king himself had told Haman, **"The silver is given to thee, the people also, to do with them as it seemeth good to thee."**

(It is as we have said that the meaning is that the matter of disclosing *Hochma* is with the intention that the people will do as seemeth good to thee, meaning that there would be room for choice. And this is called "the people also, to do with them as it seemeth good to thee." However, if there is no disclosure of *Hochma*, there is no room for choice, but the *Hassadim* that they take, it seems that it is because they have no choice.)

It means that all this came about because the king gave the order that now would be the time of disclosing *Hochma*. The intention was that the left would serve the right. By that it would become apparent that the right is more important than the left, and this is why they choose *Hassadim*.

This is the meaning of ***Megillat Esther***. There seems to be a contradiction in terms here, since ***Megilla*** **(Scroll)** means that it is *Galui* (revealed) to all, while ***Esther*** means that there is *Hastara* (Concealment). However, we should interpret that the whole disclosure is in order to give room to choose concealment.

Now we can understand what our sages wrote, **"On *Purim*, one must intoxicate until one cannot tell between the cursed Haman and the blessed Mordecai."** The matter of Mordecai and Esther was prior to the Second Temple, and the building of the temple signifies the extension of *Hochma*, and ***Malchut*** is called "The Temple."

This is the meaning of Mordecai sending Esther to go to the king and ask for her people, and she replied, "all the king's servants," etc., "who is not called, there is one law for him, that he be put to death," etc., "but I have not been called to come in unto the king these thirty days."

It means that it is forbidden to extend the discernment of *GAR de Hochma* below, and one who does extend *GAR* (which are three *Sefirot*, each comprising ten, which are thirty), is sentenced to death, because the left line causes separation from the life of lives.

"Except such to whom the king shall hold out the golden scepter, that he may live." Gold means *Hochma* and *GAR*. It means that only by the awakening of the Upper One can one remain alive, meaning in *Dvekut* (adhesion), called life, but not by the awakening of the lower one.

Although Esther is *Malchut*, who needs *Hochma*, it is only by the awakening of the Upper One. However, if she extends *Hochma* she loses herself entirely. In that regard, Mordecai had told her, "(if) then will relief and deliverance arise to the Jews from another place," meaning by completely revoking the left line, and the Jews will have only the right line, which is *Hassadim*, then **"thou and thy father's house will perish."**

In the form of "Father founded the daughter," then she must have *Hochma* within her. But it must be more eating than drinking. However, if the Jews have no counsel, they will have to revoke the left line, and thus her whole self would be annulled. It is about that that she said, **"if I perish, I perish."**

In other words, if I go, I am lost, because I might come to severance, as when the lower one awakens it induces separation from the life of lives. And if I do not go "then will relief and deliverance arise to the Jews from another place," meaning in another way. They would revoke the left line entirely, as Mordecai had told her. This is why she took the path of Mordecai by inviting Haman to the feast, which means that she extended the left line as Mordecai had told her.

Afterwards she incorporated the left in the right and thus there could be disclosure of Lights below, and also to remain in a form of *Dvekut*. This is the meaning of *Megillat Esther*, meaning although there is disclosure of the Light of *Hochma*, she still takes the form of concealment that is there (because Esther is *Hester*–Concealment).

In the matter of him not knowing, it is explained in *The Study of the Ten Sefirot* (Part 15, *Ohr Pnimi*, item 217, par. "He writes") that although it illuminated Lights of *Hochma*, it is impossible to receive without the Light of *Hassadim*, as this induces separation. However, a miracle was made where by fasting and crying they extended the Light of *Hassadim*, and then they could receive the Light of *Hochma*.

However, there is no such thing before the end of correction. But since this discernment is from the discernment of the end of correction, at which time it will already be corrected, as it is written in the Holy *Zohar*: "SAM is destined to become a Holy Angel," it follows, that then there will be no difference between Haman and Mordecai, that Haman too will be corrected. And this is the meaning of, **"On *Purim*, one must intoxicate until one cannot tell the cursed Haman from the blessed Mordecai."**

It should also be added with regard to the words that they were hanged, that it is an indication to the hanging on the tree, meaning they understood that it is the same sin as the sin of *Etz ha Daat* (The Tree of Knowledge), as there too the blemish was in the *GAR*.

Regarding "sat in the king's gate," it can be added that this implies that he was sitting and not standing, since sitting is called *VAK*, and standing is called *GAR*.

## 38. THE FEAR OF GOD IS HIS TREASURE

I heard on March 31, 1947

A treasure is a vessel in which the possession is placed. Grain, for example, is placed in the barn, and precious things are placed in a more heavily guarded place. Thus, every received thing is called by its correlation to the Light, and the vessel must be able to receive the things. It is as we learn that there is no Light without a vessel, and this applies even in corporeality.

Yet, what is the vessel in spirituality, in which we can receive the spiritual bounty that the Creator wants to give, which will match the Light? That is, as in corporeality, where the vessel needs a correlation with the object that is placed in it?

For example: we cannot say that we have treasures of wine, which we poured in new sacks to keep the wine from turning sour, or that we have taken a lot of flour in barrels. Instead, there is a conduct that the container of wine is barrels and jars, and the container for the flour is sacks and not barrels, etc..

Thus, there is a question, what is the spiritual container, the vessels from which we can make a big treasure of the Upper Bounty?

There is a rule that the cow wants to feed more than the calf wants to eat. This is because His wish is to do good to His creatures, and the reason for the *Tzimtzum* (Restriction), we must believe, is for our own good. And the reason must be that we do not have the right vessels where the bounty can be, like the corporeal vessels, which must be right for what is placed there. Hence, we must say that if we add the vessels, there will be something to hold the added bounty.

The answer that comes to that is that, in His treasury, the Creator has only the treasure of fear of God (*Berachot* 33).

Yet, we should interpret what fear is, that it is the vessel, and the treasure is made of this vessel, and all the important things are placed in it. He said that fear is as it is written about Moses: our sages said (*Berachot* p.7), "The reward for 'And Moses hid his face for he was afraid to look,' he was rewarded with 'the similitude of the Lord doth he behold.'"

Fear refers to one's fear of the great pleasure that exists there, that one will not be able to receive it in order to bestow.

The reward for that, for having had fear, is that thus he had made for himself a vessel in which to receive the Upper Bounty. This is man's work, and besides that, we attribute everything to the Creator.

Yet, it is not so with fear, because the meaning of fear is to not receive. And what the Creator gives, He gives only to receive, and this is the meaning of, "everything is in the hands of God except the fear of God."

This is the vessel that we need. Otherwise we will be considered fools, as our sages said, "Who is a fool? He who loses what he is given." It means that the *Sitra Achra* (Other Side) will take the abundance from us if we cannot aim in order to bestow, because then it goes to the vessels of reception, which is the *Sitra Achra* and impurity.

This is the meaning of, "And ye shall observe the feast of unleavened bread." Observing means fear. And although the nature of the Light is that it keeps itself, meaning that the Light leaves before one wants to receive the Light into the vessels of reception. Yet one must do it by himself, as much as one can, as our sages said, "You will observe yourselves a little from below, and I will observe you a lot from Above."

The reason we attribute fear to people, as our sages said, "Everything is in the hands of God, but the fear of God," is because He can give everything except fear. This is because what the Creator gives **is more love, not fear**.

Acquiring fear is through the power of Torah and *Mitzvot*. It means that when one engages in Torah and *Mitzvot* with the intention to be rewarded with bringing contentment to one's Maker, that aim that rests on the acts of *Mitzvot* and the study of Torah brings one to attain it. Otherwise one might stay. Although one keeps Torah and *Mitzvot* in every item and detail, one will still remain merely in the degree of Holy Still.

It follows that one should always remember the reason that obligates one to engage in Torah and *Mitzvot*. This is what our sages meant by, **"that your Holiness will be for My Name."** It means that I will be your cause, meaning that your entire work is in wanting to delight Me, meaning that all your deeds will be in order to bestow.

Our sages said (*Berachot* 20), "Everything there is in keeping, there is in remembering." This means that all those who engage in keeping Torah and *Mitzvot* with the aim to achieve "remembering," by way of, **"When I remember Him, He will not suffer me to sleep."** It follows, that the keeping is primarily in order to be awarded remembering.

Thus, one's desire **to remember that the Creator** is the cause for **keeping** Torah and *Mitzvot*. This is so because it follows that the reason and the cause to keep the Torah and *Mitzvot* is the Creator, as without it one cannot cleave to the Creator, since "He and I cannot dwell in the same abode," due to the disparity of form.

The reason that the reward and punishment is not revealed, that we must only believe in reward and punishment, is because the Creator wants everyone to work for Him, and not for themselves. This is discerned as disparity of form from the Creator. If the reward and punishment were revealed, one would work because of self-love, meaning so that the Creator would love him, or because of self-hate, meaning for fear that the Creator would hate him. It follows that the reason for the work is only the person, not the Creator, and the Creator wants that He will be the compelling reason.

It turns out that fear is precisely when one recognizes one's lowness, and says that his serving the King, meaning that one's wish to bestow upon Him, is considered a great privilege, and it is more valuable than he can say. It is according to the rule that with an important personality, what is given to him is considered receiving from him.

To the extent that one feels one's lowness, to that extent one can begin to appreciate the greatness of the Creator, and the desire to serve Him will awaken. However, if one is proud, the Creator says, "he and I cannot dwell in the same abode."

This is the meaning of, "A fool, an evil, and a rude go together." The reason is that since one has no fear, meaning one cannot lower oneself before the Creator and say that it is a great honor for him to be able to serve Him without any reward, one cannot receive any wisdom from the Creator, and he remains a fool. Then, he who is a fool is wicked, as our sages said, "One does not sin unless **folly** entered him."

## 39. AND THEY SEWED FIG-LEAVES

I heard on *Shavat*, 26, February 16, 1947

The leaf refers to the shade that it puts on the light, meaning on the sun. There are two shades: one comes from the side of *Kedusha* (Sanctity), and the other comes due to a sin.

Thus, there are two kinds of concealment of the Light. As the shade conceals the sun in corporeality, so there is concealment on the Upper Light, called "sun," which comes from the side of *Kedusha*, namely **because of a choice**. This is as it is written about Moses, "And Moses hid his face; for he was afraid to look."

The shade comes because of **fear**, and fear means that one is afraid to receive the bounty, that he may not be able to aim in order to bestow. It follows that the shade comes because of *Kedusha*, meaning that one wants to cleave to the Creator.

In other words, *Dvekut* (Adhesion) is called bestowal, and he is afraid that perhaps he will not have the ability to bestow.

It turns out that he is adhered to *Kedusha*, and this is called "a shade that comes from the side of *Kedusha*."

There is also a shade that comes because of a sin. It means that the concealment comes to one, not because he does not want to receive, but to the contrary, it is because one wants to receive in order to receive. This is the reason why the Light leaves, since the whole difference between *Kedusha* and *Klipa* (Shell) is that the *Kedusha* wants to bestow and the *Klipa* wants only to receive, and not to bestow at all. For this reason that shade is considered to come from the side of the *Klipa*.

There is no counsel to exit that state, except as it is written, "and they sewed fig-leaves together, and made themselves girdles." Girdles refer to forces of the body that joined in the form a shade of *Kedusha*. It means that although now they do not have Light, since the abundance departed due to the sin, they still **overcome in serving the Creator by mere force, above reason**, which is called **"by force."**

It is written, "And they heard the voice of the Lord, etc., **and the man and his wife hid themselves**," meaning **they went into the shade.** This is the meaning of "and Moses hid his face," meaning *Adam ha Rishon* (The First Man) did the same as did Moses.

"And said unto him: **'Where art thou?' And he said: 'I heard Thy voice in the garden, and I was afraid, because I was naked; and I hid myself.'**" Naked means stripped off the Upper Light.

The Creator asked, what is the reason that you came to the shade, called, **"and I hid myself"** for I am naked? Is it because of a shade of *Kedusha* or because of a sin? The Creator asked him: "Hast thou eaten of the tree, whereof I commanded thee that thou shouldest not eat?" meaning because of a sin.

But when the shade comes because of a sin, it is called "images, image makers, and sorcerers," which is "God hath made even the one as well as the other." This is because as there are forces in *Kedusha* to make changes, and to show signs and omens, so there are forces in the *Sitra Achra*. This is why **the righteous do not use these forces**, because of "one as well as the other," so **as not to give strength to the *Sitra Achra* to do as they do.**

Only **on exceptional occasions does the Creator not give the *Sitra Achra* the same force that is in *Kedusha*.** It is like Elijah on Mt. Carmel, who said, "Hear me" so they will not say that it is witchcraft, meaning that there is the strength for concealment of the Upper Light.

Hence, girdles that come from the side of the fig leaves, which is from the sin of the Tree of Knowledge, these leaves, meaning this shade that comes due to the sin, since the cause is not from the side of *Kedusha*, when they choose to take shade by themselves, but they take the shade **because they have no other counsel**, this can work only to **exit the state** of descent. Afterwards, however, the work must begin anew.

## 40. FAITH IN THE RAV, WHAT IS THE MEASURE

I heard in 1943

It is known that there is a right path and a left path. **Right** comes from the word **the right**, referring to the verse, "And he believed in the Lord." The Targum says, **right**, when the Rav says to the disciple to take the right path.

Right is normally called "wholeness," and left, "incompleteness," that corrections are missing there. In that state the disciple must believe the words of his Rav, who tells him to walk in the right line, called "wholeness."

And what is the "wholeness" by which the disciple should walk? It is that one should depict to oneself as if one has already been rewarded with whole faith in the Creator, and already feels in his organs that the Creator leads the whole world in the form of "Good that Doeth Good," meaning that the whole world receives only good from Him.

Yet, when one looks at oneself, he sees that he is poor and indigent. In addition, when he observes the world, he sees that the entire world is tormented, each according to his degree.

One should say to that, **"They have eyes and see not."** It means that as long as one is in multiple authorities, called **they**, they do not see **the truth**. What are the multiple authorities? As long as one has two desires, even though one believes that the entire world belongs to the Creator, but something belongs to man, too.

In fact, one must annul one's authority before the authority of the Creator, and say that one does not want to live for oneself, and the only reason that one does want to exist is in order to bring contentment to the Creator. Thus, by that one annuls one's own authority completely, and then one is found in the single authority, being the authority of the Creator. Only then can one see the truth, how the Creator leads the world by the quality of benevolence.

But as long as one is in multiple authorities, meaning when he still has two desires in both mind and heart, one is unable to see the truth. Instead, one must go above reason and say, "they have eyes," but they do not see the truth.

It follows that when one regards oneself, and wants to know if one is now in a time of descent or a time of ascent, one cannot know that either. It means that one thinks that he is in a state of descent, and that too is incorrect, because he might be in a state of ascent now, meaning seeing his true state, how far he is from the Holy Work. Thus, one has now come closer to the truth.

And it might be to the contrary, that now one feels that one is in a state of elation, when in fact one is now controlled by receiving for self, called "a descent."

Only one who is already in single authority can discern and know the truth. Hence, one must trust the opinion of one's Rav and believe what his Rav tells him. It means that one should go as his Rav told him to do.

And although one sees many arguments, and sees many teachings that do not go hand in hand with the opinion of his Rav, one should nevertheless trust the opinion of one's Rav and say that what he understands and what he sees in other books that do not cohere with his Rav's opinion, one should say that as long as he is in multiple authorities, he cannot understand the truth. One cannot see what is written in other books, the truth that they say.

It is known that when one is still not purified, one's Torah becomes **a potion of death** to him. And why does it say, "Not rewarded, his Torah becomes a potion of death to him"? This is because all the teachings that one learns or hears will not bring him any benefit to make one able to be imparted the discernment of **life**, which is *Dvekut* (Adhesion) with the Life of Lives. On the contrary, one is drawn constantly farther from the Life of Lives, since all that one does is only for the needs of the body, called "receiving for oneself," which is considered separation.

This means that through one's deeds, one becomes more separated from the life of lives, and this is called **"the potion of death,"** since it brings him death and not life. It means that one becomes ever farther from bestowal, called "equivalence of form with the Creator," by way of, "As He is Merciful, so are you merciful."

We must also know that when one is engaged in the right, the time is right to extend Upper Bounty, because "the blessed adheres to the blessed." In other words, since one is in a state of completeness, called "blessed," in that respect one presently has equivalence of form, since the sign of completeness is if one is in gladness. Otherwise, there is no completeness.

It is as our sages said, "Divinity does not stay but only out of gladness of a *Mitzva*." The meaning is that the reason that it brings one joy is **the *Mitzva***, meaning that the Rav had **commanded** him to take the right line.

It follows that one keeps the commandments of the Rav, that he was allotted a special time to walk on the right and a special time to walk on the left. Left contradicts the right, since left means when one calculates for oneself and begins to examine what he has already acquired in the work of God, and he sees that he is poor and indigent. Thus, how can one be in wholeness?

Still, one goes above reason because of the commandment of the Rav. It follows that one's entire wholeness was built on above reason, and this is called **"faith."** This is the meaning of, "in every place where I cause My Name to be mentioned I will come unto thee and bless thee." **"In every place"** means although one is still not worthy of a blessing, nonetheless, I gave My blessing, because you make **a place**, meaning **a place of gladness**, in which **the Upper Light can be.**

## 41. WHAT IS GREATNESS AND SMALLNESS IN FAITH

I heard on the evening following Passover holiday,
March 29, 1945

It is written, "and they believed in the Lord, and in His servant Moses." We must know that the Lights of *Pesach* (Passover) have the power to impart the Light of faith. Yet, do not think that the

Light of faith is a small thing, because greatness and smallness depend only on the receivers.

When one does not work by way of truth, one thinks that he has too much faith, and with the measure of faith he has, he can dispense to several people, and then they will be fearing and whole.

However, one who wants to serve the Creator in truth, and constantly examines himself, if he is willing to work devotedly **"and with all thy heart,"** he sees that he is always deficient in faith, meaning that he is always short of it.

Only when one has faith can one feel that one is always seated before the King. When one feels the greatness of the King, one can discover the love in two ways: in a good way, and in a way of harsh judgments. Hence, the one who seeks the truth is the one who needs the Light of faith. If such a person hears or sees some way to obtain the Light of faith, then one is happy as though he had found a great fortune.

Hence, those people who seek the truth, on the holiday of *Pesach*, which is capable of the Light of faith, we read in the *Parasha* (Torah portion), "and they believed in the Lord, and in His servant Moses," because then is a time that can impart that.

## 42. WHAT IS THE ACRONYM *ELUL*[3] IN THE WORK

I heard on *Elul* 15, August 28, 1942

In order to understand that, we must understand several other things.

1. The matter of the Kingship, memories, and the rams' horns, and what is the meaning of what our sages said, "annul your will before His will, so that He will annul His will before your will."

3 *ELUL* is an acronym for the verse "I am my beloved's and my beloved is mine."

2. The words of our sages, "Evil–at once to death, and righteous at once to life."
3. The verse, "The sons of Gershon: Libni and Shimei."
4. The words of the Holy *Zohar*: "*Yod* is a black point that has no white in it."
5. *Malchut* of the Upper becomes *Keter* to the lower.
6. What is, gladness testifies if the work is in wholeness.

All these things apply in the preparation of the month of *Elul*.

To understand all the above, we must understand the purpose of creation, which is said to be because He wishes to do good to His creatures. And because of the *Tikkun* (Correction), so that there will not be a matter of "bread of shame," a *Tzimtzum* (Restriction) was made. And from the *Tzimtzum* extended the *Masach* (Screen), by which the vessels of reception are turned into bestowal.

And when the vessels are prepared to be in order to bestow, the hidden and treasured Light for the creatures is received immediately. It means that one receives the delight and pleasure that was in the Thought of Creation, to do good to His creatures.

With that we can interpret what is written, "Annul your will before His will," meaning annul the will to receive in you before the will to bestow, which is the Creator's will. This means that one will revoke self-love before the love of God. This is called "annulling oneself before the Creator," and it is called *Dvekut* (Adhesion). Subsequently, the Creator can shine in your will to receive because it is now corrected in the form of receiving in order to bestow.

This is the meaning of, "so that He will annul His will before your will." It means that the Creator annuls His will, meaning the *Tzimtzum* (Restriction) that was because of the disparity of form. Now, however, when there is already equivalence of form, hence now there is expansion of the Light into the desire of the lower that has been corrected in order to bestow, for this is the purpose of creation, to do good to His creatures, and now it can be carried out.

Now we can interpret the verse, **"I am my beloved's."** It means that by the 'I' annulling my will to receive before the Creator in the form of all to bestow, it obtains **"and my beloved is mine."** It means that **My beloved**, which is the Creator, "is mine," He imparts me the delight and pleasure found in the Thought of Creation. Thus, what was hidden and restricted before has now become disclosure of the Face, since now the purpose of creation has been revealed, which is to do good to His creatures.

We must know that the vessels of bestowal are called *YH* (*Yod*, *Hey*) of the name *HaVaYaH* (*Yod*, *Hey*, *Vav*, *Hey*), which are pure vessels. This is the meaning of, "All who receive, receive in the purer vessel." In that state one is awarded, "and my beloved is mine," and He imparts abundance upon him, meaning he is rewarded with the revelation of the Face.

Yet, there is a condition to that: it is impossible to obtain disclosure before one receives the discernment of *Achoraim* (Posterior), discerned as concealment of the Face, and to say that it is as important to him as the disclosure of the Face. It means that one should be in gladness as though one has already acquired the disclosure of the Face.

However, one cannot persist and appreciate the concealment like the disclosure, except when one works in bestowal. At that time one can say, "I do not care what I feel during the work because what is important for me is that I want to bestow upon the Creator. If the Creator understands that He will have more contentment if I work in a form of *Achoraim*, I agree."

However, if one still has flickers of reception, one comes to thoughts, and it is then hard for him to believe that the Creator leads the world in a manner of "good that doeth good." This is the meaning of the letter *Yod* in the name *HaVaYaH*, which is the first letter, called "a black point that has no white in it," meaning it is all darkness and concealment of the Face.

It means that when one comes to a state where one has no support, **one's state becomes black, which is the lowest discernment in the Upper World, and that becomes the *Keter* to the lower one**, as the vessel of *Keter* is a vessel of bestowal.

The lowest discernment in the Upper is *Malchut*, which has nothing of its own, meaning that she does not have anything. And only in this manner is it called *Malchut*. It means that if one assumes the Kingdom of Heaven—**which is in a state of not having anything—gladly,** afterwards, it becomes ***Keter***, which is a vessel of bestowal and the purest *Kli*. In other words, the reception of *Malchut* in a state of darkness subsequently becomes a *Kli* of *Keter*, which is a vessel of bestowal.

It is like the verse, **"For the ways of the Lord are right, and the just do walk in them; but transgressors do stumble therein."** This means that transgressors, those who are controlled by the vessels of reception, must fall and be crouching under their load when they come to that state.

The righteous, however, meaning those who are in the form of bestowal, are elevated by that, meaning by that they are imparted vessels of bestowal. (Wicked should be interpreted as those whose heart is still not set on obtaining vessels of bestowal, and righteous is interpreted as those whose heart is already set on obtaining vessels of bestowal, but are as yet unable).

It is as the Holy *Zohar* writes, that the Holy Divinity told Rashbi (Rabbi Shimon Bar-Yochay), **"There is no place to keep from you,"** and this is why she appears to him. This is the meaning of what Rashbi said, "because of that, and His desire is upon me," and this is, "I am my beloved's and my beloved is mine," and then he administers to the **VH** (*Vav*, *Hey*).

This is the meaning of "the Name is incomplete, and the throne is incomplete until the ***Hey*** bonds with the ***Vav***." The *Hey* is called "the will to receive," which is the last and final vessel in which the ***Vav*** will dispense into the ***Hey***, and then it will be the end of correction.

This is the meaning of "righteous–at once to life." It means that the person himself should say in which book he wants his name to be written. Is it in the book of the righteous, meaning that he wants to be given the will to bestow, or not. Since one has many discernments regarding the will to bestow, meaning at times one says, "Yes, I want to be given the will to bestow, but not revoke the will to receive altogether." He rather wants two worlds for himself, meaning he wants the will to bestow for his own delight as well.

However, only those who wish to turn their vessels of reception to be only in bestowal and not to receive anything for themselves are written in the book of the righteous. It is so that there will not be room for one to say, "If I had known that the will to receive had to be revoked, I would not have prayed for it," (so that he will not say afterwards, "This is not what I had sworn to").

Hence, one must unreservedly say what one means by being registered in the book of the righteous, so that he will not complain afterwards.

We must know that in the work, the book of the righteous and the book of the wicked are in one person. It means that one must make a choice and clearly know what one wants, because wicked and righteous relate to the same person.

Hence, one must say if he wants to be written in the book of the righteous, to be immediately for life, meaning cleave to the Life of Lives, that he wants to do everything for the Creator. In addition, when one comes to be written in the book of the wicked, where all those who wish to be receivers for themselves are registered, one says that they should be written there to death at once, meaning that the will to receive for oneself will be revoked in him, as if it had died.

Yet, sometimes one is doubtful. In other words, one does not want that one's will to receive will be immediately revoked in him. It is hard for one to decide at once that all his fractions of reception will be put to death instantaneously, meaning he does not agree that all his desires for reception will be annulled in him at once.

Instead, one wants that one's fragments of reception will be annulled in him gradually and slowly, not all at once, meaning that the vessels of reception will operate some, and some the vessels of bestowal. It follows that this person has no firm and clear view.

A firm view is that, on the one hand, he claims, it is all mine, meaning all for the purpose of the will to receive. On the other hand, he claims that it is all for the Creator, and this is called a firm view. Yet, what one can do if the body disagrees with one's view of wanting to be entirely for the Creator?

In that state you can say that this person does everything he can to be entirely for the Creator, meaning he prays to the Creator to help him be able to execute all his desires only for the Creator. It is for that that we pray, "Remember us for life and write us in the book of life."

This is why he writes, ***"Malchut,"*** meaning that one will take upon oneself the discernment of the black point that has no white in it. This is the meaning of "Annul your will" so that your remembrance will rise before Me and then His will, will be annulled before your will. With what? With a horn, meaning with the horn of the mother, meaning the matter depends on repentance.

In other words, if one accepts the blackness, one should also try that it will be in an honorable manner, and not in a disgraceful manner. This is called "the horn of the Mother," meaning that one will consider it handsome and respectable.

Accordingly, we should interpret what is written, "The sons of Gershon: Libni and Shimei." If one sees that he has been expelled from the work, one should know that this is due to **Libni**,[4] meaning because he specifically wants whiteness. In other words, if one is given the whiteness, meaning that everything one does will shine, which means that one will feel a good taste in the Torah and in the prayer, then one is willing to listen and engage in Torah and *Mitzvot*.

This is the meaning of **"Shimei."**[5] It means that it is precisely through a form of "whiteness" that one can hear. However, during the work one sees a shape of black, and cannot agree to hear of taking upon himself this work. Hence, one must be expelled from the King's Hall, for reception of the Kingdom of Heaven must be unconditional surrender.

However, when one says that he is willing to take upon himself the work on condition that there will be a shape of white, meaning that the day will shine for him, and he does not agree if the work appears to him in a black form, this person has no place in the King's Hall. This is because those who wish to work in order to bestow are admitted into the King's Hall, and when one works in order to bestow, he does not mind what he feels during the work.

Rather, even in a state where one sees a shape of black, one is not impressed by it, but he only wants the Creator to give him

4 A word that sounds like the Hebrew *Lavan* (White).

5 A word that sounds like the Hebrew *Shmi'a* (Hearing).

strength to be able to overcome all the obstacles. It means that one does not ask of the Creator to give him a shape of white, but to give him the strength to overcome all the concealments.

Hence, those people who want to work in order to bestow, if there is always a state of whiteness, the whiteness allows one to continue in the work. This is because, while it shines, one is able to work even in the form of reception for oneself.

Hence, one will never have the ability to know if one's work is in purity or not, and this causes one to never be able to be awarded *Dvekut* (Adhesion) with the Creator. For this reason one is given a form of blackness from Above, and then one sees if one's work is in purity.

In other words, if one can be in gladness in a state of blackness, too, it is a sign that one's work is in purity, because one must be glad and believe that from Above he was given a chance to be able to work in order to bestow.

This is as our sages wrote, "All who are greedy are cross." It means that one immersed in self-reception is cross, since he is always lacking. He forever needs to fulfill his vessels of reception.

However, those who want to walk in the path of bestowal should always be in gladness. This means that in any shape that comes upon him, one should be in gladness, since he has no intention to receive for himself.

This is why he says that either way, if one is really working in order to bestow, one should certainly be glad that he has been granted bringing contentment to his Maker. And if one feels that his work is still not to bestow, he should also be in gladness because for himself, one says that he does not want anything for himself. He is happy that the will to receive cannot enjoy this work, and that should give him joy. However, if one thinks that one will also have something for himself from this work, one permits the *Sitra Achra* (Other Side) to cling to his work, and this causes him sadness, and anger, etc..

## 43. THE MATTER OF TRUTH AND FAITH

I heard

Truth is what one feels and sees in one's eyes. This discernment is called "reward and punishment," meaning that nothing can be gained without labor. It is like a person who sits in his home and does not want to do anything to provide for his sustenance. He says that since the Creator is good that doeth good, and provides for all, hence He will certainly send him his needs, while he himself is required to no action.

Of course, if this person behaves in this manner, he will certainly starve to death. Reason, too, necessitates it, so it appears to the eyes, and this is indeed the truth, meaning that he will die of starvation.

But at the same time one must believe above reason that one could obtain all one's needs without any exertion and trouble, because of private Providence. In other words, the Creator does and will do every deed, and one does not help Him in anything, but the Creator does everything, and one cannot add or subtract.

Yet, how can these two things go hand in hand, since one contradicts the other? One discernment is called what one's mind attains, meaning that without man's help, meaning that without preceding labor and exertion, nothing will be attained. This is called "truth," because the Creator wanted one to feel that way. This is why this path is called "the path of truth."

Let it not perplex you that, if these two ways are in contradiction, how is it possible that this state is true? The answer is that the truth does not refer to the way and to the state. Rather, truth refers to the sensation that the Creator wanted one to feel like that; this is "truth." It follows that the matter of truth can be said precisely about the Creator, meaning about His will, that He wants one to feel and see this way.

Yet, at the same time, one must believe that even though one does not feel and does not see with one's mind's eye that the Creator can help him obtain all the profits that can be gained without any exertion, it is only with respect to private Providence.

The reason that one cannot attain the matter of private Providence before one attains the matter of reward and punishment is that private Providence is an eternal thing, and one's mind is not eternal. Hence, something eternal cannot clothe in something not eternal. Thus, once one has been awarded the discernment of reward and punishment, the reward and punishment become a *Kli* (Receptacle) where private Providence can clothe.

Now we can understand the verse, "O Lord, do save, O Lord, do succeed." "Do save" refers to reward and punishment. One must pray that the Creator will provide one with labor and exertion by which one will have reward. At the same time one should pray for success, which is private Providence, meaning that one will be rewarded with all the profits in the world without any labor and exertion.

We also see this in corporeal possessions (discerned by their separation in places, meaning in two bodies, whereas in spiritual matters everything is examined on a single body but in two times). There are people who obtain their possessions specifically through great exertion, energy, and great wit, and at the same time we see the opposite, that people who are not so witty, who do not have that much energy, and do not make great efforts, succeed and become the greatest owners of property and possessions in the world.

The answer is that these corporeal things extend from their Upper Roots, meaning from reward and punishment and from private Providence. The only difference is that in spirituality it appears in one place, meaning in one subject, but one-by-one, meaning in one person but in two states. And in corporeality it is in one time, but in two subjects, meaning at one time and in two different people.

## 44. MIND AND HEART

I heard on *Tevet* 10, February 1, 1928

One must examine if the faith is in order, meaning if one has fear and love, as it is written, "If I am a father, where is my honor, and if I am a Lord, **where is my fear**?" And this is called **"Mind."**

We must also see that there will not be any desires for self-gratification, that even a thought to want for himself will not arise in him, but all his desires will be only to bestow upon the Creator. This is called **"heart,"** which is the meaning of "The Merciful One wants the heart."

## 45. TWO DISCERNMENTS IN THE TORAH AND IN THE WORK

I heard on *Elul* 1, September 5, 1948

There are two discernments in the Torah, and there are two discernments in the work. The first is the discernment of **fear**, and the second is the discernment of **love**. Torah is called a state of wholeness, meaning we do not speak of the state one's work is in, but we speak with respect to the Torah in and of itself.

The first is called "love," meaning that one has a desire and craving to know the ways of the Creator and His hidden treasures, and for that one makes every effort and exertion to obtain his wish. One regards everything in the Torah that one extracts from one's study as having been granted a priceless thing. According to the appreciation from the importance of the Torah, so one gradually grows until one is slowly shown the secrets of the Torah, according to one's exertion.

The second discernment is fear, meaning that one wants to be a servant of the Creator. Since "He who does not know the commandment of the Upper One, how will he serve Him?" one fears and dreads not knowing how to serve the Creator.

When one learns in this way, every time one finds a flavor in the Torah, and can use it, one is elated and excited according to the appreciation of the importance from having been granted something in the Torah. And if one persists in this way, one is gradually shown the secrets of the Torah.

Here there is a difference between external teachings and the wisdom of the Torah: In exterior teachings, the elation lessens the intellect, since emotion is opposite to intellect. Thus, the elation diminishes the understanding of the mind.

However, in the wisdom of the Torah, the elation is an essence, like the ratio. The reason for it is that the Torah is life, as it is written, "wisdom preserveth the life of him that hath it," as wisdom and life are the same thing.

Hence, as the wisdom appears in the mind, so the wisdom appears in the emotion, because the Light of life fills all the organs. (It seems to me that this is why one should see that one is always thrilled with the wisdom of the Torah, since in the elation there is a great distinction between an exterior teaching and the wisdom of the Torah.)

It is likewise, **in the work**, considered the left line, because it is discerned as reception. The matter of reception means that one wants to receive because one feels a lack, and a lack is regarded as three discernments: 1) the want of the individual; 2) the want of the public; 3) the want of the *Shechina* (Divinity).

Any want is regarded as wanting to fulfill the deficiency; hence it is considered reception, and left line. Torah, however, means that one works not because one feels a lack that must be corrected, but that one wants to bestow contentment upon one's Maker.

(It is like a prayer, and praise, and gratitude. When one engages in a way that one feels oneself in wholeness and does not see any shortcoming in the world, this is called **"Torah."** However, if one engages while feeling some shortcoming, this is called **"work."**)

Also, two discernments must be made during the work: 1) due to **love of God**, when one wants to cleave to the Creator, when one feels that this is the place where one can bring out the measure of love one feels, and love the Creator; 2) because of fear, when one has **fear of God**.

## 46. THE DOMINATION OF ISRAEL OVER THE *KLIPOT*

I heard

Concerning the domination of Israel over the *Klipot* (Shells), and vise-versa, the domination of the *Klipot* over Israel. First we must understand what is "Israel" and what is "The Nations of the World."

It is explained in several places that Israel means "Internality," called "The Anterior *Kelim* (Vessels)," with which one can work in order to bestow contentment upon one's Maker. "The Nations of the World" are called "Externality," "The Posterior *Kelim*," whose sustenance comes solely from reception and not from bestowal.

The domination of the nations of the world over Israel is in that they cannot work in a form of bestowal and in the Anterior

*Kelim*, but only in the Posterior *Kelim*. They entice the workers of the Creator to extend the Lights below in the Posterior *Kelim*.

The domination of Israel means that if they give power so that each and every one will be able to work in order to bestow contentment upon his Maker, meaning only in Anterior *Kelim*, even if they extend *Hochma* (Wisdom), it is only in a form of "A path to travel through," and not more.

## 47. IN THE PLACE WHERE YOU FIND HIS GREATNESS

I heard

"In the place where you find His greatness, there you find His humbleness." It means that one who is always in true *Dvekut* (Adhesion), sees that the Creator lowers Himself, meaning the Creator is present in the low places.

One does not know what to do, and therefore it is written, "that is enthroned on high, that looketh down low upon heaven and upon the earth?" One sees the greatness of the Creator and then "That looketh down low," meaning one lowers the heaven to the earth. The advice that is given to that is to think that if this desire is from the Creator, we have nothing greater than that, as it is written, "He raiseth up the poor out of the gutter."

First, one must see that one has a want. If he does not, he should pray for it, why does one not have it? The reason one does not have a want is due to the diminution of awareness.

Hence, in every *Mitzva* (Precept/Commandment), one must pray, why does one not have awareness that one is not keeping the *Mitzva* in wholeness? In other words, the will to receive covers so that one will not see the truth.

If one would see that one is in such a low state, then one would certainly not want to be in that state. Instead, one should exert in one's work every time until one comes to repentance, as it is written, "He bringeth down to the grave, and bringeth up."

It means that when the Creator wants the wicked to repent, He makes the netherworld so low for him that the wicked himself does not want to be so. Hence, one needs to pray pleadingly that the Creator will show him the truth by adding to him the Light of the Torah.

## 48. THE PRIMARY BASIS

I heard on the evening after Shabbat, *Vayera*,
November 8, 1952

The primary basis is a path that is known to all. The care and the guard regarding the intellect is because it is built on the foundation of a question. If one encounters the known question, one must be armed and protected to stand guard and instantaneously reply with the known answer.

In other words, the whole structure is built on questions and answers, when one who is on the path of the Creator, and is rewarded with building the structure of Divinity. And when one has no place for questions and answers, he is called "standing."

The Creator has prepared a place even to those who have already been granted the permanent clothing of Divinity, and are already on the path of degrees, who no longer have a place for the above work. In this place they have a free basis where faith can be.

Although it is difficult to understand how such a thing can be in high degrees, the Creator Himself can do such a thing. This is the meaning of the correction of the middle line, and the prohibition on reception from the left line.

At the same time, we see that *Hochma* appears only in *Malchut*. And even though *Malchut* is an opposite attribute from *Hochma*, still, the place for the appearance of *Hochma* is precisely here in *Malchut*.

This is the meaning of, "and let this ruin be under thy hand." Our sages said that one does not stand on a law unless he has failed in it. **Law** means a discernment of *Malchut* (and this is the meaning of the bride; when going to the bride it is called "law"[6]). It is built solely on obstacles, meaning on a time of questions. When one has no questions, one does not have the name **"Faith"** or **"Divinity."**

## 49. THE MOST IMPORTANT IS THE MIND AND THE HEART

I heard on Thursday, *Vayera*, November 6, 1952

There should be a preparation on the discernment of "mind," in that work which refers to the discernment of faith. This means that if one is neglectful in the work of faith, one falls into a state of wanting only knowledge, which is a *Klipa* (Shell), which is against the Holy *Shechina* (Divinity). Hence, one's work is to strengthen the discernment of "mind" every time.

Similarly, if one feels negligence in the work of the heart, one needs to strengthen the work that relates to the discernment of "heart," and perform opposite operations, meaning affliction of the body, which is the opposite of the will to receive. The difference between negligence in the work of the mind and the work of the heart is that there is an evil *Klipa* (shell) against the mind that can prompt a state of "pondering the beginning."

Hence, one must perform opposite actions, meaning in every renewal of the discernment of "mind," he will take upon himself remorse for the past and acceptance of the future. One

6 In Hebrew, the words "bride" and "law" are written with the same letters, except in a different order.

can receive the source that causes it from the discernment of "still." And the matter of the clothing of faith is a perpetual and eternal thing. Hence, one will always have it as a measurement if one's work is clean or not, since the clothing of *Shechina* departs only due to a flaw, either in the mind or in the heart.

## 50. TWO STATES

I heard on *Sivan* 20

There are two states to the world. In the first state the world is called "pain," and in the second state it is called "Holy *Shechina* (Divinity)." It is so because before one is endowed with correcting one's deeds to be in order to bestow, one feels the world only in the form of pains and torments.

However, afterwards one is rewarded with seeing that the Holy *Shechina* is clothed in the entire world, and then the Creator is considered to be filling the world. Then the world is called "Holy *Shechina*," which receives from the Creator. This is called "the unification of the Creator and Divinity." As the Creator gives, so the world is now occupied solely in bestowal.

It is like a sad tune. Some players know how to perform the suffering about which the tune is composed, because all melodies are like a spoken language where the tune interprets the words that one wants to say out loud. If the tune evokes crying in the listeners to the extent that each and everyone cries because of the suffering that the melody expresses, it is then called "a tune," and everyone loves to hear it.

However, how can people enjoy suffering? Since the tune does not point to present suffering, but to the past, meaning torments that have already past, were sweetened, and received their fill, for that reason people like to hear them. It indicates to the sweetening of the judgments, that the pains one had were sweetened. This is why these sufferings are sweet to hear, and then the world is called "Holy Divinity."

The important thing that one should know and feel is that there is a leader to the city, as our sages said, "Abraham the Patriarch said, 'There is no city without a leader.'" One must not think that everything that happens in the world is incidental and that the *Sitra Achra* causes one to sin and say that everything is incidental.

This is the meaning of *Hammat* (vessel of) *Keri* (semen). There is a *Hammat* filled with *Keri*. The *Keri* brings one to think that everything is *Bemikreh* (incidental). (Even when the *Sitra Achra* brings one such thoughts as to say that everything is incidental, without guidance, this is also not by chance, but the Creator wanted it this way.)

However, one must believe in reward and punishment, and that there is a judgment and there is a judge, and everything is conducted by Providence of reward and punishment. This is because sometimes when some desire and awakening for the work of God comes to a person, and he thinks that it comes to him by chance, he should know that here, too, he made an effort that preceded the hearing. He prayed to be helped from Above to be able to perform an act with intent, and this is called raising MAN.

Yet, one has already forgotten about that and did not consider it doing, since one did not receive an instantaneous answer to the prayer, so as to say, "for You hear the prayer of every mouth." Still, one should believe that the order from Above is that the response for the prayer may come several days and months after one prays.

One should not think that it is by chance that one has received this present awakening. Sometimes one says, "Now that I feel that I do not lack anything and I have no concerns, my mind is clear and sound now, and for that reason I can focus my mind and desire on the work of God."

It follows that one can say that his entire engagement in the work of God is, "his power and the might of his hand hath gotten him that wealth." Thus, when one can engage and attain spiritual needs, one should believe that this is the answer to the prayer. What one has prayed for before, that prayer has now been answered.

Also, sometimes when reading some book, and the Creator opens one's eyes and he feels some awakening, then too one's regular conduct is to relate it to chance. However, it is all guided.

Although one knows that the whole Torah is the names of the Creator, how can one say that through the book one is reading came some kind of sublime sensation? One must know that one often reads the book and knows that the whole Torah is the names of the Creator, but nevertheless receives no luminescence and sensation. Instead, everything is dry and the knowledge that one knows does not help him at all.

Hence, when one studies in a certain book and hangs his hope in Him, one's study should be on the basis of faith, that one believes in Providence and that the Creator will open his eyes. At that time one becomes needy of the Creator and thus has contact with the Creator. By that one can attain adhesion with Him.

There are two forces that contradict each other, an Upper Force and a Lower Force. The Upper Force is, as it is written, "Every one that is called by My Name, and whom I have created for My glory." This means that the whole world was created only for the glory of the Creator. The Lower Force is the will to receive that argues that everything was created for it, both corporeal and spiritual things, all is for self-love.

The will to receive argues that it deserves this world and the next world. Of course, the Creator is the winner, but this is called "the path of pain." It is called "a long way." But there is a short way, called "the path of Torah." It should be everyone's intention–to shorten time.

This is called **"I will hasten it."** Otherwise it will be **"in its time,"** as our sages said, **"rewarded–I will hasten it; not rewarded–in its time,"** "that I place upon you a king such as Haman, and he will force you to reform."

The Torah begins from *Beresheet* (In the beginning), etc. "Now the earth was unformed and void, and darkness," etc., and ends, "in the sight of all Israel."

In the beginning we see that the land is "unformed and void, and darkness," but then when they correct themselves to bestow, then they are rewarded with "and God said, let there be light etc." until the Light appears "in the sight of all Israel."

## 51. IF YOU ENCOUNTER THIS VILLAIN

I heard after the holiday of Passover, April 27, 1943

"If you encounter this villain, draw him to the seminary, etc. and if not, remind him of the dying day." It means that he will remind him that the work should be in the place where he is not present, which is after one's skin. This is called "working outside one's body," that he has not a single thought about his own body.

## 52. A TRANSGRESSION DOES NOT PUT OUT A *MITZVA*

I heard on the eve of Shabbat, *Iyar* 9, May 14, 1943

"A transgression does not put out a *Mitzva* (Commandment)," and a *Mitzva* does not put out a transgression. It is the conduct of the work that one must take the good path. But the bad in a person does not let him take the good path.

However, one must know that one does not need to uproot the evil, as this thing is impossible. Rather, one must only hate the evil, as it is written, "Ye that love the Lord, hate evil." Thus, it is only hatred that is needed, since it is the conduct of hate to separate the adhered.

For this reason, evil has no existence of its own. Rather, the existence of evil depends on love for the evil or the hate for the evil. It means that if one has love for evil then one is caught in the authority of the evil. If one hates the evil, one exits their premises and one's evil has no dominion over that person.

It follows that the primary work is not in the actual evil, but in the measure of love and the measure of hate. And for this reason transgression prompts transgression. We must ask, "Why one deserves such a punishment?" When one falls from one's work, one must be aided to rise from the fall. Here, however, we see that more obstacles are added to one, so that one would fall lower than one's first fall.

But in order for one to feel hatred for the evil, one is given more evil, so as to feel how the transgression departs one from the work of God. Although one did regret the first transgression, one still did not feel a measure of remorse that would bring one hatred for the evil.

Hence, a transgression prompts a transgression, and every time one regrets, and each remorse certainly instigates hatred for the evil until the measure of one's hatred for the evil is completed. At that time one is separated from the evil, since evil induces separation.

It therefore follows that if one finds a certain measure of hate at a level that prompts separation, one does not need a correction of transgression-prompts-transgression, and naturally, one saves time. When one has been rewarded, one is admitted to the love of God. This is the meaning of, "ye that love the Lord, hate evil." They only hate the evil, but the evil itself remains in its place, and it is only hatred to the evil that we need.

This extends from, "Yet Thou hast made him but little lower than God," and this is the meaning of the serpent's saying, "and ye shall be as God, knowing good and evil." It means that when one exerts and wants to understand all the conducts of Providence, such as the Creator, this is the meaning of, "A man's pride shall bring him low." It means that one wants to understand everything in the exterior mind, and if one does not understand it, one is in lowness.

The truth is that if one awakens to know some thing, it is a sign that one needs to know that thing. And when one overcomes one's own mind, what he wishes to understand, and takes everything in faith above reason, this is called the greatest lowness in the human attribute. You find that to the extent that one has a demand to know more, yet takes it in faith above reason, you find that he is in greater lowness.

Now we can understand what they interpreted about the verse (Numbers, 12:3), "Now the man Moses was very meek," humble and patient. It means that he tolerated the lowness in the highest possible measure.

This is the meaning of *Adam ha Rishon* eating from the Tree of Life prior to the sin, and that he was in wholeness. Yet, he could not walk more than the degree he stood on, since he did not feel any want in his state. Hence, he naturally could not discover all the Holy Names.

For this reason he made, "He is terrible in His doing toward the children of men," that he would eat from the tree of knowledge of good and evil. And through this sin, all the Lights departed from him, hence, he was naturally compelled to start his work anew.

And the writing says about it that he was expelled from the Garden of Eden because if he had eaten from the Tree of Life he would have lived forever. This is the meaning of the internality of the worlds. If one enters there, one remains there forever. It means that once more one would remain without any want. And to be able to go and reveal the Holy Names, which appear by the correction of good and evil, he therefore had to eat from the Tree of Knowledge.

It is similar to a person who wants to give his friend a big barrel filled with wine, but his friend has only a small cup. What does he do? He pours wine into that cup and takes the cup home, where he pours it. After that he begins to go with the cup once more and once more fills it with wine. Then, once more he goes to his house, until he receives all the wine-barrels.

I had heard another parable that he had told of two friends, one of which became a king and the other became very poor, and he had heard that his friend became a king. The poor went to his friend the king, and told him of his bad state.

The king gave him a letter to the minister of the treasury that for two hours he would receive as much money as he wanted. The poor came to the treasury with a small box and entered and filled that small box with money.

When he came out, the minister kicked the box and all the money fell to the floor. It continued similarly time and time again, and the poor man was crying, "Why are you doing this to me?" Finally, he said, all the money that you took throughout this whole time is yours and you will take it all. You did not have the receptacles to take enough money from the treasury, and this is why that trick was played on you.

## 53. THE MATTER OF LIMITATION

I heard on the eve of Shabbat, *Sivan* 1, June 4, 1943

The matter of limitation is to limit the state one is in and not want *Gadlut* (Greatness). Instead, one wants to remain in one's present state forever, and this is called eternal *Dvekut* (Adhesion). Regardless of the measure of *Gadlut* that one has, even if one has the smallest *Katnut* (Smallness), if it shines forever it is considered having been imparted eternal *Dvekut*.

However, one who wants more *Gadlut*, it is considered luxury. And this is the meaning of, "any sorrow will be surplus," meaning that sadness comes to a person because he wants luxuries. This is what it means that when Israel came to receive the Torah, Moses brought forth the people to the bottom of the mountain, as it is written, "and they stood at the nether part of the mount."

(A mount (Hebrew: *Har*) means thoughts (Hebrew: *Hirhurim*)). Moses led them to the end of the thought and the understanding and the reason, the lowest degree there is. Only then, when they agreed to such a state, to walk in it without any wavering and motion, but to remain in that state as if they had the greatest *Gadlut*, and to be happy for it, this is the meaning of, "Serve the Lord with gladness." This is so because during the *Gadlut* it is irrelevant to say that He gives them work to be in gladness, since during the *Gadlut* gladness comes by itself. Instead, the work of gladness is given to them for the time of *Katnut*, so that they will have joy although they feel *Katnut*. And this is a great work.

This is called the main part of the degree, which is a discernment of *Katnut*. This discernment must be permanent, and the *Gadlut* is only an addition. Also, one should yearn for the main part, not for the additions.

## 54. THE PURPOSE OF THE WORK

What I heard on *Shevat* 16, February 13, 1941

It is known that the servitude is essentially to bestow contentment upon the Maker. Yet, one must know the meaning of bestowing, as this is commonly used, and it is known that habit wears off the taste. Therefore, we must thoroughly clarify the meaning of the word **to bestow.**

The thing is that the will to receive too is incorporated in the will to bestow of the lower one (but the will to receive can be used with corrections), or else there is no connection between the giver and the receiver. This is because it is impossible that one will give and the other will give nothing in return, and that there will be a state of partnership.

Only when they both show love to one another is there a connection and friendship between them. But if one shows love and the other shows no response, such a love is unreal and has no right to exist. Our sages stated about the verse, **"and say unto Zion: 'Thou art My people'"** (Isaiah 51), do not say *Ami* (My people), but *Imi* (with Me),[7] "to be My partner" (*Zohar Beresheet* p.5), meaning that the creatures are in partnership with the Creator.

It follows that when the lower one wants to bestow upon the Creator, then the lower one too should receive from the Creator. This is called partnership, when the lower one gives, and the Upper One gives too.

However, the will to receive should crave to cleave unto Him and receive His abundance, and sustenance, and goodness; and that was the purpose of creation, to do good to His creatures.

However, because of the breaking that occurred in the world of *Nekudim*, the will to receive fell into the domination of the

7 Both words consist of the same letters in Hebrew, and when there are no punctuation marks, as in the Bible, they look the same.

*Klipot* (Shells), by which two discernments were made in the *Kli* (Vessel). The first is that it developed a relation to the separated pleasures, and the work of exiting the authority of the *Klipot* is called "the work of purification." The second discernment that occurred due to the breaking is the detachment from spiritual pleasures.

In other words, one becomes distant from spirituality, and has no desire for spirituality. The correction for that is called *Kedusha* (Sanctity), where the order of the work is to crave His greatness. In that state the Creator shines for one in these vessels. However, we must know that to the extent that one has *Kelim* (plural for *Kli*) of **purity**, called "hate evil," to that extent one can work in ***Kedusha***, as it is written, "ye that love the Lord, hate evil."

It follows that there are two discernments, the first is purity, and the second is *Kedusha*. **Kedusha** is called the *Kli*, being the preparation to receive His goodness, by way of, to do good to His creatures. However, this *Kli* is attributed to the lower one, meaning that it is for us to repair. In other words, it is for us to crave the good, and this means engaging extensively in His greatness and one's own lowness.

Yet, the abundance that should appear in the *Kli* of ***Kedusha*** is in the hands of the Creator; He is the One who imparts the lower one with bounty. At that time the lower one cannot help in that in any way, and this is called, "The secret things belong unto the Lord our God."

The Thought of Creation, called "to do good to His creatures," begins from *Ein Sof* (No End). For this reason we pray to *Ein Sof*, meaning to the connection that exists between the Creator and the creatures. This is the meaning of what is written in the writings of the Ari, that we must pray to *Ein Sof*.

It is so because *Atzmuto* (His Self) has no connection with the creatures, as the beginning of the connection starts in *Ein*

*Sof*, where His Name is, which is the root of creation. This is the meaning of what is written in the Yerushalmi,[8] that one who prays will pray in the Name, meaning where there is His Name, and His Name and *Ein Sof* are called in the words of the legend, **"A tower filled with goodly matters."** This is why we pray to the Name, to receive the benefit that has been prepared for us in advance.

This is why *Keter* is called "His desire to do good to His creatures," and the benefit itself is called *Hochma* (Wisdom), which is the essence of the abundance. This is why *Keter* is called *Ein Sof* and "Emanator." However, *Hochma* is not called "emanated" yet, since there is still no *Kli* in *Hochma*, and it is considered a Light without a *Kli*.

Hence, *Hochma*, too, is discerned as the Emanator because there is no attainment in the Light without a *Kli*, and the whole difference between *Keter* and *Hochma* is that there, the root of the emanated is more disclosed.

## 55. HAMAN FROM THE TORAH, FROM WHERE

I heard on *Shevat* 16, February 13, 1941

Haman from the Torah, from where? "Hast thou eaten of the tree, whereof I commanded thee that thou shouldest not eat?" (Genesis 3:11). We must understand what is the connection between Haman and *Etz ha Daat* (Tree of Knowledge). *Etz ha Daat* is considered the state of greatness of reception, which is not in *Kedusha* (Sanctity) and must be brought into the *Kedusha* through corrections.

The discernment of Haman is also the state of greatness of reception, as it is written, that Haman said, "Whom would

8 A section of the Talmud.

the king delight," the King of the world, "to honor besides myself?" It means that it is discerned as the state of greatness of reception, and this is discerned as, "And his heart was lifted up in the ways of the Lord."

## 56. TORAH IS CALLED INDICATION

I heard on *BeShalach* 1, February 2, 1941

Torah is called "indication," from the words "shot through."[9] It means that when one engages in the Torah, one feels one's remoteness to the extent of one's exertion. In other words, one is shown the truth, meaning he is shown his measure of faith, which is the whole basis of the truth.

The basis of keeping Torah and *Mitzvot* is on one measure of faith, since then it appears to one that one's whole basis is built only on the upbringing one received. This is because rearing is sufficient for one to keep Torah and *Mitzvot* in all its intricacies and details, and everything that comes through rearing is called "faith within reason."

Even though this is against one's mind, meaning reason necessitates that according to one's addition in the Torah, so one should feel closer to the Creator. However, the Torah always shows one more of the truth. When one searches for the truth, the Torah brings one closer to the truth and one sees one's measure of faith in the Creator.

This is so that one would be able to ask for mercy and to pray for the Creator to bring him genuinely closer to Him, which means that he will be awarded faith in the Creator. Then one will be able to give praise and gratitude to the Creator for having been granted being brought closer to Him.

9 In Hebrew the same word is used for shooting and for indicating something.

However, when one does not see the measure of one's remoteness and thinks that he is constantly adding, you find that he builds his buildings on a rickety foundation, and one has no place to pray for the Creator to bring him closer to Him. It follows that one has no place for exertion to be imparted whole faith, since one exerts only for that which one needs.

Hence, as long as one is not worthy of seeing the truth, it is the opposite. The more one adds in Torah and *Mitzvot*, one adds in the measure of one's wholeness and does not see any deficit in himself. Therefore, one has no place to exert and pray to be granted faith in the Creator in truth, because when one feels corruption, you should say correction.

However, when one engages in Torah and *Mitzvot* in truth, the Torah indicates the truth to him, because the Torah has that power to show one's true state of faith (and this is the meaning of, "be known").

When one engages in the Torah and sees the truth, meaning one's measure of remoteness from spirituality, and one sees that he is such a low creature, that there is not a worse person on earth than him, then the *Sitra Achra* (Other Side) comes to one with a different argument: In fact, one's body is really very ugly, and it is true that there is not an uglier person in the world than him.

She tells him that so he will despair, since she is afraid that he will notice and come to correct his state. For this reason, she agrees to what one says, that he is an ugly person, and lets him understand that if he had been born with higher skills and better qualities, he could have overcome his evil and correct it, and would have been able to achieve *Dvekut* (Adhesion) with the Creator.

The answer to that should be that what she says to him is brought in *Massechet Taanit* (p.20), that Rabbi Elazar, son of Rabbi Shimon, came from a fenced tower from the house of his rabbi. He was riding his donkey and strolling along the riverbank, feeling great joy. And his mind was crude, as he had been studying much Torah.

A person who was very ugly came by his way. He told him: "Hello rabbi," but he did not reply. He told him: "Vain, how ugly is that man, perhaps all your town's men are as ugly as you?" He replied, "I do not know, but go and tell the craftsman who made me, How ugly is this vessel that you have made?" Because he knew that he himself had sinned, he descended from the donkey.

According to the above, we can see that since he had learned a lot of Torah, through it he was granted seeing the truth about the distance between him and the Creator, meaning the measure of his remoteness and nearness. This is the meaning of his mind being crude, meaning that he saw the complete form of one who is proud, which is his will to receive, and then he could see the truth that it was him who was most ugly. How did he see the truth? By learning much Torah.

Thus, how will he be able to cleave to Him, since he is such an ugly person? This is the reason why he asked if all the people were as ugly as him, or that he was the only ugly one but the rest of the people in the world were not ugly.

What was the answer? "I don't know." It means that that they do not feel, hence they do not know. And why do they not feel? It is for the simple reason that they were not rewarded with seeing the truth, since they lack Torah, so the Torah will show them the truth.

To that Elijah replied to him: "go to the craftsman who made me," because he saw that he had come into a state from which he could not ascend. For this reason Elijah appeared and told him, "go to the craftsman who made me." In other words, since the Creator created you so ugly, He must have known that it is with these *Kelim* (Vessels) that the goal can be achieved. So do not worry, go forward and succeed.

## 57. WILL BRING HIM AS A BURNED OFFERING TO HIS WILL

I heard on *Yitro* 1, February 5, 1944

About the verse, **"will bring him as a burned offering to His will,"** our sages said, "How so? He is he coerced until he says 'I want.'" We must also understand what we pray, "Let there be a will," since more than the calf wants to eat, the cow wants to feed, so why do we need to pray, "Let there be a will Above"?

It is known that in order to extend abundance from Above, one must precede an awakening from below. We must understand **why** we need an awakening from below. Because of that we pray that there will be a will Above. It means that we must evoke a desire from Above to administer below.

It is not enough that we have a desire, but there has to be a good will on the part of the Giver too. Even though there is a general desire to do good to His creatures, He still awaits for our desire to awaken His desire.

In other words, if we are unable to evoke His desire, it is a sign that the desire on the part of the receiver is still incomplete. Hence, precisely by praying that there will be a will Above, our desire is made to be a genuine desire, to be a fitting *Kli* (Vessel) to receive the abundance.

At the same time, we must say that all that we do, both bad and good, everything extends from Above (which is the meaning of Private Providence), that the Creator does everything. Yet, at the same time we must regret the bad deeds, though it too extends from Above.

The mind necessitates that we must not regret, but justify the judgment, that we deserve the bad deeds. Nevertheless, it is to the contrary; we must regret not being permitted to do good deeds, which is certainly as a result of a punishment, meaning that we are unworthy of serving the King.

If everything is guided, how can we say that we are unworthy, since there is no act below? For this purpose we are given bad thoughts and desires that distance us from the work of God, that we are not worthy of serving Him. For this reason there is a prayer that comes on that, that this is a place of correction to be worthy and capable of receiving the work of the King.

Now we can see why there is a prayer for some trouble. This trouble must have come as a punishment, and punishments must be corrections, since there is a rule that the punishment is a correction. Thus, why do we pray to the Creator to take our corrections away?

Our sages say about the verse, "then thy brother should be dishonored before thine eyes," since the beaten is your brother. **We must know that the prayer corrects a person even more than punishment**. Thus, when prayer appears instead of punishment, the affliction is lifted and the prayer is placed in its place, to correct the body.

This is the meaning of what our sages said, "Rewarded–through the Torah; was not rewarded–through affliction." We must know that the path of Torah is a more successful way and yields more profit than the path of pain. This is because the *Kelim* (Vessels) that will be fit to receive the Upper Light are broader, and can yield *Dvekut* (Adhesion) with Him.

This is the meaning of, "He is coerced until he says, 'I want.'" It means that the Creator says, "I want the deeds of the lower ones."

The meaning of prayer is what our sages said, "The Creator craved the prayer of the righteous," where by the prayer, the

*Kelim* are made fit for the Creator to later give the abundance, since there is a fit *Kli* to receive the abundance.

## 58. JOY IS A "REFLECTION" OF GOOD DEEDS

I heard on *Sukkot* Inter 4

Joy is a "reflection" of good deeds. If the deeds are of *Kedusha* (Sanctity), hence joy appears. However, we must know that there is also a discernment of a *Klipa* (Shell). In order to know if it is *Kedusha*, the scrutiny is in the reason. In *Kedusha*, there is reason, and in the *Sitra Achra* (other side) there is no reason, since another god is sterile and does not bear fruit. Hence, when one comes by gladness, one should delve in words of Torah in order to discover the mind of the Torah.

We must also know that gladness is discerned as sublime luminescence that appears by MAN[10], which is good deeds. The Creator sentences one where one is. In other words, if one takes upon himself the burden of the Kingdom of Heaven for eternity, there is an immediate sublime luminescence on that, which is considered eternity, too.

Even if one evidently sees that one will soon fall from one's degree, He still sentences one where one is. It means that if one has now made up one's mind to take upon himself the burden of the Kingdom of Heaven for eternity, it is considered wholeness.

However, if one takes upon himself the burden of the Kingdom of Heaven and does not want that state to remain in him forever, this thing and this deed is not considered wholeness, and naturally, the Upper Light cannot come and rest on it. This is because it is whole and eternal, and it is not about to change. With a person, however, even if he wants, the state one is in will not be eternal.

---

10 abb. for *Mayin Nukvin* (Female Waters).

## 59. ABOUT THE ROD AND THE SERPENT

I heard on *Adar* 13, February 23, 1948

"And Moses answered and said: 'But, behold, they will not believe me,'" etc. "And the Lord said unto him: 'What is that in thy hand?' And he said: 'A rod.' And He said: 'Cast it on the ground…' and it became a serpent; and Moses fled from before it" (Exodus 4).

We must understand that there are not more than two degrees, either *Kedusha* (Sanctity) or *Sitra Achra* (Other Side). There is no intermediary state, but the same rod itself becomes a serpent, if thrown to the ground.

In order to understand that, we will precede with the words of our sages, that He had put His *Shechina* (Divinity) on trees and rocks. Trees and rocks are called things of inferior importance, and specifically in this manner He placed His *Shechina*. This is the meaning of the question, "What is that in **thy hand**?"

A **hand** means attainment, from the words, "and if a hand attains." A **rod** means that all one's attainments are built on the discernment of inferior importance, which is faith above reason.

(This is because faith is regarded as having inferior importance, and as lowness. One appreciates the things that clothe within reason. However, if one's mind does not attain it, but resists one's mind, then one should say that the faith is of superior importance to one's mind. It follows that at that time one lowers one's mind, and says that what he understands within reason, that he resists the path of the Creator, that faith is more important than his mind. This is because all the concepts that contradict the path of the Creator are worthless concepts.

Rather, "that have eyes, and see not, that have ears, and hear not." It means that one annuls everything that one hears and sees, and this is called going above reason. And thus it seems to a person as lowness and smallness.

However, with the Creator, faith is not considered lowness. This is because one who has no other counsel and must take the path of faith considers faith as lowness. However, the Creator could have placed His *Shechina* on something other than trees and rocks.

Yet, He chose this way, called faith, specifically. He must have chosen it because it is better and more successful. You find that for Him faith is not regarded as inferior importance. Quite the contrary, this path has many merits, but it appears low to the eyes of the creatures.)

If the rod is thrown to the ground and one wants to work with a higher discernment, meaning within reason, degrading the above reason, and this work seems low, one's Torah and the work immediately become a serpent. This is the meaning of the primordial serpent, and this is the meaning of, "Any one who is proud, the Creator tells him: 'He and I cannot dwell in the same abode.'"

The reason is, as we have said, that He has placed His *Shechina* on trees and rocks. Hence, if one throws the discernment of the rod to the ground, and raises oneself to work with a higher attribute, this is already a serpent. There is no middle; it is either a serpent, or *Kedusha*, since all the Torah and the work that one had from the discernment of a rod, all has now entered the discernment of serpent.

It is known that the *Sitra Achra* has no Lights. Hence, in corporeality too, the will to receive has only deficiencies, but not fulfillments of the deficiencies. And the vessel of reception remains forever in deficit, without fulfillment, because one who has one hundred, wants two hundred etc., and one does not die with half one's wish in one's hand.

This extends from the Upper Roots. The root of the *Klipa* (Shell) is the vessel of reception, and they have no correction in the six thousand years. The *Tzimtzum* (Restriction) is placed upon them, and hence, they do not have Lights and abundance.

This is why they entice one to draw Light to their degree. And the Lights that one receives by being adhered with *Kedusha*, since abundance shines in *Kedusha*, when they seduce one to draw abundance to their state, they receive that Light. Thus, they have dominion over a person, meaning they give him satisfaction in the state he is in so that he will not move away.

Hence, one cannot move forward through this dominion, because one has no need for a higher degree. Since one has no need, one cannot move from one's place, even a slight movement.

In that state one is unable to discern if one is advancing in *Kedusha* or the other way around. This is because the *Sitra Achra* gives one power to work more strongly, since now one is within reason, and can therefore work not in a state of lowness. It follows that thus one would remain in the authority of the *Sitra Achra*.

In order for one to not remain in the authority of the *Sitra Achra*, the Creator had made a correction where if one leaves the discernment of the rod, one immediately falls into the discernment of the serpent. One immediately falls into a state of failures and has no power to strengthen, unless one accepts the discernment of faith, called lowness, once more.

It follows that the failures themselves cause one to take upon himself the discernment of rod once more, which is the discernment of faith above reason. This is the meaning of what Moses had said, "But, behold, they will not believe me." It means that they will not want to take upon themselves the path of working in faith above reason.

In that state the Creator had told him, "What is that in thy hand? A rod." "Cast it on the ground," and then, "it became a serpent." It means that there is no intermediary state between the rod and the serpent. It is rather to know if one is in *Kedusha*, or in the *Sitra Achra*.

It turns out that in any case, they do not have any choice other than to assume the discernment of faith above reason, called "a rod." This rod should be in the hand; the rod should not be thrown. This is the meaning of the verse, "The rod of Aaron was budded."

It means that all the budding one had in serving the Creator was based specifically on Aaron's rod. This means that He wanted to give us a sign to know if we are walking on the path of truth, or not. He gave us as sign to know only the basis of the work, meaning what basis one is working on. If one's basis is the rod, it is *Kedusha*, and if the basis is within reason, this is not the way to achieve *Kedusha*.

However, in the work itself, meaning in the Torah and in the prayer, there is no distinction between one who serves Him and one who does not serve Him. This is because it is the opposite there: if the basis is within reason, meaning based on knowing and receiving, the body gives fuel for work, and one can pray and study more persistently and more enthusiastically, since it is based on within reason.

However, when one takes the path of *Kedusha*, whose basis is bestowal and faith, one requires great preparation so that *Kedusha* will shine for him. Without the preparation, the body does not give one the strength for work, and one must always exert extensively, since man's root is reception, and within reason.

Hence, if one's work is based on earthliness, one can always be alright. However, if one's basis for the work is on the discernment of bestowal and above reason, one needs perpetual efforts so as not to fall into one's root of reception, and within reason.

One must not be neglectful for a minute, otherwise one will fall into one's root of earthliness, called "dust," as it is written, "for dust thou art, and unto dust shalt thou return." And that was after the sin of the Tree of Knowledge.

One examines if one is advancing in *Kedusha* or to the contrary, since another god is sterile and does not bear fruit. The Holy *Zohar* gives us that sign, that specifically on the basis of faith, called "a rod," is one imparted "be fruitful and multiply" in the Torah. This is the meaning of "the rod of Aaron was budded": the budding and growing come specifically through the rod.

Therefore, as one rises from one's bed daily and washes oneself to purify one's body from the filth of the body, so one should wash oneself from the filth of the *Klipa*, to examine oneself if one's discernment of rod is in completeness.

This should be a perpetual examination, and if one is distracted from it, one immediately falls to the authority of the *Sitra Achra*, called self-reception. One becomes immediately enslaved to them, as it is known that the Light creates the *Kli*, hence, as much as one works in order to receive, to that extent one needs only a desire to receive for oneself, and becomes remote from matters concerning bestowal.

Now we can understand the words of our sages, "Be very very humble." What is that fuss that it says, "very very"? It is because one becomes needy of the creatures, by having been honored once. At first one receives the honor not because he wanted to enjoy the honor, but for other reasons, such as the glory of the Torah, etc.. One is certain of this scrutiny since one knows about himself that he has no desire for honor whatsoever.

It follows that it is reasonable to think that one is permitted to receive the honor. However, it is still forbidden to receive because the Light makes the vessel. Hence, after one has received the honor, one becomes needy of the honor, and one is already in its dominion, and it is hard to break free from the honor.

As a result, one acquires one's own reality and it is now hard to annul before the Creator, since through the honor one has become a separate entity, and in order to obtain *Dvekut* (Adhesion) one must annul one's reality completely. Hence the "very, very." "Very" is that it is forbidden to receive honor for oneself, and the other "very" is that even when one's intention is not for self, it is still forbidden to receive.

## 60. A *MITZVA* THAT COMES THROUGH TRANSGRESSION

I heard on *Tetzve* 1, February 14, 1943

A *Mitzva* that comes through transgression means that if one takes upon oneself the work in order to receive a reward, it is then divided into two things:

- **A.** The reception of the work, which is called a *Mitzva*.
- **B.** The intention: to receive a reward. It is called a sin because reception moves one from *Kedusha* (Sanctity) to *Sitra Achra* (Other Side).

The whole basis and the reason that gave one the strength to work was the reward; hence, a *Mitzva* **'that comes,'** meaning that one was brought to perform the *Mitzva*, this is the transgression. This is why it is called a "*Mitzva* **that comes**"; that which brings the *Mitzva* is the transgression, which is only the reward.

The advice for it is to do one's work in the form of, "without seeing more," that one's whole aim of the work will be to increase the glory of heaven in the world. This is called working in order to raise Divinity from the dust.

The matter of raising Divinity means that **the Holy Divinity is called "the collective of the souls."** It receives the abundance from the Creator, and dispenses to the souls. The administrator and what transfers the abundance to the souls is called "the unification of the Creator and divinity," at which time the abundance extends to the lower ones. However, when there is no unification, there is no extension of abundance to the lower ones.

To make it clearer, because the Creator wanted to delight His creatures, therefore, as He thought of dispensing the abundance, He also thought of the reception of the abundance. That is, that the lower ones would receive the abundance. And both were in potential. This means that afterwards, souls will come and they will receive the actual abundance.

Also, the receiver of the abundance in potential is called "Holy Divinity," since the thought of the Creator is a whole reality, and He does not need an actual deed. Hence the lower one... (discontinued)

## 61. ROUND ABOUT HIM IT STORMETH MIGHTILY

I heard on *Nisan* 9, April 18, 1948

Our sages say about the verse, "and round about Him it stormeth mightily," that the Creator is particularly meticulous with the righteous. He asked: If they are generally righteous, why do they deserve a great punishment?

The thing is that all the borders we speak of in the worlds are from the perspective of the receivers, meaning the lower ones limit and restrict themselves to some degree, and thus remain below. Above, they agree to everything that the lower ones do, hence, to that extent the abundance extends below. Hence, by their thoughts, words and actions, the lower ones induce the abundance to come down from Above in this manner.

It turns out that if the lower one regards a minor act or word as if it is an important act, such as considering a momentary cessation in adhesion with the Creator as breaking the most serious prohibition in the Torah, then there is consent Above to the opinion of the lower one and it is considered Above as though he had broken a serious prohibition. Thus, the righteous says that the Creator is particularly meticulous with him, and as the lower one says, so it is agreed Above.

When the lower one does not feel a slight prohibition as a serious one, from Above they also do not regard the trifle things he breaks as great prohibitions. Hence, such a person is treated as though he is a small person, meaning his precepts are considered small, and his sins are considered small, too. They are both weighed as the same and he is generally considered a small person.

However, one who regards the trifle things and says that the Creator is very meticulous about them is considered a great person, and both his sins and his precepts are great.

One can suffer when committing a transgression to the extent that he feels pleasure when performing a good deed. There is a parable about that: A man did a terrible crime against the kingship and was sentenced to twenty years imprisonment with hard labor. The prison was outside the country in some desolate place in the world. The sentence was executed right away and he was sent to the desolate place at the end of the world.

Once there, he'd found other people who were sentenced by the kingdom to be there as he was, but he became sick with amnesia and forgot that he had a wife and children, friends and acquaintances. He thought that the whole world is nothing more than meets the eye in the desolate place with the people who are there; and that he was born there and did not know of more than that. Thus, his truth is according to his present feeling and he has no regard for the actual reality, only according to his knowledge and sensations.

There he was taught rules and regulations so that he would not break the rules once more, keep himself from the felonies written there, and know how to correct his actions so as to be brought out of there. In the books of the king, he learned that one who breaks this rule, for example, is sent to a desolate land far from any settlement. He is impressed by the harsh punishment, and has grievances at why such harsh punishments are given.

Yet, he would never think that he himself is one who broke the rules of the state, that he has been sentenced harshly and the verdict has been executed. In addition, since he became sick with amnesia, he will never feel his actual state.

This is the meaning of "and round about him it stormeth mightily": One must consider his every move, that he himself had already broken the king's commandment, and has already been banished from the settlement. Now, through many good deeds, his memory begins to work and he begins to feel how far he has become from the settled place of the world.

He begins to engage in repentance until he is delivered from there and brought back to the settled place, and this work comes specifically by one's work. He begins to feel that he has grown far from his origin and root until he is endowed adhesion with the Creator.

## 62. DESCENDS AND INCITES, ASCENDS AND COMPLAINS

I heard on *Adar Aleph* 19, February 29, 1948

Descends and incites, ascends and complains. One must always examine oneself, if one's Torah and work do not descend to the abyss. This is because one's greatness is measured by one's measure of *Dvekut* (Adhesion) with the Creator, meaning on one's **measure of annulment before the Creator**.

In other words, one's self-love does not merit reference, but one wishes to annul one's self completely. This is because in one who works in order to receive, the measure of one's work is the measure of the greatness of one's self. At that time one becomes a being, an object, and a separate authority. In that state it is difficult for one to annul before the Creator.

However, when one works in order to bestow, and when one completes one's work, meaning that he has corrected one's entire vessels of reception for oneself from what he has from the root of his soul, then he has nothing more to do in the world. It follows that one should think and concentrate on that point only.

The sign that one is walking on the path of truth if one is in the form of "descending and inciting," meaning that one's entire work is in a state of descent. In that state one is in the authority of the *Sitra Achra* (Other Side), and then he ascends and complains, meaning one feels oneself in a state of ascent, and complains about others. Yet, one who works in purity always complains about oneself, and sees others in a better degree than he feels himself.

## 63. I WAS BORROWED ON, AND I REPAY

I heard on the eve after Shabbat, 1938

Understand what our sages said, "I was borrowed on, and I repay." It means that the purpose of making the heaven and earth is the Light of the Shabbat. This Light should come to disclosure to the lower ones, and this purpose appears through Torah and *Mitzvot* and good deeds.

*Gmar Tikun* (end of correction) means when this Light appears in its completeness through an awakening from below, meaning preceded by Torah and *Mitzvot*. Yet, before *Gmar Tikun* there is also a discernment of Shabbat, called "A likeness of the next world," when the Light of Shabbat shines in both the individual and the public as a whole.

This Light of Shabbat Comes by credit, meaning without preceding exertion, though afterwards one will pay off for all the credit. In other words, afterwards one will give all the exertion that one had to give before one was imparted the Light, he will pay afterwards.

This is the meaning of "I was borrowed on," meaning draw the Light of Shabbat by credit, and I will pay, from the verse, "and let the hair of the woman's head go loose."[11] It means that the Creator will reveal this Light only if Israel will borrow, meaning extend. Although they are still not worthy, by credit, one can still draw.

## 64. FROM *LO LISHMA* TO *LISHMA*

I heard on *Vayechi*, *Tevet* 14, December 27, 1947

From *Lo Lishma* one comes to *Lishma*. If we pay close attention, we can say that the period of ***Lo Lishma*** is the more important time, since it is easier to unite the act with the Creator.

This is so because in ***Lishma*** one says that he did this good deed because he serves the Creator in wholeness, and all his actions are for the Creator. It follows that he is the owner of the act.

However, when one engages in ***Lo Lishma***, one does not do the good deed for the Creator. It turns out that one cannot

11 In Hebrew, the same word is used for letting loose and for paying off.

come to Him with a complaint that he deserves a reward. Thus, for him the Creator is not in debt.

Hence, why did he do that good deed? Only because the Creator provided him an opportunity that this SAM would compel him and force him to do it.

For example, if people come to one's house, and one is ashamed of being idle, one takes a book and studies Torah. Thus, who is one studying Torah for? It is not for the *Mitzva* of the Creator, to be favored in the eyes of the Creator, but for the guests who have come into his authority, to find grace in the eyes of man. Thus, how then can one seek reward from the Creator for this Torah, which he engaged in for the guests?

It follows that for him, the Creator did not become debited, and instead, he can charge the guests, that they would pay him a reward, meaning honor him for studying Torah. However, one cannot debit the Creator in any way.

When one performs self-examination, and says that finally, I engage in the Torah, and tosses off the cause, meaning the guests, and says that now he is working only for the Creator, then one should immediately say that everything is conducted from Above. It means that the Creator wanted to grant him engagement in the Torah, and he is not worthy of receiving an element of truth. He is unworthy of receiving the truth, hence the Creator provided him a false cause, and through this cause one engages in the Torah.

It follows that the Creator is the operator, and not the individual. Then, moreover, one should praise the Creator that even in a state of lowness that he is in, the Creator does not leave him and gives him power, meaning fuel to want to engage in words of Torah.

You find that if one pays attention to this act, one notices that the Creator is the operator, in the form of, "He alone does and will do all the deeds." Yet, one does not put any action in the good deed. Although one makes that *Mitzva*, he does not do it for a *Mitzva*, but for another cause (man), and the cause extended from the separation.

The truth is that the Creator is the cause and He is the reason that compels him. But the Creator is robed in him in another clothing, and not in a clothing of a *Mitzva*, but for another fear or another love. It follows that during the *Lo Lishma*, it is easier to attribute the good deed and say that the Creator is the doer of the good deed, and not man.

This is simple, because one does not want to do the thing for a *Mitzva*, but for another cause. However, in ***Lishma***, one knows in oneself that he is working because of the *Mitzva*.

This means that he himself was the cause, meaning because of a *Mitzva*, but not because the Creator did not place the idea and the desire to make the *Mitzva* in his heart, but he himself chose it. The truth is that it was all done by the Creator, but private Providence cannot be attained by a person prior to attaining the matter of reward and punishment.

## 65. ABOUT THE REVEALED AND THE CONCEALED

I heard on, *Tevet* 29, January 18, 1942

It is written, "The secret things belong unto the Lord our God; but the things that are revealed belong unto us and to our children forever, that we may do all the words of this law." We should ask, "What does the text come to tell us, that the secret things belong unto the Lord?" We should not say that concealed means unattainable and that revealed means attainable. We can see that there are people with knowledge in the concealed part, as there are people who have no knowledge in the revealed part.

And it cannot be said that this means that there are more people with knowledge in the revealed part than in the concealed part. (If so, you have given only a part of the whole picture).

The thing is that in this world, we see that there are actions that are revealed as actions to our eyes. This means that man's hand is involved there. Alternatively, there are actions where we see that an act is done, but man cannot do anything there. Rather, a hidden force operates there.

It is as our sages said: "There are three partners in man–the Creator, his father, and his mother." The revealed part is the commandment to be fruitful and multiply. This act is done by the parents. And if the parents do their things properly, the Creator puts a soul in the newborn. This means that his parents do the revealed part, as they can only do the revealed part, but the hidden part–placing the soul in the newborn–here the parents cannot do a thing; only the Creator Himself does that thing.

Similarly, with the *Mitzvot*, we must do only the revealed part, as only here we can act, that is, engage in Torah and *Mitzvot* by way of "that **fulfill** His word." However, the hidden part, meaning the soul in the keeping of Torah and *Mitzvot*, there one cannot do a thing. And when one keeps the Torah and *Mitzvot* in action, called "doing," one should pray to the Creator that He will do the concealed part, meaning place a soul in the practical part of our share.

The practical part is called "a candle of a *Mitzva*," which are only candles, which must be lit by the "Torah, Light." The Light of the Torah ignites the *Mitzva* and gives the soul and the liveliness in the practical part, as with the newborn, where there are three partners.

And this is the meaning of "the things that are revealed belong unto us," meaning that we must work in the form of "whatsoever thy hand attaineth to do by thy strength, that do."

It is only here that we can act; but obtaining the soul and vitality depend on the Creator.

And this is the meaning of "The secret things belong unto the Lord our God." The Creator promises that if we do the share that is revealed to us, acting on the conditions of the Torah and *Mitzvot* in the practical part, the Creator will put a soul into our actions. However, before we are awarded the concealed, called "a soul," our revealed part is like a body without a soul. Thus, we must be awarded the hidden part, and this is only in the hands of the Creator.

## 66. THE GIVING OF THE TORAH

I heard during a meal on the eve of *Shavuot* (Pentecost), 1948

The issue of the giving of the Torah that occurred on Mount Sinai does not mean that the Torah was given once and then the giving was stopped. Rather, there is no absence in spirituality, since spirituality is an eternal matter, unending. But since, from the perspective of the giver, we are unfit to receive the Torah, we say that the cessation is by the Upper One.

However, then, at the foot of Mount Sinai, the whole of Israel were ready to receive the Torah, as it is written, "there Israel encamped before the mount, as one man in one heart." At that time, the whole public was prepared; they had but one intention, which is a single thought about the reception of the Torah.

However, there are no changes from the perspective of the Giver–He always gives. It is written in the name of the Baal Shem Tov that every day must one hear the ten commandments on Mount Sinai.

The Torah is called the "potion of life" and the "potion of death." We must understand how two opposites can be said about a single subject.

We must know that we cannot attain any reality as it is in itself. Rather, we attain everything according to our sensations. And reality, as it is in itself, is of no interest to us at all. Hence, we do not attain the Torah as it is in itself, but only attain our sensations. Thus, all of our impressions follow only our sensations.

Therefore, when a person is studying Torah, and the Torah removes him from the love of God, this Torah is certainly considered "the potion of death." Conversely, if this Torah that he is learning brings him closer to the love of God, it is certainly considered "the potion of life."

But the Torah in itself, the existence of the Torah in and of itself, without consideration of the lower one who must attain it, is considered "a Light without a *Kli*," where there is no attainment whatsoever. Hence, when we speak of the Torah, it refers to the sensations that a person receives from the Torah, and only they determine the reality for the creatures.

When one works for oneself, it is called *Lo Lishma* (not for Her Name). But from *Lo Lishma* we arrive at *Lishma* (for Her Name). Hence, if one has not yet been rewarded with the reception of the Torah, one hopes to be rewarded with the reception of the Torah in the following year. But when one has been awarded the wholeness of *Lishma*, one has nothing more to do in this world, since he has already corrected everything to being in the wholeness of *Lishma*.

For this reason, each and every year there is the time of reception of the Torah, since that time is ready for an awakening from below. This is because it is the awakening of the time when the Light of the giving of the Torah was revealed in the lower ones. Hence, there is an awakening from Above, which gives strength to the lower ones to be able to perform the qualifying act to receive the Torah, as then, when they were ready to receive the Torah.

Therefore, if one marches on a path where the *Lo Lishma* will bring him the *Lishma*, he marches on the path of truth. Then one should hope that he will eventually be rewarded with achieving Lishma, and will be awarded the reception of the Torah.

Yet, caution is required, to constantly keep the goal before one's eyes, or he will march on an opposite line, as the root of the body is reception for itself. Thus, it always draws to its root, which is reception in order to receive, the opposite of the Torah, called "the tree of life." This is why the body considers the Torah "the potion of death."

## 67. DEPART FROM EVIL

I heard after the holiday of *Sukkot* (the Tabernacles Feast), October 5, 1942, Jerusalem

We must take caution with "depart from evil," to keep the four covenants.

1) The covenant of the eyes, which is to caution from looking at women. And the prohibition is not necessarily because it might lead to a thought. The evidence of that is that the prohibition applies also to an old man of one hundred years. Rather, the real reason is that it extends from a very high root: the caution is because if one is not cautious, one might come to look upon the Holy *Shechina* (Divinity).
2) The covenant of the tongue, to be watchful with truth and falsehood. The scrutinies that exist now, after the

> sin of *Adam ha Rishon*, are scrutinies of true and false. However, prior to the sin of the tree of knowledge the scrutinies concerned bitter and sweet. Yet, when the scrutiny is in truth and falsehood, it is entirely different. At times it begins sweet and ends bitter. Hence, it follows that there is a reality of bitter which is nonetheless true.

For this reason we must be careful with changing our words. Although one thinks that one is only lying to one's friend, we should know that the body is like a machine: as it is accustomed to walk, so it continues to walk. Therefore, when it is accustomed to falsehood and deceit, it is then impossible to walk by another way, and this forces man to proceed with falsehood and deceit when one is alone, too.

It turns out that one must deceive oneself and cannot tell oneself the truth at all, because he does not find any special preference to the truth.

We might say that he who thinks that he is deceiving his friend, is really deceiving the Creator, since besides man's body there is only the Creator. This is because it is the essence of creation that man is called "creature" only with respect to himself. The Creator wants man to feel that he is a separated reality from Him; but except for that, it is all "the whole earth is full of His glory."

Hence, when lying to one's friend, one is lying to the Creator; and when saddening one's friend, one is saddening the Creator. For this reason, if one is accustomed to speak the truth, it will help him with respect to the Creator. That is, if one had promised something to the Creator, he will try to keep his promise, since he is not used to changing his word, and by that he will be rewarded with "the Lord is thy shade." If one keeps and does what he says, the Creator, too, will keep "blessed is he who says and does" in return.

There is a sign in the covenant of the tongue, to not speak of everything that is possible, since by speaking one reveals what is in one's heart, and this gives a hold to the externals. This is so because as long as one is not perfectly clean, when he reveals something of his interior, the *Sitra Achra* (other side) has power to complain Above, and mock one's work. She says, "What kind of work is he giving upward, since his whole intention in this work is only downward?"

This answers a great question: it is known that "a *Mitzva* induces a *Mitzva*"; so why do we often see that one often falls from one's work? As we have said above, the *Sitra Achra* defames and complains about one's work, and then comes down and takes one's soul. That is, since she has already defamed Above, and said that his work was not clean, but that he is working in the form of reception for oneself, she comes down and takes the spirit of one's life by asking, "What mean you by this service?" Hence, even when one is awarded some illumination of the spirit of life, he loses it again.

The advice for it is to walk humbly, so she will not know about his work, by way of "he does not reveal from the heart to the mouth." Then the *Sitra Achra* cannot know of one's work, as she only knows what is revealed by word or action; this is what she can grip.

And we should know that pain and suffering comes primarily through those who slander. Hence, we should be as careful as we can with speaking. Moreover, we should know that even when speaking mundane words, this still reveals the secrets of one's heart. This is the meaning of "My soul failed me when he spoke." This is the covenant of the tongue, with which we must take caution.

And the keeping should especially be during the ascent, since during the descent it is hard to walk in great degrees and cautions.

## 68. MAN'S CONNECTION TO THE *SEFIROT*

I heard on *Adar* 12, February 17, 1943

**Prior to the sin of *Adam ha Rishon*:**

1. His *Guf* (body) was from *Bina de Malchut de Malchut de Assiya*;
2. And he had *NRN* from *Beria* and *NRN* from *Atzilut*.

**After he sinned:**

His *Guf* fell into the discernment of the serpent's skin, which is the *Klipa* (shell) of *Behina Dalet*, called "the dust of this world." Clothed within it is the inner *Guf* of the Noga Shell, which is half good and half bad. And all the good deeds that he does are only with this *Guf* of Noga. And through engaging in Torah and *Mitzvot*, he brings this *Guf* back to being entirely good, and the *Guf* of the serpent's skin is departed from him. And then he is awarded *NRN* of *Kedusha*, according to his actions.

**Man's NRN Connection to the *Sefirot*:**

The essence of man's *NRN* is from *Behinat Malchut* of the three *Sefirot*, *Bina* and *ZON* in each of the worlds from *ABYA*. If he is awarded the *NRN* of *Nefesh*, he receives from the three *Behinot Malchut de Bina* and *ZON de Assiya*. If he is awarded *NRN de Ruach*, he receives from the three *Behinot Malchut de Bina* and *ZON de Yetzira*. And if he is awarded *NRN de Neshama*, he receives from the three *Behinot Malchut de Bina* and *ZON de Beria*. And if he is awarded *NRN de Haya*, he receives from the three *Behinot Malchut de Bina* and *ZON de Atzilut*.

And this is what our sages said, that man thinks only from within the thoughts of his heart, that **the whole body is considered "heart."** And even though man consists of four discernments of still, vegetative, animate, and speaking, they are all registered in the heart.

Since after the sin, the *Guf* of *Adam ha Rishon* fell into the serpent's skin, which is the *Klipa* of *Behina Dalet*, called "the dust of this world," hence, when he calculates, all his thoughts are of his heart, meaning his *Guf* from the *Behina* of the serpent's skin.

And when he prevails through his engagement in Torah and *Mitzvot*–the only remedy–if he aims to bestow contentment upon his Maker, the Torah and *Mitzvot* purify his body. This means that the serpent's skin departs from him. Then, the previous act of the Torah and *Mitzvot*, called "the Noga Shell," considered the "inner *Guf*," which was half good and half bad, has now become all good. This means that now he has achieved equivalence of form.

And then he is awarded the *NRN* of *Kedusha*, according to his deeds. That is, in the beginning he attains *NRN de Nefesh* from the world *Assiya*. Latterly, when he examines all the discernments that belong to the world *Assiya*, he is awarded *NRN de Ruach* of the world *Yetzira*, until he achieves *NRN de Haya de Atzilut*.

Thus, a different structure is made within his heart every time: where there was previously the inner *Guf* from the Noga Shell, which was half good and half bad, this *Guf* is now turned into all good, through the cleansing he had received from the Torah and *Mitzvot*.

Accordingly, when he had a body from the serpent's skin, he had to think and calculate his thoughts only from within the thoughts in his heart. This means that all his thoughts were only about how to fulfill the desires to which the *Klipa* compels him. He had no counsel to think thoughts and aim intentions, only what sat within his heart, which was then in the form of the serpent's skin, the worst *Klipa*.

Also, when he is rewarded through his engagement in Torah and *Mitzvot*, even in *Lo Lishma* (not for Her Name), when he asks and demands of the Creator to help him by engaging in Torah and *Mitzvot* in the form of "whatsoever thy hand attaineth to do by thy hand, that do," and he awaits mercy from Above, that the Creator will thus help him achieve *Lishma*, that the whole reward that he is asking for his work is that he will be rewarded with working in order to bring contentment to his Maker, as our sages said, "the Light in it reforms it."

In that state the body of the serpent's skin is purified, meaning that that body is separated from him, and he is awarded an entirely different structure—the structure of *Nefesh de Assiya*. He also adds further until he achieves a structure from *Nefesh* and *Ruach de Bina* and ZA and *Malchut de Atzilut*.

But even then one has no option to think other thoughts, but only according to what the structure of *Kedusha* dictates. This means that he has no room to think thoughts against his own structure, but he must think and act only with the intention to bring contentment to his Maker, as his structure of *Kedusha* necessitates.

All the above means that one cannot correct one's thought, but should only aim the heart—make one's heart straight to the Creator. Then all of his thoughts and actions will naturally be to bestow contentment upon his Maker. And when he corrects his heart to have a heart and desire of *Kedusha*, the heart will then be the *Kli* in which to place the Upper Light. And when the Upper Light shines in the heart, the heart will strengthen and he will add and supplement continuously.

Now we can interpret our sages' words, "Great is the study that yields action." It means that through the Light of the Torah, he is led into action, as **the Light in it reforms it. This is called "an act."** This means that the Light of the Torah builds a new structure in his heart.

Thus, the previous *Guf*, which came to him from the serpent's skin, has been separated from him and he has been awarded a sacred *Guf*. The inner *Guf*, called "the Noga Shell," which was half good, half bad, has become all good, and now the *NRN* is in it, which he attains through his actions, as he adds and supplements.

Before he is awarded a new structure, although he tries to cleanse his heart, the heart is still unchanged. In that state it is considered that he is in the form of "that fulfill His word." Yet, we must know that the beginning of the work is specifically in the form of "that fulfill His word."

But this is not completeness, since he cannot cleanse his thoughts in that state, since he cannot be saved from thoughts of transgression, as his heart is of a *Guf* of *Klipa*, and one thinks only from the thoughts in one's heart. Rather, only the Light in it reforms it. At this time the separating *Guf* departs from him, and the inner *Guf*, the Noga Shell, which was half bad, becomes all good. In that state, the Torah brings one into action through the making of a new structure. And this is called "an act."

## 69. FIRST WILL BE THE CORRECTION OF THE WORLD

I heard on *Sivan*, June, 1943

He said that first will be the correction of the world, then will be the complete redemption, the coming of the Messiah. This is the meaning of "but thine eyes shall see thy Teacher," etc., "and the whole earth shall be full of the knowledge." This is the meaning of what he wrote, that first the interior of the worlds will be corrected, and subsequently the exterior of the worlds. But we must know that the externality of the worlds is a higher degree than the correction of the internality.

And the root of Israel is from the interior of the worlds. This is the meaning of "for ye were the fewest of all peoples." However, by correcting the interior, the exterior is corrected, too, though in small pieces. And the exterior will be corrected every time (until many pennies accumulate into a great sum), until all the exterior is corrected.

The main difference between the internal and the external is, for example, when one performs a certain *Mitzva*, not all the organs agree to it. It is like a person who fasts. We say that only his interior agreed with the fast, but his exterior is feeling discomfort by the fast, since the body is always in opposition to the soul. Thus, the difference between Israel and the nations of the world should only be made concerning the soul; but concerning the body, they are equal: Israel's body, too, cares only for its own benefit.

Hence, when individuals in the whole of Israel are corrected, the whole world will naturally be corrected. It follows that the nations of the world will be corrected to the extent that we correct ourselves. This is the meaning of what our sages said, "Rewarded–sentences himself and the whole world to a scale of merit." And they did not say, "sentences the whole of Israel," but "the entire world to a scale of merit." In other words, the internal will correct the external.

## 70. WITH A MIGHTY HAND AND WITH FURY POURED OUT

I heard on *Sivan* 25, June 28, 1943

To understand what is written, "with a mighty hand, ...and with fury poured out, will I be king over you," we should understand that there is a rule that there is no coercion in spirituality, as it is written, "thou hast not called upon Me, O Jacob, neither hast thou wearied thyself about Me, O Israel." There is a known interpretation by the Sayer of Duvna; hence, what does “with a mighty hand, ...and with fury poured out, will I be king over you” mean?

He said that we should know that of those who want to enter God’s work in order to truly cleave unto Him and enter the King’s Palace, not every one is admitted. Rather, one is tested–if he has no other desires but only a desire for *Dvekut* (adhesion), he is admitted.

And how is one tested if he has only one desire? One is given obstructions. This means that he is sent alien thoughts and alien messengers to obstruct him so he would leave this path and follow the path of the populace.

And if one overcomes all the difficulties and breaks all the bars that block him, and little things cannot turn him off, then the Creator sends him great *Klipot* and chariots, to deflect one from admittance into adhesion with Him alone, and with nothing else. This is considered that the Creator is rejecting him with a mighty hand.

If the Creator does not show His mighty hand, it will be hard to turn him off, since he has a strong desire to cleave only to the Creator and to nothing else.

But when the Creator wants to repel one whose desire is not so strong, He turns him off with a slight thing. By giving him a great desire for corporeality, he already leaves the holy work entirely, and there is no need to repel him with a mighty hand.

Yet, when one overcomes the hardships and the obstructions, one is not easily repelled, but with a mighty hand. And if one overcomes even the mighty hand, and does not want to move from the place of *Kedusha* (Sanctity) whatsoever, and wants to cleave specifically onto Him in truth, and sees that he is being repelled, then one says that fury is poured out on him. Otherwise, he would be allowed inside. But because fury is poured out on him by the Creator, he is not admitted into the King’s Palace, to cleave onto Him in truth.

It follows that before one wants to move from one's place, and breaks in and wants to enter, it cannot be said that one feels that fury is poured out on him. Rather, after all the rejections that he is rejected, when he does not move from his place, meaning when the mighty hand and the fury poured out have already been revealed upon him, then "will I be king over you." This is so because only through bursting and great efforts does the Kingdom of Heaven become revealed to him, and he is allowed into the King's Palace.

## 71. MY SOUL SHALL WEEP IN SECRET

I heard on *Sivan* 25, June 28, 1943

"My soul shall weep in secret for your pride," for the pride of Israel. He asks, "Is there crying before the Creator, because 'strength and gladness are in His place'"? We must understand the matter of weeping Above. Weeping is in a place where one cannot help oneself. Then one weeps that the other will help him. The meaning of "in secret" is concealments and the contradictions that appear in the world.

And this is the meaning of "my soul shall weep in secret," since "all is in the hands of God, but for the fear of God."

Our sages said about that, that there is weeping in the inner homes. This means that when the Light shines only in the interior and there is no disclosure of Light outwardly, for lack of *Kelim* in the lower ones so they can receive, then there is weeping. However, in the outer homes, when the Light can be revealed outwardly, when the abundance becomes revealed below, to the lower ones, then "strength and gladness are in His place," and everything is seen. Yet, when He cannot bestow upon the lower ones it is called "weeping," since He needs the *Kelim* of the lower ones.

## 72. CONFIDENCE IS THE CLOTHING FOR THE LIGHT

I heard on *Nisan* 10, March 31, 1947

Confidence is the clothing for the Light, called "life." This is because there is a rule that there is no Light without a *Kli* (vessel). It follows that the Light, called "Light of life," cannot clothe, but must dress in some *Kli*. The *Kli* where the Light of life is clothed is usually called "confidence." It means that he sees that he can do every difficult thing.

Thus, the **Light is felt and recognized in the *Kli* of confidence**. Because of that, one's life is measured by the measure of confidence that appears there. One can measure the magnitude of vitality in oneself according to the confidence in himself.

For this reason, one can see in oneself that as long as his level of vitality is high the confidence shines on every single thing, and he sees nothing that can obstruct him with what he wants. This is because the Light of life, which is a force from Above, shines on him and he can work with superhuman powers, since the Upper Light is not limited like corporeal forces.

However, when the Light of life leaves him, which is considered that he has descended from his previous level of vitality, then he becomes clever and inquisitive. He begins to calculate the profitability of everything, is it worthwhile to do it or not. And he becomes temperate, and not lively and sizzling as before he began to decline in his level of vitality.

However, one does not have the wisdom to say that all this cleverness and wit with which he now thinks of everything are because he'd lost the spirit of life he had then. Instead, he thinks that now he has become smart, not as he was before he'd lost the Light of life. Rather, then he was reckless and careless.

However, he should know that all the **wisdom** that he has now acquired came to him because he has lost the spirit of life that he had had before. Before, he measured all the acts with the Light of life that the Creator gave him. But now that he is in decline the evil inclination has the power to come to him with all their "just arguments."

The counsel for it is that one should say that now he cannot speak to his body and argue with it. Rather, he should say, "Now I am **dead** and I am awaiting the revival of the dead." Then he must begin to work above reason, meaning say to his body, "Everything you say is true, and I have nothing rational to answer you. However, I hope that I will begin to work anew. Now I take upon myself Torah and *Mitzvot*, and now I am becoming a proselyte, and our sages said, 'a proselyte who has converted is like an newborn infant.' Now I await the salvation of the Creator; He will certainly help me and I will come once more into the path of holiness. And when I have **power in holiness**, then I will have what to answer you. But in the meantime I must go above reason for I am still without the mind of holiness. Hence, you can win with your intellect and there is nothing I can do but believe in our sages who said that I should keep Torah and *Mitzvot* with faith above reason. I must certainly believe that by the power of faith we will be helped from Above, as our sages said, 'He who comes to purify is aided.'"

## 73. AFTER THE *TZIMTZUM*

I heard in 1943

After the *Tzimtzum* (restriction), the Upper Nine became the place of *Kedusha*, and *Malchut*, over which there was the *Tzimtzum*, became the place of the worlds. And there are two discernments to be made: 1) a vacant place, which is a place for the *Klipot*, whose essence is the desire to receive only for themselves; and 2) a free place, meaning a place that became free for inserting what one chooses—*Kedusha* or the opposite.

Had it not been for the *Tzimtzum*, the whole of reality would have been in the form of Simple Light. Only after the *Tzimtzum* occurred was there room for choosing to do bad or good.

The bounty extends into that place through choosing the good. And this is the meaning of what is written in the writings of the Ari, that the Light of *Ein Sof* shines to the lower ones.

*Ein Sof* is called "the desire to do good to His creations." And although we discern many worlds, ten *Sefirot*, and other names, it all extends from the *Ein Sof*, called "the Thought of Creation."

The names, *Sefira* and "world," are because the abundance that pours off the *Ein Sof* descends through that *Sefira* and world. This means that since the lower ones cannot receive His bounty without preparation and correction, in order for the lower ones to be able to receive, corrections were made, by which there was ability to receive. This is called *Sefirot*.

In other words, each *Sefira* has its unique correction. Because of that there are many discernments. But they are only with respect to the receivers, since when the lower one receives the abundance from *Ein Sof*, it receives through a special correction, which adapts it to receive the bounty. This is the meaning of receiving through a special *Sefira*; although there are no changes whatsoever in the bounty itself.

Now you will understand the matter of the prayer that we pray to the Creator, which is the Light of *Ein Sof*, being the connection that the Creator has with the creatures, called "His desire to do good to His creations." And even though there are many names with the aim of the prayer, the interpretation is that the bounty will pour forth through the corrections in the souls. This is because precisely through the corrections in the souls will the abundance be in the hands of the receivers.

## 74. WORLD, YEAR, SOUL

I heard in 1943

It is known that there is no reality without someone who senses the reality. Hence, when we say "*Nefesh de Atzilut*," it means that we are sensing a certain measure of attainment in the Upper Abundance, a measure which we call *Nefesh*.

And world refers to the "common" within that attainment, meaning that all the souls have a common form so anyone who attains that degree attains that name, *Nefesh*. This means that it is not necessarily that a specific individual attains that name and in that form, but that anyone who achieves that degree–which is certainly through the preparation of *Kedusha* and purity–the abundance appears to him in that form, called *Nefesh*.

We can understand that from a corporeal example, applied in this world. For example, when one says to another, "Now I am going to Jerusalem," when he says the name of the city, everyone knows and recognizes that city. They are all certain of the place he is speaking of, since those who have already been to that city know what this is about.

## 75. THERE IS A DISCERNMENT OF THE NEXT WORLD, AND THERE IS A DISCERNMENT OF THIS WORLD

I heard during a meal celebrating a circumcision, Jerusalem

There is a discernment of "the next world," and there is a discernment of "this world." The next world is considered "faith," and this world is considered "attainment."

It is written about the next world, "they shall eat and they shall delight," meaning that there is no end to the satiation.

This is so because everything that is received by faith has no limits. However, what is received through attainment already has limits, since everything that comes in the *Kelim* of the lower one, the lower one limits it. Hence, there is a limit to the discernment of this world.

## 76. WITH ALL THY OFFERINGS THOU SHALT OFFER SALT

I heard on *Shevat* 30, January-February,
celebrating the completion of Part Six, Tiberias

"With all thy offerings thou shalt offer salt," meaning the covenant of the salt. The covenant corresponds to the mind. It is generally accepted that when two people do good to each other, when love acts between them, they certainly do not need to make a covenant. But at the same time, we can see that precisely when love acts, it is the usual time to make covenants. Then he said that the making of the covenant is for afterwards.

This means that the agreement is made now so that later, if there is a state where each of them thinks that the other's heart is not whole with one's friend, they will have an agreement. This agreement will obligate them to remember the covenant that they had made, in order to continue the old love in this state, too.

And this is the meaning of "with all thy offerings thou shalt offer salt," meaning that all the *krevut*[12] in the work of God should be about the covenant of the King.[13]

---

12 In Hebrew *Krevut* means «nearing» but also «battles.»

13 In Hebrew, the words *Melach* (salt) and *Melech* (king) are spelled and pronounced very similarly.

## 77. ONE LEARNS FROM ONE'S SOUL

I heard on *Elul* 8, August 24, 1947

"One learns from one's soul."

It is known that the whole Torah is studied primarily for the needs of the soul, meaning for those who've already been awarded a discernment of a soul. However, they must still crave and search the words of Torah of others who attained, to learn new ways from them, which the previous ones have invented in their innovations in the Torah. Thus, it will be easy for them to advance in the High Degrees, meaning that through them they will advance from degree to degree.

But there is a Torah that is forbidden to disclose, since each soul should make that scrutiny by itself, and not have that scrutiny done for it by another. Hence, before they make the scrutiny themselves, it is forbidden to disclose to them the words of Torah.

This is why the great ones hide many things. And except for this part, there is great benefit to the souls by what they receive from others' innovations of the Torah. And "one learns from one's soul" how and what to receive, and to be assisted by others' innovations in the Torah, and what he himself should innovate.

## 78. THE TORAH, THE CREATOR, AND ISRAEL ARE ONE

I heard on *Sivan*, June, 1943

"The Torah, the Creator, and Israel are one."

Hence, when one is studying Torah, he should study *Lishma*. This means that he studies with the intention that the Torah will teach him, meaning as is the name of the Torah, which means "instruction." And because "the Torah, Israel, and the Creator are one," the Torah teaches one the ways of the Creator, how He is clothed in the Torah.

## 79. *ATZILUT* AND *BYA*

I heard on *Tamuz* 15, *Pinechas* 1, July 18, 1943

*Atzilut* is considered from the *Chazeh* up, which is only vessels of bestowal. *BYA* means reception in order to bestow, the ascent of the lower *Hey* to the place of *Bina*.

Because man is immersed in the will to receive in order to receive, one cannot do a thing without having reception for oneself in there. For this reason our sages said, "from *Lo Lishma* one comes to *Lishma*." This means that we begin the engagement in Torah and *Mitzvot* in order to "give us the wealth of this world," and afterwards, "give us the wealth of the next world."

And when studying this way, one should achieve studying *Lishma*, for the Torah. This means that the Torah will teach him the ways of the Creator. And he should first make the sweetening of *Malchut* in *Bina*, which means that he elevates *Malchut*, called "will to receive," to *Bina*, which is considered bestowal. That is, that all of one's work will be only in order to bestow.

And then it becomes dark for him. He senses that the world has grown dark on him, since the body gives strength to work only in the form of reception, and not in the form of bestowal. In that state, one has but one counsel: to pray to the Creator to open his eyes so he can work in the form of bestowal.

And this is the meaning of "who stands for the question?" It refers to *Bina*, called *Mi* (water) and the question comes from the verse, "asking about the rains," meaning prayer. Since they arrive at the state of "water of *Bina*," there is room to pray for it.

## 80. CONCERNING BACK TO BACK

I heard

*Panim* and *Achor* (face and back).

*Panim* means reception of bounty or bestowal of bounty.

Negation is called *Achoraim* (posterior), meaning neither receiving nor giving.

Hence, in the beginning of the work, one is in a state of *Achor be Achor* (back to back) because he still has the vessels of the desire to receive. If he extends abundance into these *Kelim*, he could blemish the Light, since he is considered opposite in value, since the Lights come from the root, and the root only bestows.

For this reason, the lower ones use the *Kelim* of *Ima*, called *Achoraim*, meaning that they do not want to receive, so as not to blemish. And the Emanator, too, does not bestow upon them, for the above reason, that the Lights guard themselves so the lower ones do not blemish them. This is why it is called *Achor be Achor*.

To explain what is written in several places, that "wherever there is a deficiency, there is suction for the *Klipa*." We might say that the reason for it is that this place is still not clear of *Aviut*. Otherwise, the Light would have illuminated in perfection, since the Upper Light never stops. If there is a place that is corrected with a *Masach*, the Upper Light is immediately gripped there. And since there is a place of deficiency, meaning absence of the Upper Light, there is certainly a discernment of *Aviut* (thickness/will to receive), whose entire grip is in the will to receive.

## 81. CONCERNING RAISING MAN

I heard

It is known that because of the breaking, sparks of *Kedusha* fell into *BYA*. But there, in *BYA*, they cannot be corrected, and hence must be elevated to *Atzilut*. And by doing good deeds and *Mitzvot* with the aim to bring contentment to one's Maker and not to oneself, these sparks rise to *Atzilut*. Then they are integrated in the *Masach* of the Upper One, at the *Rosh* of the degree, where the *Masach* remains in its eternity. And at that time there is a *Zivug* (spiritual coupling) on the *Masach* by the *Hitkalelut* (mixture/integration) of the sparks, and the Upper Light spreads through all the worlds according to the measure of the sparks that they have raised.

This is similar to the *Hizdakchut* (purification) of the *Partzufim* of *Akudim*. We learned that during its *Hizdakchut*, when the Light departs because of it, the *Masach* of the *Guf* ascends along with the *Reshimot* to *Peh de Rosh*. The reason is that when the lower one stops receiving, it is considered that it has been purified of its *Aviut* (will to receive). Hence, the *Masach* can rise back to *Peh de Rosh*, as its whole decline into the degree of *Guf* was because the Light expanded from Above downward, into the vessels of reception.

Also, the *Rosh* is always discerned as being from below upward, meaning in resistance to the expansion. And when the *Guf* stops receiving the Lights from Above downward because of the absence of the *Masach* that had been purified by the *Bitush* (beating) of the internal and the external, it is considered that the *Masach de Guf* has been purified of its *Aviut*, and ascended to the *Rosh* with the *Reshimot*.

Additionally, when one engages in Torah and *Mitzvot* in order to bestow and not to receive, through it, the sparks rise to the *Masach* in the *Rosh*, in the world of *Atzilut* (and they rise degree-by-degree until they arrive at the *Rosh de Atzilut*). And when they are integrated in that *Masach*, and the level of Light appears according to the size of the *Masach*, more Light is added in all the worlds. And man, too, who caused that betterment Above, receives illumination by having improved Above, in the worlds.

## 82. THE PRAYER ONE SHOULD ALWAYS PRAY

What I heard in private on *Vayera*, November 1952

Faith is discerned as *Malchut* interpreted in the mind and the heart, that is, bestowal and faith. And opposite faith there is the discernment of the "foreskin," which is knowing, whose way is to appreciate the discernment of the foreskin. Faith, however, called "the Holy *Shechina* (Divinity)," is in the dust. This means that this work is considered disgraceful, and everyone escapes walking on this path. But only this is called "the path of the righteous and *Kedusha*."

The Creator wants His names to be revealed only in this manner, as in this manner it is certain that they will not blemish the Upper Lights, since the whole basis is bestowal and *Dvekut* (adhesion). Also, the *Klipot* cannot suck from this discernment, since their whole suction is from knowing and receiving.

And where there is darkness, the Holy *Shechina* cannot receive the Upper Lights into it, so the Lights do not fall into the *Klipot*. Because of that there is the sorrow of the *Shechina*, meaning that the Upper Lights are detained from being drawn into it, so it can bestow upon the souls.

And this depends on the lower ones alone. The Upper One can only dispense the Upper Light; but the force of the *Masach*, so the lower one does not want to receive anything in the vessels of reception, depends on the work of the lower ones; that is, the lower ones must make that scrutiny.

## 83. CONCERNING THE RIGHT VAV, THE LEFT VAV

I heard on *Adar* 19, February 24, 1943

There is the discernment of *Ze* ('this' in male form) and the discernment of *Zot* ('this' in female form). Moses is considered *Ze*, which is the King's best-man. The rest of the prophets are considered *Zot* or *Koh* (the letters *Chaf* and *Hey*), which is the meaning of *Yadecha* (thy hand), a left *Vav*. There also is the discernment of the right *Vav*.

And this is the meaning of "the gathering *Zayins*," which gather two *Vavs*. This is the meaning of "and one that contains them," which is the thirteen, considered a complete degree.

There is a right *Vav* and there is a left *Vav*. The right *Vav* is called "the tree of life," and the left *Vav* is called "the tree of knowledge," where there is the place of the guarding. The two *Vavs* are called "the twelve *Challahs*,"[14] two rows, six in a row, which is the meaning of the thirteen *Tikkunim* (corrections), which are twelve, and one that contains them, called "luck and cleansed."

It also contains the thirteenth correction, called "shall not be cleansed," which is the meaning of the gathering *Zayins*. The ***Zayin*** is *Malchut*; she contains them. Before one is rewarded with "shall not turn back to folly," she is called "shall not be cleansed." And those who have already been rerwarded with not turning back to folly are called "cleansed."

This is the meaning of "will reveal its flavors in twelve roars, which are a sign in his sky, twice and weak" (in the song *I will Prepare for a Meal*). It is also written, "she will be crowned with *Vavs* and gathering *Zayins*" (in the song *I will Praise with a Song*). We should interpret the crowning with the *Vavs*, that the connection through two *Vavs* is the meaning of the twelve roars (which are the twelve *Challahs*) that are a sign in the sky.

A sign is called *Yesod*, and it is called "twice and weak." This means that the *Vavs* have been doubled: the left *Vav* is called "the tree of knowledge," the place of the guarding. Then they became weak (called "light"), and then a room was made through which it was easy to pass. Had it not been for the doubling with the

14 Braided bread (traditionally served during the Sabbath).

tree of knowledge, they would have had to work with the right *Vav*, discerned as "the tree of life." And then, who could elevate himself and receive the *Mochin*?

However, with the left *Vav*, discerned as the keeping, one is always in this form. And by merit of the keeping, when he assumes above reason, his work is then desirable. This is why it is called "weak," light, meaning it is easy to find a place for work.

This means that in any state one is in, one can be the Creator's worker, since he does not need anything, but does everything above reason. It turns out that one does not need any *Mochin*, with which to be the servant of the Creator.

Now we can interpret what is written, "set up a table before me, against my enemies." A table means, as it is written, "and sendeth her out of his house, and she **departeth** out of his house, and goeth" (Deuteronomy 24:1-2). A *Shulchan* (table) is like *VeShlacha* (and sendeth her), meaning exit from the work.

We should interpret that even during the exits from the work, meaning in a state of decline, one still has a place to work. This means that when one prevails above reason during the declines, and says that the descents, too, were given to him from Above, the **enemies** are thus canceled. This is so because the enemies thought that through the declines the person will reach utter lowness and escape the campaign, but in the end the opposite occurred—the enemies were cancelled.

This is the meaning of what is written, "the table that is before the Lord," that precisely in this manner does he receive the face of the Creator. And this is the meaning of subduing all the judgments, even the greatest judgments, since he assumes the burden of the Kingdom of Heaven at all times. That is, he always finds a place for work, as it is written that Rabbi Shimon Bar-Yochai said, "there is not a place to hide from Thee."

## 84. WHAT IS "SO HE DROVE THE MAN OUT OF THE GARDEN OF EDEN LEST HE WOULD TAKE OF THE TREE OF LIFE"

I heard on *Adar* 24, March 19, 1944

It is written, "and said unto him: 'Where art thou?' And he said: 'I heard Thy voice,'" etc., "'and I was afraid, because I was naked; and I hid myself.'...lest he put forth his hand, and take also of the tree of life," etc.. "So He drove out the man."

We should understand Adam's fear, which was so much that he had to hide because he saw himself being naked. The thing is that before he ate from the tree of knowledge, his nourishment came from *Bina*, which is the world of freedom. Afterwards, when he ate from the tree of knowledge, he saw that he was naked. This means that he was afraid lest he would take the Light of Torah and use it in the form of "the herdsmen of Lot's cattle."

"The herdsmen of Lot's cattle" means that there is faith above reason, called "the herdsmen of Abraham's cattle." In other words, one who has been rewarded with attainment of the Light of Torah does not take it as the basis of one's work, saying that now he no longer needs strengthening in faith in the Creator, since he already has the foundation of the Light of the Torah. This is called "the herdsmen of Lot's cattle," considered "the cursed world," which is considered a curse. This is the opposite of faith, which is a blessing.

Rather, he said, he says that now he sees that if he goes with faith above reason, he is given the Light of the Torah from Above, to show him that he is marching on the path of truth. And it is not that he takes it as support, that his work will be within reason, from which one comes into the discernment of the vessels of reception, on which there was the *Tzimtzum* (restriction). This is why it is called "the place of the curse," since Lot means the cursed world.

And in that regard the Creator told him, "Why are you afraid to take these Lights for fear that you will blemish them? Who told thee that thou was naked? It must be because you have eaten off the tree of knowledge, and this brought you the fear. When you were previously eating off every tree in the garden, meaning when you were using the Lights by way of 'herdsmen of Abraham's cattle,' you had no fear at all." Hence he drove him out, "lest he put forth his hand, and take also of the tree of life."

The fear was that he would repent and enter the tree of life. But what is the fear? Since he had sinned in the tree of knowledge, he must now correct the tree of knowledge.

This is the meaning of "He drove him out of the garden of Eden," to correct the sin of the tree of knowledge. And afterwards he will have the ability to enter the garden of Eden.

The garden of Eden means the ascent of *Malchut* into *Bina*, where she receives *Hochma*, as Eden means *Hochma*. And then *Malchut*, called "garden," receives *Hochma* in the form of "Eden," and this is "the garden of Eden."

## 85. WHAT IS THE FRUIT OF GOODLY TREES, IN THE WORK

I heard on *Sukkot* inter 1, September 27, 1942

It is written, "And ye shall take you on the first day the fruit of goodly trees, branches of palm-trees, and boughs of thick trees, and willows of the brook" (Leviticus 23:40).

And we should interpret "fruit of goodly trees": A tree is considered righteous, called "tree of the field." "Fruit" is the progeny of the tree, meaning the progeny of the righteous, which are the good deeds, which should be in the form of adornment in his tree.

"From year to year" means a whole year, which are "six months with oil of myrrh, and six months with sweet odors." The wicked, however, are "like the chaff which the wind driveth away."

"Branches of palm-trees" are two spoons, which are the two *Heys*, the first *Hey* and the last *Hey*, by which one is awarded "one golden pan of ten shekels, full of incense."

The spoons mean coercion, that one assumes the Kingdom of Heaven coercively. This means that despite reason's disagreement, one goes above reason. This is called "coercive mating." *Tmarim* (palm-trees) comes from the word *Morah* (fear), which is fear (by way of "and God hath so made it, that men should fear before Him").

And because of that it is called *Lulav* (palm branch). This means that before one is rewarded, he has two hearts. And this is called *Lo Lev* (no heart), meaning that the heart is not devoted solely to the Creator. And when he is rewarded with the discernment of *Lo* (to Him), meaning a heart to the Creator, this is the *Lulav*.

Also, one should say, "When will my actions reach the actions of my fathers?" Through it, one is rewarded with being a branch of the holy patriarchs, and this is the meaning of "boughs of thick trees," which are the three myrtles.

Yet, at the same time one should be in the form of "willows of the brook," tasteless and scentless. And one should delight in this work, even though he feels no flavor or fragrance in this work. And then this work is called "the letters of Thy Unified Name," by which we are awarded complete unification with the Creator.

## 86. AND THEY BUILT STORE-CITIES

I heard from my father, *Shevat* 3, January 31, 1941

The writing says (Exodus 1): "And they built for Pharaoh store-cities,[15] Pithom and Raamses." We should ask, "Pithom and Raamses means that they are beautiful cities, while the words *Arei Miskenot* imply poverty and meagerness, and they also imply danger?" And we must also understand what Abraham the Patriarch asked, "Whereby shall I know that I shall inherit it" (Genesis 15; 8)? What did the Creator reply? It is written, "And He said unto Abram: Know of a surety that thy seed shall be a stranger in a land that is not theirs, and shall serve them, and they shall afflict them four hundred years."

The literal meaning is hard to understand, since the question was that he wanted guarantees on the inheritance, and there is no apparent guarantee in the Creator's answer, that your seed will be in exile, which means that this was a sufficient answer for him. Moreover, we see that when Abraham had a long argument with the Creator regarding the people of Sodom, he kept saying "perhaps." Here, however, when the Creator said that his seed will be in exile, he immediately received it as a sufficient answer, and did not argue and said, "perhaps?" Instead, he accepted it as a guarantee on the inheritance of the land.

We must understand this answer, and we must also understand what the meaning is that the *Zohar* interprets about the text, "Pharaoh drew nigh," saying that he drew them toward repentance. Can it be that evil Pharaoh would want to bring them closer to repentance?

In order to understand all that, we must understand what our sages said (*Sukkah*, 52; 71): "Rabbi Yehuda says: 'At the end of days, the Creator brings the evil inclination and slaughters

15 Translator's note: the word combination "store-cities" is not used in Hebrew, but the words *Arei Miskenot*, implying poverty and (phonetically) danger.

it before the righteous and before the wicked. To the righteous it seems like a high mountain, and to the wicked it seems as a thread of a hair's breadth. These cry and those cry. The righteous cry, saying 'How could we conquer such a high mountain?' and the wicked cry, saying 'How could we not conquer this thread of a hair's breadth?'"

This verse is perplexing through and through:

1. If the evil inclination has already been slaughtered, how are there still wicked?
2. Why do the righteous cry? Quite the contrary, they should have been happy!
3. How can there be two opinions in reality when they have both arrived at the state of truth? This verse speaks of the end of days, which is certainly a state of truth, so how can there be such a difference in reality between a thread of a hair's breadth and a high mountain?

He explains this with the words of our sages (there): "Rabbi Assi says: 'In the beginning, the evil inclination seems like spider-web, and in the end, it seems like cart-ropes,' for it is said, 'Woe unto them that draw iniquity with cords of vanity, and sin as it were with a cart rope' (Isaiah 5)."

There is a great rule we must know. Our work, which was given to us so as to be a basis for faith above reason, is not because we are unworthy of a high degree. Hence, this was given to us so as to take it all in a vessel of faith. It appears to us as ignominy and worthlessness, and we are anxious for the time when we can rid ourselves of this burden, called "faith above reason." However, it is a great and very important degree, whose sublimity is immeasurable.

The reason it appears to us as ignominy is because of the will to receive in us. Thus, we must discern a *Rosh* (Head) and a *Guf* (Body) in the will to receive. The *Rosh* is called knowing, and the

*Guf* is called receiving. Because of that, we consider everything that is against knowing as low and beastly.

Now we can interpret what Abraham the Patriarch asked, "Whereby shall I know that I shall inherit it?" How would it be possible for them to accept the burden of faith, since it is against reason, and who can go against reason? Thus, how will they come to be granted the Light of faith, since perfection depends on that alone?

The Creator answered him, "Know of a surety etc. that they will be in exile." This means that He had prepared a *Klipa* (shell), which is the evil inclination, an evil person, Pharaoh king of Egypt. The letters of the word **Pharaoh** are like the letters of the word **Oref**[16] (back of the neck).

The Ari wrote (*Shaar HaKavanot* for Pesach) that Pharaoh is considered the *Oref* of **Egypt.**[17] He would suck out the abundance that comes to the lower ones with his question (Exodus 5; 2), "Who is the Lord that I should hearken unto His voice?" By this very question, they are at the hands of the *Klipot* (shells), as the RAMBAM says (*Hilchot Deot*), regarding not turning to idol gods, that with this approach alone, meaning with the very question, the prohibition on turning to them is already broken.

The evil inclination wishes to suck abundance from the *Kedusha* (Sanctity). Thus, what does it do to suck abundance from the *Kedusha*? The writing tells us, "and Pharaoh drew nigh." The *Zohar* interprets that he brought them nigh to repentance. It asks: How can we say that Pharaoh brought them close to repentance, if the conduct of the *Klipot* is to turn one away from the Creator?

We must understand this by what is written in the *Zohar* ("Introduction to the Zohar" and the *Sulam* Commentary):

16 In Hebrew.

17 The Ari divides the Hebrew word for Egypt—*Mitzraim*—into two words: *Metzar Yam*, meaning Narrow Sea.

"Transgression is concealed within you, like the serpent that strikes and hides its head inside its body." Also, in the *Sulam*: "Like, etc. Since that transgression is concealed, the force of the serpent that strikes the people of the world and brings death to the world is still in full power and cannot be revoked. It is like a serpent that bites a human and immediately brings its head to its body, and then it is impossible to kill it."

There is yet another saying in the *Zohar*, that the serpent bows its head and strikes with its tail. This means that sometimes it lets one take upon himself the burden of faith above reason, which is the bowing of the head, but it strikes with tail. The tail can be interpreted as the end, that it bowed its head so as to ultimately receive in order to receive. In other words, it first gave one permission to accept faith so that afterwards it would take everything into its own authority, for the *Klipa* knows that there is no way to receive abundance except through *Kedusha*.

This is the meaning of Pharaoh bringing them near. It is explained that he deliberately brought Israel to repentance, so as to afterwards take everything from them into his own authority. This is why the Ari wrote that Pharaoh sucked all the abundance that came down to the lower ones. He sucked from the *Oref* and from the throat, which is considered the head of the body, meaning it would take everything in its vessels of reception.

This is the meaning of "And they built *Arei Miskenot*," meaning that this was for **Israel**. In other words, all their work during the exile was taken into Pharaoh's custody, and Israel remained poor. We should also interpret ***Miskenot*** from the word ***Sakana*** (danger), meaning that they were in great danger of remaining in that state for the rest of their lives. However, to Pharaoh, the work of Israel was **Pithom and Raamses**, meaning very beautiful cities.

Thus, the meaning of "And they built *Arei Miskenot*," (to Israel), and Pithom and Raamses, to Pharaoh. This is because all the work of Israel fell into the *Klipot*, and they saw no blessing in their work.

When they prevailed in their work in faith and bestowal, they did see fertility; and the moment they fell into knowing and receiving, they immediately fell into the hands of the *Klipa* of Pharaoh. Finally, they came to a determined resolution that the work must be in faith above reason and bestowal.

However, they saw that they were unable to come out of Pharaoh's power by themselves. This is why it is written, "And the children of Israel sighed by reason of the bondage," since they were afraid that they might stay in exile for all time. Then, "their cry came up unto God," and they were awarded exodus from the exile in Egypt.

It turns out that before they saw the situation, that they are in the hands of the *Klipot*, and were hurting and afraid that they would remain there forever, they had no need for the Creator's help from vessels of reception, if the shortcoming and detriment caused by them is unfelt, which is all that obstructs them from cleaving to the Creator. This is because otherwise one has a higher regard to work in the form of knowledge and reception, and faith is considered lowness. They choose knowledge and reception, since this is what man's exterior mind necessitates.

Hence, they were given the exile to feel that they do not progress toward nearness to the Creator, and all their work sinks in the *Klipa* of Egypt. Finally, they saw that they have no other choice but to resolve to a work of lowness, which is faith above reason, and yearn for bestowal. Otherwise they feel that they are in the dominion of the evil inclination.

It turns out that the faith that they have taken upon themselves was because they saw that otherwise they would have no counsel, and hence agreed to a work of ignominy. This is considered "conditional work," when they have accepted this work so they do not fall into the net of the *Klipot*. This is why they had taken this work upon themselves.

However, if the reason is revoked, the love for this work is revoked, too. In other words, if the evil inclination is cancelled, and there is no one that brings them thoughts of not turning to idol gods, then the love for the work in ignominy is revoked.

Now we can understand what our sages wrote: "In the beginning, the evil inclination seems like spider-web, and in the end, it seems like cart-ropes." We know that there is a discernment of "coercive," "mistaken," and "deliberate." The will to receive that is imprinted in man is considered "coercive," since one cannot revoke it, and it is therefore not considered a sin, but a **misdeed**, as it is written, "Woe unto them that draw iniquity with cords of vanity." It cannot be rejected or hated, since he does not feel that it will be a sin.

However, afterwards, it turns out like "sin, as it were with cart-ropes," and the *Klipot* were then made of this will to receive, which have a complete structure, as it is written, "God hath made even one as well as the other." This is where the evil inclination comes from, meaning everything comes out of this thread.

Since it already showed itself to be a sin, then everyone knows to guard themselves from this **thread**, and they understand that there is no other counsel if they want to enter *Kedusha*, except to resolve to work in lowness, meaning faith and bestowal. Otherwise they see that they are under the authority of the *Klipa* of Pharaoh, King of Egypt.

It follows that the benefit in the exile was the feeling that the will to receive is a sin, and this is the reason to decide that there is no other counsel but to try and acquire vessels of bestowal. This is also the meaning of the Creator's answer to Abraham the Patriarch about his request for guarantees for the inheritance of the land: "Know of a surety that thy seed etc. and they shall afflict them etc." Through the exile they would come to discover that the thread is a sin, and then they would accept the real work of detaching themselves from the sin.

This is the meaning of what Rabbi Yehuda said, that in the future death shall be swallowed up forever, meaning the Creator will slaughter the evil inclination, and all that will be left of it is but the tiny thread, which is not even felt as a sin. (The thread which is like a hair's breadth is something that cannot be seen in the eye.)

Yet, some evil and righteous do remain, and they all want to cleave to Him. The wicked have not yet corrected their thread, when the evil inclination still existed, and they could feel that it is a sin. Now, however, when there is no evil inclination, all that is left is but the tiny thread, and they have no reason to make them turn their vessels of reception into vessels of bestowal, since a thread of a hair's breadth is unfelt. But nevertheless, they cannot yet cleave to Him because there is disparity of form there, and He and I cannot dwell in the same abode.

Their correction is to be dust under the feet of the righteous. This means that since the evil inclination has been cancelled, the righteous have no reason to have to go with faith above reason. Hence, since they have no reason, who would make them?

They see that the wicked are left with the thread and did not correct the thread while there was evil inclination; and it was the time to correct it since then the will to receive was evidently a sin, whereas now it does not seem like sin, but like a thread. Hence, if there is no reason, there is no place to correct.

Yet, there is also no place for adhesion, since the disparity of form remains, and all their correction is that the righteous walk on them. This means that they now see that there is no fear from the net of the *Klipot*, since the evil inclination has been slaughtered.

Thus, why do they now have to work in faith above reason? Now they see that the wicked cannot reach adhesion because they now have no reason, meaning an evil inclination that will be distinguished as a sin, yet they remain outside for there is still disparity of form. Hence, when the righteous see this, they understand how good it was for them that they had a reason to work in bestowal.

They thought they were engaged in bestowal only because of the evil inclination, but they see that the sin they saw was for their own good. In other words, this is the real work, and it is not because of fear of falling into the hands of the *Klipot* that they do this work. The evidence for that is that they see that the wicked who did not correct the thread, and now have no reason to, and remain outside, and cannot come to adhesion with the Creator.

It follows that the righteous receive the strength to go from strength to strength through the wicked, and the wicked have become dust under the feet of the righteous, and the righteous walk on the discernments that remain as wicked.

Hence, in retrospect, this work specifically is important. And it is not because of necessity, as they first thought, while there was evil inclination. Now they see that even without the evil inclination it is worthwhile to work in bestowal and faith.

Regarding "these cry and those cry," it is known that weeping is *Katnut* (smallness, infancy), *VAK*. There is a differentiation between *GAR* and *VAK*. *Mochin de VAK* (Light of *VAK*) illuminate from the past, meaning they take sustenance from what they have been through. *Mochin de* GAR, however, shine in the present by uniting the *Zivug* (spiritual coupling).

This is the meaning of the righteous crying and saying, "How could we conquer such a high mountain?" Now they see what was prior to the slaughtering of the evil inclination, that its dominion was indeed great, as it is written, "God hath made even one as well as the other." They received great mercy by the Creator, who gave them the power to defeat the war against the inclination, and they now rejoice in the miracle that they had then, meaning in the past. This is called *Mochin de Katnut.*

The wicked cry because now there is no way for them to cleave to Him, even though they now see that it is only a tiny thread. But since there is no evil inclination, they have no reason to turn the vessels of reception to bestowal; they can only see that they are on the outside; this is why they cry.

However, their correction is in becoming dust under the feet of the righteous. In other words, by the righteous seeing that now there is no evil inclination, the wicked still cannot attain adhesion. Thus, they say about their thoughts that they had followed the path of bestowal only because of the evil inclination, they see that this is the actual vessel. This means that even if there hadn't been an evil inclination, still this path is true, and that the path of faith is a wonderful path.

Now we understand why wicked remain after the slaughtering of the evil inclination; it is so that they become dust under the feet of the righteous. If wicked had not remained, there would not be anyone to show this great thing, that the path of faith is not because of conditional love. Meaning, it is not because of the evil inclination that the path of faith should be followed, but this is unconditional love, since now there is no longer any evil inclination, and still, only through faith can adhesion with the Creator be acquired.

I heard on another occasion: The reason we specifically need faith is the pride in us. It is then difficult for us to accept faith.

Meaning, although faith is a sublime and wonderful degree, which the lower one cannot attain and understand its preciousness and sublimity, it is only because of our pride, meaning the will to receive. We imagine it as low and beastly, and for that reason we were given the evil person.

I heard another time: We see that when we do not want to accept faith, we fall from our state. We rise and fall every time, until we resolve that there is no other counsel but to set faith permanently. This was in order to receive faith, and this is "And they built *Arei Miskenot*" (for Israel), for Pharaoh.

## 87. SHABBAT *SHEKALIM*

I heard on *Adar* 26, March 7, 1948

On Shabbat *Shekalim* (name of weekly portion), when he began the *Kidush* ... he said, "There was a custom among the *Admorim* (rabbis, heads of congregations) in Poland, that all the rich men would come to their rabbis on Shabbat *Shekalim*, to receive *Shekalim* (coins) from their rabbis."

And he said that it implies that there cannot be obliteration of Amalek without *Shekalim*. This is so because before one receives *Shekalim*, there is still no *Klipa* (shell) of Amalek. Rather, when taking *Shekalim*, the great *Klipa* called "Amalek" arrives, and the work of obliterating Amalek begins. However, prior to that, there is nothing to erase.

And he added an explanation to it, concerning what the Sayer of *Kuznitz* said about what is said in the closing prayer: "You have separated man from the beginning and You will recognize him to stand before You." The sayer asked about it: "How is it possible to stand without a *Rosh* (head, but also beginning)? It means that he has separated the *Rosh* from the man, and how can such a thing be?" The explanation is, "When thou takest the sum of the children of Israel," by which we extend the discernment of *Rosh*. If we give the half *Shekel*, through it we are awarded the *Rosh*.

And he later asked ... "Why does he prepare for the *Kidush* more drinking that eating? This is not the right order, since the order should be eating more than drinking, as drinking comes only to complement the eating, by way of 'And thou shalt eat and be satisfied, and bless.' However, it is not so when drinking is more than eating." And he interpreted that eating implies *Hassadim* (mercy) and drinking implies *Hochma* (wisdom).

And he said further, that the Shabbat prior to the month of *Adar* contains the whole of the month of *Adar*. Hence, "when *Adar* enters, there is much gladness." And he said that there is a difference between a Shabbat and a good day. Shabbat is called "love," and a good day is called "gladness." The difference between gladness and love is that love is an essence, and gladness is only an outcome, born off some cause. The cause is the essence, and the outcome is only a progeny of the essence. Hence, Shabbat is called "love and good will" and a good day is called "gladness and joy."

He also explained concerning what Rabbi Yochanan Ben Zakai replied to his wife, that I was like a minister before the King, and he, Rabbi Hanina Ben Dosa, like a slave before the King; this is why he could pray. It seems as though it should have been the opposite–that the minister would have more strength to induce his opinion on the King, and not the slave.

However, a "minister" is one who has already been awarded private Providence. In that state, one sees no room for prayer, since everything is good. But a slave is one who is at the degree of reward and punishment, and then he has room to pray because he sees that he has more to correct.

And he adds an explanation from an article that is presented (*Baba Metzia* 85a). It is written there that a calf was being led to the slaughter. It went, put its head in the rabbi's lap and wept. He told it, "Go, this is what you were made for." They said, "Since he does not pity, suffering shall come upon him."

"This is what you were made for" means private Providence, that there is nothing to add or to subtract, since there the sufferings, too, are considered merits. This is why he extended sufferings upon him.

And the *Gemarah* says that he was rid of the suffering through an act, by saying, "and His mercies are over all His works." One day, the rabbi's maid was sweeping the house. There were rat young there, and she was sweeping them away. He told her, "Leave them!", it is written, "and His mercies are over all His works." Since he attained that a prayer, too, remains in eternity, he now had room for prayer. This is why the sufferings departed from him.

At the end of Shabbat, he said an interpretation about what the Holy *Zohar* says about the verse, "For the Lord hath chosen Jacob unto Himself." Who chose whom? And the Holy *Zohar* replies, "The Lord chose Jacob" (*Beresheet*, 161b). And he said that the question of the Holy *Zohar* is if the Creator chose Jacob. It follows that Jacob did not do anything, but all was under private Providence. And if Jacob did choose, it means that Jacob is the doer, meaning an issue of reward and punishment.

And he replied that in the beginning, one should begin on the path of reward and punishment. When he completes that phase of reward and punishment, one is rewarded with seeing that everything is under private Providence, that "He alone does and will do all the deeds." However, before one completes one's work in reward and punishment it is impossible to understand private Providence.

And on Sunday night, after the lesson, he explained the matter of Jacob's cunningness, that it is written about Jacob, "Thy brother came with guile." There was certainly no issue of falsehood here. Otherwise, the text would not say about Jacob, the "elect" patriarch, that he was a liar.

Rather, the guile means that when one performs an act of wisdom without intending for wisdom, but to educe some benefit that he needs, and sees that it cannot be obtained directly, hence, he performs an act of wisdom, to obtain the needed thing. This is called "wisdom."

This is the meaning of the verse, "be guile with reason," meaning wisdom through reason. This means that the wisdom he wants to obtain is not for wisdom's sake, but for another thing, which forces him to extend wisdom. In other words, he must extend to complement the *Hassadim*.

This is because before the *Hassadim* obtain *Hochma*, they are discerned as *Katnut* (smallness). However, afterwards, when he extends *Hochma*, but still prefers *Hassadim* to *Hochma*, it is apparent that the *Hassadim* are more important than *Hochma*. This is called *Gar de Bina*, which means that he uses the *Hassadim* because of a choice.

This is the meaning of *Hochma* through *Daat*, that *Hochma* appears in the form of *Vak* in *YESHSUT*. And in *AVI*, *Hochma* appears by improving the *Hassadim* and remaining in *Hassadim*. However, although *Bina* is considered "delighting in mercy," its choice of *Hassadim* is not apparent because of *Tzimtzum Bet*, where there is no *Hochma*. However, in *Gadlut* (adulthood), when *Hochma* comes, the *Hassadim* that she uses are because of choice.

## 88. ALL THE WORK IS ONLY WHERE THERE ARE TWO WAYS

I heard after Shabbat *Beshalach*, January 24, 1948

All the work is only where there are two ways, as it is written, "and he shall live by them, and he shall not die by them. And the issue of 'shall die and not breach' applies only to three *Mitzvot*: idolatry, bloodshed, and incest." And yet, we find that the first *Hassidim* would give their lives over positives.

And we should know that all the work and the labor are only when one should keep the Torah. At that time one feels the heavy load that the body does not agree to the conditions of the Torah. But when a person is rewarded, and the Torah guards him, no heaviness is sensed in the work of God. This is because the Torah guards one, as it is written, "One's soul shall teach him."

## 89. TO UNDERSTAND THE WORDS OF THE HOLY ZOHAR

I heard on *Adar* 5, February 15, 1948

To understand the words of the Holy *Zohar*, we should first understand what the Holy *Zohar* wants to say. And understanding what the Holy *Zohar* wants to say depends on one's dedication to the Torah and *Mitzvot*. The Torah and *Mitzvot* can bring cleanness to a person, to be cleaned of self love. And this is why he engages in Torah and *Mitzvot*. And to that extent we can understand the truth that the Holy *Zohar* wants to say. Otherwise, there are *Klipot* that hide and block the truth in the words of the Holy *Zohar*.

## 90. IN THE ZOHAR, BERESHEET

I heard on *Adar Bet* 17, March 28, 1948

In *The Zohar*, *Beresheet* p.165, "In the secrets of the Torah, the ministers' defenders are erected from Above. And the blaze of the flaming sword is appointed over all the armies and the camps. And in this discernment, several other discernments are interpreted to several other degrees."

And he explained that when the left line extends, it must be sweetened with the right line. It spreads in three places:

1. In *AVI*, which is the root;
2. In *Malchut*;
3. In God's angels.

In *AVI*, they are called "defenders of the ministers," and in *Malchut* they are called "the blaze of the swirling sword." And in the angels they are called "and in this discernment, several other discernments are interpreted to several other degrees."

## 91. CONCERNING THE REPLACEABLE

I heard on *Nisan* 9, April 18, 1948

In the Holy *Zohar* he explains the reason that Reuben was born to Leah, while he was thinking of Rachel during the act. The law is that if he thinks of another, the child is called "replaceable." And the Holy *Zohar* explains that since he was thinking of Rachel and he thought that it really was Rachel, and replaceable means that his thought was of Rachel and of the act, he knew that it was Leah. However, here his thought was of Rachel and of the act, he thought that it really was Rachel.

And he explained it: it is known that in spirituality, they are as seal and imprint—each degree is sealed by its Upper degree. And the conduct of seals and imprints is that they are always opposites: the imprint is always opposite from the seal. It follows that what is considered *Klipa* (shell) in *Beria*, is *Kedusha* (Sanctity) in *Yetzira*, and what is *Kedusha* in *Yetzira*, is *Klipa* in *Assiya*.

Therefore, if the righteous is united in some degree, he certainly unites with the *Kedusha* in the degree. And if, during the act, he thinks of another degree, and what is considered *Kedusha* in that degree is considered *Klipa* in another degree, it is therefore called "replaceable." That means that the offspring of this unification is replaceable because the degrees are opposite from one another.

Jacob, however, was thinking of Rachel, meaning of the *Kedusha* in the discernment of Rachel. And of the act, too, he thought that it was Rachel. Hence, both the thought was of the *Kedusha* in Rachel and the act intended to be the degree of Rachel. Therefore, there is no discernment of Leah here, to be considered replaceable.

## 92. EXPLAINING THE DISCERNMENT OF LUCK

I heard on *Sivan* 7, June 14, 1948

"Luck" is something that is above reasoning. Thus, even though it was reasonable that it would be such and such, luck made him succeed with his actions. Reasoning refers to cause and consequence, meaning that a cause makes the result come out as it does. But above reasoning, when the initial cause is not the cause of the consequence, this is called "above reasoning." We refer to it as luck causing the result.

It is known that all bestowals come from the Light of *Hochma* (Wisdom). And when *Hochma* shines, it is called "left line" and "darkness." The abundance is blocked, and this is called "ice." This is called "merit" because he is rewarded. That means that the reason that causes the Light of Wisdom is called "merit," which is cause and effect.

But "sons, life, and nourishment do not depend on man, but on luck." This means that *Hochma* is diminished specifically through the middle line, and shines precisely through the diminution, called *Masach de Hirik*. It follows that it does not shine with cause and consequence, meaning that *Hochma* shines through the left line, but precisely through the diminution. This is called "above reasoning," and this is "luck."

## 93. CONCERNING FINS AND SCALES

I heard in 1945

To understand what our sages said, "whatsoever hath scales is known to have fins. And whatsoever hath fins, it is not known if it has scales."

In the work, we should interpret the matter of *Kaskeset* (scales) as *Kushiot* (questions) that he has in the work of God. The *Kushiot* are vessels in which to receive answers, since the answers are not filled in the external mind, but specifically in the internal mind, which is the Upper Light, clothed within a person. And then the questions are settled in him.

Hence, to the extent that questions increase, to that extent does the Upper Light dress within man. This is why the scales are among the signs of purity, since through it one can come to purify oneself, by not wanting to have questions. Hence, one does whatsoever one can to purify oneself, so he can be awarded the Upper Light.

And a fin, too, is among the signs of purity. *Snapir* (fin) implies *Soneh-Peh-Ohr Elyon* (hating-mouth-Upper Light). And since he has questions, it is certainly because he has hatred towards the Upper Light. But one who has fins does not have to have questions. One may hate the Upper Light not because one has questions, but because one is simply greedy, and says, "I will not go in any case."

This is the sign of purify. That is, when he has a fish. A fish implies meat that is clothed in fins and scales. This means that the Upper Light shines in these two signs.

But one who works without any questions in the work, this is not a sign of purity, that one has no questions. This is so because one has no place in which to place the Upper Light, as one has no reason that will compel one to draw the Upper Light, as even without the Upper Light one thinks that one is just fine.

This is why when Pharaoh, King of Egypt, wanted to keep the people of Israel in his domain, he issued an order to not give *Kash* (straw), as it is written, "So the people were scattered... to gather stubble for straw." Then they would never need the Creator to deliver them from the domain of the impurity into the *Kedusha* (Sanctity).

## 94. AND YOU SHALL KEEP YOUR SOULS

I heard in 1945

In the verse, "Take ye therefore good heed unto yourselves," the care refers primarily to the spiritual soul. However, one cares for the corporeal soul even without commandments from the Torah. This is because the rule is that a *Mitzva* is primarily evident, meaning it is evident that he does what he does for the purpose of a *Mitzva* when he would not do it, were it not for a *Mitzva*. Rather, the reason he does it is because of a *Mitzva*.

Hence, with a *Mitzva* that he performs, if he would do it even if it were not a *Mitzva*, he needs special care, to find a place where he can say that he does this only because of a *Mitzva*. Then the Light of the *Mitzva* can shine on the act of the *Mitzva* that he performs. This is called "making a *Kli* with the *Mitzva*," in which the Upper Light can be. Hence, the care refers primarily to the spiritual soul.

## 95. CONCERNING REMOVING THE FORESKIN

I heard during a meal celebrating a circumcision,
1943, Jerusalem

*Malchut* in itself is called "lower *Hochma*," and with respect to its connection to *Yesod*, it is called "faith." And there is a foreskin over the *Yesod*, whose task is to separate *Malchut* from *Yesod*, and not let it connect to *Yesod*. The foreskin's power is in picturing faith as dust. This is the meaning of *Shechina* (Divinity) in the dust.

When that depicting force is removed, and instead, saying that the depicting force is dust, this is called "circumcision," when the foreskin is cut off and the foreskin is thrown to the dust.

In that state, the Holy *Shechina* comes out of the dust, and the merit of faith becomes apparent. This is called "redemption," being rewarded with raising Divinity from the dust. Hence, we must force all the work on removing the depicting force, and only faith is considered whole.

"They are meticulous with themselves as much an olive and as much as an egg." An "olive" is as the dove said, "I prefer my food as bitter as an olive from Above." And the "egg" means that it is lifeless, although a living animal emerges from it. But in the meantime, no life is seen in it. And they are meticulous with themselves and prefer to work even though the situation is like an olive.

Also, when they see that there is no vitality in the work, and all their strength to work is only because their aim is only to raise Divinity from the dust, then, through this work, they are awarded redemption. And then they see that this meal, which was previously like an olive and an egg, has now become lively and sweet and sublimely pleasant.

This is the meaning of "a converted proselyte is similar to a newly born infant." He must then keep the discernment of the covenant, too, and then he will be glad.

It follows that when the infant is circumcised, although the child is suffering, the guests and the parents are nonetheless happy, since they believe that the boy's soul is happy. Similarly, in the work of the covenant, we must be happy even though we feel a state of suffering. Nevertheless, we should believe that our soul is happy.

Our whole work should be in gladness. And the evidence to that is from the first commandment man was given. The *Mitzva* is done by the parents, and the parents and the guests are in gladness. This is how all the *Mitzvot* that one performs should be–only in gladness.

## 96. WHAT IS WASTE OF BARN AND WINERY, IN THE WORK

I heard on the eve of *Sukkot*, inside the *Sukkah*, 1942

A **barn** is male *Dinim* (judgments), as in "hidden and not defiled," when he feels that he is in a state of *Goren* (barn), meaning *Ger* (stranger) in the work.

A **winery** is female *Dinim*, as in "hidden and defiled." *Yekev* (winery) is considered *Nekev* (foramen).

And there are two kinds of *Sukkot*: 1) clouds of glory; and 2) waste of barn and winery.

A **cloud** is considered concealment, when one feels the concealment over the *Kedusha* (Sanctity). If a person overcomes the cloud, meaning the concealment that one feels, one is thus awarded clouds of glory. This is called *MAN de Ima*, and it applies during the six thousand years. It is considered a secret that still has not become a nature, called "literal."

And the waste of barn and winery are called "literal and nature," which is considered *MAN de Malchut*, erected specifically through faith, called an "awakening from below."

And *MAN de Ima* is considered an awakening from Above, which is not discerned as nature. This means that with respect to nature, when one is not ready to receive the abundance, he does not receive any bestowal.

However, from the perspective of the awakening from Above, which is above nature, the Light is indeed poured onto the lower ones, by way of "I am the Lord, that dwelleth with them in the midst of their uncleanness," as it is written in the Holy *Zohar*, "even though he has sinned, it is as if he did not sin at all."

However, with an awakening from below, the Light is not dispensed. Rather, precisely when one is qualified by nature, meaning by himself, this is called ***MAN de Nukva***, which he can correct through faith. This is called "by himself," considered the seventh millennium, called "**and one is ruined**," meaning that "she has nothing of her own," considered *Malchut*. When this is corrected, one is awarded the tenth millennium, which is *Gar*.

Such a soul is found in one of ten generations. However, there is the discernment of the seventh millennium, from the perspective of the six thousand years, called "particular," as the general and the particular are always equal. But this is considered MAN *de Ima*, called "clouds of glory."

And the purpose of the work is in the literal and the natural, since in this work he no longer has room to fall lower down, since he is already placed on the ground. This is so because he does not need greatness because for him it is always like a new thing.

This means that he always works as though he had just begun working now. And he works in the form of acceptance of the burden of the Kingdom of Heaven above reason. The basis upon which he built the order of the work was in the lowest manner, and all of it was above reason. Only one who is a real fool can be so low as to proceed without any basis on which to establish one's faith, literally with no support.

Additionally, he accepts this work with great joy, as though he had had real knowledge and vision on which to establish the certainty of faith. And to that exact measure of above reason, to that very measure as though he had reason. Hence, if he persists in this path, he can never fall. Rather, he can always be in gladness, by believing that he is serving a great King.

This is the meaning of the verse, "The one lamb thou shalt offer in the morning; and the other lamb thou shalt offer at dusk. ... according to the meal-offering of the morning, and according to the drink-offering thereof." This means that that gladness that he had while he was sacrificing his sacrifice, when it was a morning for him, as morning is called "light," meaning that the Light of the Torah was shining for him in utter clarity. In that same gladness he was making his sacrifice, meaning his work, even though for him it was like evening.

This means that even though he did not have any clarity in the Torah and the work, he still did everything gladly, since he worked above reason. Hence, he could not measure from which state the Creator derives more contentment.

This is the meaning of Rabbi Shimon Ben Menasia's preaching "a kind of matter." Matter means without reason and knowledge. "An ear that heard on Mount Sinai will not steal." This means not receiving anything for oneself, but assuming the burden of the Kingdom of Heaven without any *Gadlut* (greatness), but entirely above reason. And he went and stole some illumination for himself, meaning he said, "Now I can be a servant of the Lord because I already have reason and knowledge in the work, and I understand that it is worthwhile to be the Creator's servant. And now I no longer need faith above reason."

He tells us about that, "and he was sold to the court." "Court" refers to man's reason and knowledge, which judge a person's actions, whether or not they are worth doing. "Sold" means that he has become a stranger in the work of God, that the mind comes and asks him the known question, "What mean you by this service?" And it only comes from the angle of stealing, having received some support to the discernment of faith. Hence, he comes and wants to cancel the support with his questions. But this is only for "six," meaning "he was sold for six years," considered male *Dinim*.

"But if the servant shall plainly say: I love my master… I will not go out free," meaning he does not want to go out free without *Mitzvot*, then the correction is "his master shall bring him," meaning the Lord, "to the door, or unto the door-post," meaning give him blockage over the reception of the Kingdom of Heaven. And "his master shall bore his ear," meaning his ear is pierced. This means that another hole is made in him, so he will be able to hear once more what he had heard on Mount Sinai: "thou shalt not steal," "and he shall serve him for ever." This is because then he truly becomes a servant of the Creator.

*Sukkot* is temporary residence. This means that one who has already been awarded permanent residence and has nothing more to do, as with the matter of the first to count the iniquities, the counsel is to leave for temporary residence, as when he was on his way to the house of God, before he arrived at the permanent residence. At that time he constantly needed to reach God's Palace, and he had guests, when his work was in the form of "a passing visitor."

And now he can extend from the past work, when he was always thankful and praising the Creator by always bringing him closer, and from which he had gladness. And now, on *Sukkot*, he can extend the gladness he had then, and this is the meaning of temporary residence. This is why they said, "leave the permanent residency and dwell in temporary residency."

"The study is not the most important, but the act." This means that an act is like a substance. Rabbi Shimon Ben Menasia was preaching "a kind of matter," that the act is the most important, and the mind is but a kind of mirror.

However, the act is considered living, and the mind is considered speaking. The thing is that if there is wholeness in the act, then the act is so great that it brings with it the mind of the Torah. And the mind of the Torah is called "speaking."

## 97. WASTE OF BARN AND WINERY

I heard

***Goren* (barn)** means diminution of good deeds, when a person feels primarily *Gronot* (Hebrew: throats; sounds like *Ger'onot*—deficiencies) with the Creator. Hence, he lessens the good deeds. And afterwards he comes to a state of ***Yekev* (winery)**, which is the meaning of "And he that blasphemeth the name of the Lord."

***Sukkot*** is considered gladness, considered "rejoicing *Gevurot*," which is repentance out of love, when sins become as merits for him, and even the barn and winery are admitted into *Kedusha* (Sanctity). This is the meaning of *Sukkot's* primary discernment being **Isaac**, but that everyone is included in him (and Passover is considered **love**, which is right). This is the meaning of "Abraham begot Isaac."

This is because the father and son issue is cause and consequence, reason and result. Had there not been a discernment of Abraham first, which is the right, there could not have been the discernment of Isaac, which is the left. Rather, the left is integrated in the right, as in, "For Thou art our Father."

Abraham said, "will be destroyed over the Sanctity of Your Name." And Jacob also said that it means that the sins will be destroyed over the Sanctity of Your Name. And if it remains so, then there is a breach in the middle. In other words, the sins that were in the whole of Israel are like a breach in the *Kedusha* (Sanctity).

Isaac, however, said, "half over me and half over you," meaning the part of the sins and the part of the *Mitzvot*, that is, that both will enter *Kedusha*. And this can be through repentance out of love, when sins become as merits to him. In that state there is a breach, as it is written, "with no breach and no... outcry," but all is corrected for *Kedusha*.

This is the meaning of our sages' words: "Greater are the dung and mules of Isaac than Abimelech's money and gold." Dung is something inferior, worthless, meaning that they consider the servitude of him as dung. And afterwards arrives a state of separation. Because he does not appreciate his work, he falls into separation. And this is called "the dung and mules of Isaac." And since Isaac corrected everything in the form of repentance out of love, and his sins became as merits, the profits that had come to him through his dung and mules are greater than "Abimelech's money and gold."

His *Kesef* (money) means *Kisufim* (longing) to the Creator; and *Zahav* (gold) means *Ze Hav* (give this), concerning the craving for the Torah, meaning to achieve the Torah. And since Isaac corrected everything, meaning achieved repentance out of love, the sins, too, were considered merits for him. And then he is very rich in any case, since in keeping *Mitzvot* there is not more than 613 *Mitzvot*, but sins and transgressions are endless. Hence, Isaac became rich, as it is written, "and he have found a hundred gates." This means that he had one hundred percent in *Kedusha*, without any waste, since the waste, too, was corrected in him.

This is why the thatch of the *Sukkah* is made of waste of barn and winery. (And you can say what our sages said, that Moses became rich from waste). Hence, *Sukkot* is named primarily after Isaac, who is the rejoicing *Gevurot*, and *Sukkot* is named after Moses, too.

## 98. SPIRITUALITY IS CALLED THAT WHICH WILL NEVER BE LOST

I heard in 1948

Spirituality is called that which will never be lost. Hence, the will to receive, in the form it is in, meaning in order to receive, is called corporeality. It is so because it will be cancelled from this form and will adopt the form of in order to bestow.

A real place in spirituality is called the place of reality, since anyone who comes there, to that place, sees the same form as the other. However, an imaginary thing is not called a real place, since it is imaginary and then everyone imagines it differently.

When we refer to the seventy faces of the Torah, it means that they are seventy degrees. In each degree, the Torah is interpreted according to the degree one is in. However, a world is a reality, meaning anyone who comes to any of the seventy degrees in that world attains the same form as all the other attaining who came there.

From that extends what our sages say, who interpret the verses of the Torah. They say that this is what Abraham said to Isaac, and other similar sayings of our sages. They would say what is said, what is explained in the verses.

The question arises, "How did they know what one said to another?" But, because those who reached the degree where Abraham (or anyone) stood, they see and know what Abraham saw and knew.

For this reason they know what Abraham said. And likewise in all the sayings of our sages when they interpreted the verses of the Torah. All that was because they, too, attained the degree, and each degree in spirituality is a reality. Everyone sees the reality, as all those who come to the city of London in England see what is in the city and what is said in the city.

## 99. HE DID NOT SAY WICKED OR RIGHTEOUS

I heard on *Iyar* 21, Jerusalem

"Rabbi Hanina Bar Papa said, 'That angel, appointed on conception, its name is *Laila* (night). It takes a drop and places it opposite the Creator, and says before Him: 'Lord, what shall become of this drop, a hero or a weakling, a wise or a fool, a wealthy or an indigent?' But he did not say 'a wicked or a righteous'" (*Nida* 16b).

We should interpret according to the rule that a fool cannot be righteous, as our sages said, "One does not sin unless a spirit of folly has entered him." It is even more so with one who is a fool all his days. Hence, one who is born a fool has no choice, since he has been sentenced to be a fool. Therefore, the saying, "he did not say 'a wicked or a righteous'" is so that he would have a choice. But what is the benefit if he did not say a "a righteous or a fool"? After all, if he is sentenced to be a fool, it is the same as being sentenced to become a wicked!

We should also understand the words of our sages: "Rabbi Yochanan said, 'The Creator saw that the righteous are few, He stood and planted them in each generation, as it is written, 'for the pillars of the earth are the Lord's, and He hath set the world upon them.''" And Rashi interprets: "'He hath set the world upon them'—He dispersed them in all the generations to be an infrastructure and existence and foundation for the sustenance of the world" (*Yoma* 38b).

"They are few" means that they are growing fewer. Hence, what did he do to propagate them? "He stood and planted them in each generation." We should ask, "What is the benefit of planting them in each generation, by which they multiply?" We must understand the difference between all the righteous being in a single generation or being dispersed through all the generations, as Rashi interprets. Does being in many generations propagates the righteous?

To understand the above, we must expand and interpret our sages' words, that the Creator sentences the drop to be a wise or a fool. This means that one who is born weak, without the strength to overcome his inclination, and is born with a weak desire and untalented, since during the preparation, when beginning in the work of God, one must be qualified to receive the Torah and the wisdom, as it is written, "will give wisdom to the wise," he asked, "If they are already smart, why do they still need wisdom? It should have been 'will give wisdom to the fools.'"

And he explains that a sage is one who longs for wisdom, although he still does not have wisdom. Rather, because one has a desire, and a desire is called a *Kli*, thus, those who have a desire and craving for wisdom, this is the *Kli* in which wisdom shines. It therefore follows that a fool means one without a desire for wisdom, and whose whole desire is only for one's own needs. In terms of bestowal, a fool is completely incapable of achieving any bestowal whatsoever.

Therefore, one who is born with such qualities, how can he achieve the degree of a righteous? It follows that he does not have a choice. Therefore, what is the benefit from saying, "he did not say, 'a righteous or a wicked'?" So he would have a choice. After all, since he was born weak and unwise, he is no longer capable of having a choice, since he is completely incapable of any overcoming and craving for His wisdom.

To understand that, meaning that there can be choice even for a fool, the Creator made a correction, which our sages call, "the Creator saw that the righteous were few; He stood and planted them in each generation." And we asked, "What is the benefit of that?"

Now we will understand this matter. It is known that as it is forbidden to bond with the wicked even when one does not do as they do, as it is written, "nor sat in the seat of the scornful." This means that the sin is primarily because he sits among the scornful, even though he sits and learns Torah and keeps *Mitzvot*. Otherwise, the prohibition would be due to the cancellation of Torah and *Mitzvot*. But rather, the sitting itself is forbidden, since man takes the thoughts and desires of those that he likes.

And vise versa: if one does not have any desire and craving for spirituality, if he is among people who have a desire for spirituality, if he likes these people, he, too, will take their strength to prevail, and their desires and aspirations, although by his own quality, he does not have these desires and cravings and the power to overcome. But according to the grace and the importance he ascribes to these people, he will receive new powers.

Now we can understand the above words: "The Creator saw that the righteous are few." This means that not any person can become a righteous, for lack of the qualities for it, as it was written, that he is born a fool or a weakling; he, too, has a choice and his own qualities are no excuse. This is because the Creator planted the righteous in every generation.

Hence, a person has the choice of going to a place where there are righteous. One can accept their authority, and then he will receive all the powers that he lacks by the nature of his own qualities. He will receive it from the righteous. This is the benefit in "planted them in each generation," so that each generation would have someone to turn to, to cleave to, and from whom to receive the strength needed to rise to the degree of a righteous. Thus, they, too, subsequently become righteous.

It follows that "he did not say 'a wicked or a righteous'" means that he does have a choice: he can go and cleave to the righteous for guidance, and through them receive strength, by which they, too, can later become righteous.

However, if all the righteous were in the same generation, the fools would have no hope of approaching the Creator, and hence, would not have a choice. But by dispersing the righteous in each generation each person has the power of choice, to approach and draw near to the righteous that exist in every generation. Otherwise, one's Torah must be a potion of death.

We can understand that from a corporeal example. When two people stand one opposite the other, the right hand side of the one is opposite the left hand side of the other, and the left hand side of the one is opposite one's friend right hand side. There are two ways: the right–the way of the righteous, which is only to bestow, and the left–whose interest is only to receive for themselves, by which they are separated from the Creator, who is only to bestow. Thus, they are naturally separated from the Life of Lives.

This is why the wicked in their lives are called "dead." It therefore follows that when one has not yet been awarded *Dvekut* (adhesion) with the Creator, they are two. Then, when one learns Torah, which separates him from Him, his Torah becomes a potion of death to him. This is because he remains separated, as he wants his Torah to clothe his body. This means that he wants the Torah to increase his body, and this makes his Torah the potion of death.

However, when a person becomes adhered to Him, a single authority is made, and that person unites in His uniqueness. Then, the right side of the person is the right side of the Creator, and then the body becomes a clothing for one's soul.

The way to know if one is marching on the path of truth is that when one engages in bodily needs, one should see that he does not engage in them more than is necessary for the needs of one's soul. And when one thinks that one has more than he needs to clothe for the needs of one's soul, it is like a clothing that a person puts over one's body. At that time he is meticulous to keep the clothing not longer and wider, but precisely dressing his body. Similarly, when engaging in one's bodily needs, one should be meticulous to not have more than one needs for one's soul, meaning to clothe one's soul.

To come to adhesion with the Creator, not all who wish to take the Lord may come and take, since it is against man's nature, who was created with a will to receive, which is self love. This is why we need the righteous of the generation.

When a person clings to a genuine Rav, whose only wish is to do good deeds, but one feels that he cannot do good deeds, that the aim will be to bestow contentment upon the Creator, by cleaving to a real Rav and wanting the Rav's fondness, he does things that his Rav likes, and hates the things his Rav hates. Then he can have *Dvekut* with his Rav and receive his Rav's powers, even that which he does not have from birth. This is the meaning of planting the righteous in each generation.

However, according to this, it is hard to see why plant the righteous in each generation. We said that it was for the fools and the weak. But he could have resolved to another counsel: to not create fools! Who made him say that this drop will be a weakling or a fool? He could have created everyone smart.

The answer is that the fools, too, are needed, since they are the carriers of the will to receive. They see that they have no counsel of their own by which to draw near to the Creator, so they are as those about whom it is written, "And they shall go forth, and look upon the carcasses of the men... for their worm shall not die, neither shall their fire be quenched; and they shall be an abhorring unto all flesh." They have become ashes under the feet of the righteous, by which the righteous can acknowledge the good that the Lord has done for them, by creating them wise and strong, by which He has brought them closer to Him.

Hence, now they can give thanks and praise the Creator, since they see the lowly state they are in. And this is called "ashes under the feet of the righteous," meaning that righteous walk by it, and thus give thanks to the Creator.

But we must know that the lower degrees are needed, too. The *Katnut* (smallness) of a degree is not considered superfluous, saying that it would be better if the degrees of *Katnut* were born immediately with the *Gadlut* (greatness).

It is like a physical body. There are certainly important organs, such as the mind, the eyes, etc., and there are organs that are not so important, such as the stomach, the intestines, and the fingers, and the toes. But we cannot say that an organ that performs a not-so-important task is redundant. Rather, everything is important. It is the same in spirituality: we need the fools and the weaklings, too.

Now we can understand what is written, that the Creator said, "Return unto Me, and I will return unto you." It means that the Creator says, "Return," and Israel say the opposite: "bring us back, Lord, and then we shall return."

The meaning is that during the decline from the work, the Creator says "Return" first. This brings a person an ascent in the work of God, and one begins to cry, "Bring us back." However, during the decline, one does not cry, "Bring us back." On the contrary, he escapes the work.

Therefore, one should know that when he cries, "bring" us back, it stems from an awakening from Above, since the Creator previously said "Return," by which one has ascension, and can say "bring us back."

This is the meaning of, "And it came to pass, when the ark set forward, that Moses said: 'Rise up, O Lord, and let Thine enemies be scattered." Setting forward [the Hebrew word is traveling] means when advancing in servitude of the Creator, which is a time of ascension. Then Moses said "Rise." And when they rested he said "Return." And during the rest from the work of God, we need the Creator to say, "Return," meaning "Return unto Me," meaning that the Creator gives the awakening. Hence, one should know when to say "rise" or "Return."

This is the meaning of what is written in *Parashat Akev*, "And thou shalt remember all the way... to know what was in thy heart, whether thou would keep His commandments, or no." "Would keep His commandments" is discerned as "Return." "Or no" is discerned as "rise," and we need both. And the Rav knows when to "rise" and when to "Return," since the forty-two paths is a matter of ascents and descents that unfold in the work of God.

## 100. THE WRITTEN TORAH AND THE ORAL TORAH

I heard on *Mishpatim*, 1943

The written Torah is considered "awakening from Above" and the oral Torah is an awakening from below. And together they are called, "six years he shall serve; and in the seventh he shall go out free."

This is so because the essence of the work is specifically where there is resistance. And it is called *Alma* (Aramaic: world) from the word *He'elem* (concealment). Then, when there is concealment, there is resistance, and then there is room for work. This is the meaning of the words of our sages, "Six thousand years the world, and one ruined." This means that the concealment will be ruined and there will be no more work. Rather, the Creator makes him wings, which are covers, so he would have work.

## 101. A COMMENTARY ON THE PSALM, "FOR THE LEADER UPON ROSES"

I heard on *Adar Aleph* 23, February 28, 1943

**For the leader**, one who has already won.

**Upon *Shoshanim* (roses)**, meaning the Holy *Shechina* (Divinity), which concerns the inversion from mourning to a good day and *Sasson* (joy). And since there are many states of ascents and descents, called *Shoshanim*, from the words "blunt its *Shinaim* (teeth)," the questions of the wicked should not be answered, but rather, blunt its teeth. And from the multiple beatings, meaning from the proliferation of blunting its teeth, we come to roses. Hence there are many discernments of *Sasson* (Joy) in it, which is why it is spoken of in plural tense, "roses."

**Of the sons of Korah**, from the word *Karachah* (bold), meaning that the hair has gone bold. *Se'arot* mean *Hastarot* (concealments), from the word *Se'ara* (storm). It is known that "reward is according to the effort." This means that when there are *Se'arot*, it is a place for work. And when corrected, hair comes over the storm, by way of, "This is the gate of the Lord." And when one has corrected all the storms, and has no more concealments, then he hasn't any room for work, and therefore has no place for reward.

It follows that when a person comes to the state of *Korah*, he can no longer extend faith, called "the gate to the Lord." This is so because if there is no gate, one cannot enter the King's palace, since it is the foundation, since the entire structure is built on faith.

"Sons of Korah" comes from the word *Bina*. They understood that *Korah* is considered left, from which Hell extends. This is why they wanted to continue their past friendship, from the time they were in the form of "O Lord, I have heard the report of Thee, and am afraid" (*Zohar*, *Beresheet*, 4:7). This means that with the strength they had extended from the past, they could endure the states and go from strength to strength. This is the meaning of "the sons of Korah died not." That is, they understood that if they remained in a state of *Korah*, they would not be able to continue living, so they did not die.

***Maskil* (learned) A Song of loves**, meaning that they have learned that the measure of friendship with the Creator is complete.

**My heart overfloweth**. The overflowing in the heart is by way of, "does not reveal from heart to mouth." This means that there is nothing to elicit off the mouth, which is only reception in the heart, as in, whispered in the lips.

**A goodly matter**–faith is called "a goodly matter."

**I say: "My work is concerning a king."** When he receives the Light of faith, he says, "My work is concerning a king," and not for myself. And then he is awarded, **my tongue is the pen of a ready writer**, when he is awarded the discernment of the written Torah, which is the meaning of the tongue of Moses.

**Thou art fairer than the children of men**, when he says to the Holy *Shechina* that her beauty is from people. This means that what people think of her, which is considered insignificant, precisely out of that is beauty born.

**Grace is poured upon thy lips**. Grace belongs particularly where praise cannot be told, but we still want it. Then we say that it is graceful.

**Upon thy *Sefataim* (lips)** means at the *Sof* (end), meaning that he saw from the end of the world to its end.

## 102. AND YOU SHALL TAKE YOU THE FRUIT OF GOODLY TREES

I heard on *Ushpizin de Yosef*

In the verse, "And ye shall take you... the fruit of citrus trees," meaning a righteous, called a "tree bearing fruit," this is the whole difference between *Kedusha* (Sanctity) and the *Sitra Achra* (other side), that "another God is sterile and does not bear fruit." However, a righteous is called *Hadar* (citrus) because he bears fruit, he *Dar* (lives) in his tree from year to year. This is why it is written about Josef, "he was the one who *Mashbir* (sold) to all the people of the land," for he *Shover* (brakes) them with the fruits that he had, and the fruits that they did not have. Thus, everyone felt his state, whether he was from the good side or to the contrary.

And this is the meaning of "And Joseph sustained... with bread, according to the want of their little ones." The "little ones" are considered *Gar*, as in "and they shall be for frontlets between your eyes," which is the *Tefillin* of the head. For this reason Josef, the son of his old age is called "a wise son." This is the meaning of "did send me before you to preserve life," which is the "Light of *Haya*," considered *Gar*.

This is the meaning of the verse, "I have given to thee one **portion** above thy brethren, which I took out of the hand of the Amorite with my sword and with my bow." (His sons took two parts. And according to Rashi, "portion" means smooth). That is, through his sons, as sons are called "fruits." And he gave this to Josef.

This is the meaning of what is written about Saul, "from his shoulders up he was higher than any of the people." And this is the meaning of "Thou hast a mantle, be thou our ruler." And this is the meaning of "The little ones, why do they come? To give reward to those who bring them." He asked, "Why do they need wisdom if the important thing is not the study but the act?" And he replied, "to give reward to those who bring them," since wisdom yields action.

On the matter of the dispute between Saul and David, there was no flaw in Saul. This is why he was one year old when he reigned, and did not need to prolong the kingship, since he had completed everything in a short time. David, however, needed to rule forty years. David was the son of Judah, the son of Leah, the hidden world. And Saul was of Benjamin, the son of Rachel, the revealed world, and hence opposite from David. For this reason David said, "I am all peace," meaning I attain everyone and I love everyone, "but when I speak, they are for war."

And Avishalom was the opposite of David. This is the meaning of the sin of Jeroboam the son of Nebat: the Creator held onto his clothes and said unto him: "You and Me and the son of *Yishai* (Jesse) will walk in the garden of Eden." And he asked, "Who is leading?" And the Creator told him: "the son of *Yishai* is leading." Then he replied, "Don't want."

The thing is that the order of degrees is that the hidden world comes first, and then the revealed world. This is the meaning of "I have enough," "I have everything." "Enough" is *Gar*, and "everything" is *Vak*. This is also the meaning of "how shall Jacob stand? for he is small?" And this is the meaning of Josef taking the seniority from him. Afterwards, he was given everything, since he had *Gar*, too, which came to him through Josef, by way of "And Joseph sustained."

This is the meaning of "Leah was hated," from whom all hatreds and disputes among wise disciples extend. This is also the meaning of the dispute between Shamai and Hillel, and for the future, when the two camps unite, the camp of Josef and the camp of Judah. This is the meaning of what Judah said onto Josef: "Oh my lord," as then was the unification of Judah and Josef. But Judah must be in the lead.

This explains the Holy Ari being Messiah Son of Josef. This is why he could reveal such wisdom, since he had permission from the revealed world. And this dispute extends from "And the children struggled together within her," that Esau had the good clothes that were with Rebecca.

## 103. WHOSE HEART MAKETH HIM WILLING

I heard on the eve of Shabbat, *Beresheet*, October 1942

In the verse, "of every man whose heart maketh him willing ye shall take My offering." This is the meaning of "the substance of an offering from Sanctity." In other words, how does one come to a state of offering? Through Sanctity.

This means that if one sanctifies oneself with the permitted, he thus comes to a state of offering, which is the Holy *Shechina* (Divinity), called "my offering." And this is the meaning of "of every man whose heart maketh him willing." **All of his heart**, meaning if he had given all his heart, he is then rewarded with My offering, to cleave to the Holy *Shechina*.

In the verse, "in the day of his espousals, and in the day of the gladness of his heart," **espousals** means being of inferior degree, which is lowliness. If a person takes upon himself to serve the Creator in a state of lowness, and at the same time he is happy with this work, this is an important degree. And then one is called "a bridegroom" to the Holy *Shechina*.

## 104. AND THE SABOTEUR WAS SITTING

I heard on the eve of Shabbat, *Beresheet*, October 1942

In *The Zohar*, Noah, there was a flood, and the saboteur was sitting in the midst of it. He asked, "A flood means a flood of water. This, in itself, is deadly and a saboteur. So what does it mean that the saboteur was sitting in the midst of it, in the midst of the flood? And also, what is the difference between the flood and the saboteur?"

And he replied that the flood is corporeal torments, meaning torments of the body. And within it, meaning within the torments of the body, there is yet another saboteur, who sabotages spirituality. This means that the afflictions of the body bring him alien thoughts, until these alien thoughts sabotage and kill his spirituality.

## 105. A WISE DISCIPLE BASTARD PRECEDES A HIGH PRIEST COMMONER

I heard on *Heshvan* 15, November 1, 1944, Tel-Aviv

"A wise disciple bastard precedes a high priest commoner."

A bastard means an alien God, cruel. This refers to bastardy. When one breaches the prohibition of turning unto other gods, they beget him the bastard.

Turning unto the other gods means that he mates himself with the *Sitra Achra* (other side), which is pudendum. This is called "who comes over the pudendum and begets a bastard off it."

And the rule of landlords is opposite from the rule of Torah. Hence, there is a dispute between commoners and wise disciples. And here there is a big difference if the person has begotten the bastard. A wise disciple claims that that, too, comes from the Creator; that the form that appears to him—the bastard form—he says that the Creator caused him that reason.

The wicked, however, says that it is only an alien thought that came to him because of a sin, and he needs nothing more than to correct his sins.

A wise disciple, however, has the strength to believe that this, too, meaning his present form, he must see its true essence. At the same time, he must assume the burden of the kingdom of heaven to the point of devotion.

This means that on what is considered of little importance, too, the lowest and most concealed, still, at such a time it should be ascribed to the Creator, that the Creator created such a picture of Providence in him, called "alien thoughts." And he works above reason in such a small thing as though he had great *Daat* (knowledge) in *Kedusha* (Sanctity).

And a great priest is one who serves the Creator by way of "and they are many..." meaning that they have much Torah and many *Mitzvot* and they are not lacking anything. Hence, if one connects and takes upon himself some order in the work, the rule is that a bastard who is a wise disciple comes first. This means that one assumes one's bastardy in the form of a wise disciple. "Wise" is the name of the Creator. His disciple is one who learns from the Creator. Only a wise disciple can say that everything, all the shapes that appear during the work are "for it was from the Lord."

But a commoner priest, although he serves the Lord and he is great in the Torah and in the work, but he has not been rewarded with learning from the Creator's mouth; and he is still not considered "a wise disciple."

Hence, this above state cannot help him achieve true perfection whatsoever, since he has the rule of landlords, and the rule of Torah is only one who learns from the Creator. Only a wise disciple knows the truth, that the Creator causes all the reasons.

Now we can understand the words of our sages, "Rabbi Shimon Ben Menasia was studying all the *Etin* ('the' (in plural form)) in the Torah." *Et* means including. This means that every day he added Torah and *Mitzvot* more than in the day before. And since he came to "Thou shalt fear the Lord thy God," meaning that he could not increase, but came to a point where he could not add, but God forbid, to the contrary.

And Rashi interprets, Ben Menasia means that he understood the *Menusa* (fleeing), which means fleeing and retreat from the campaign. Also, *Ben*[18] *Haamsuny*, meaning that he understood the truth, and which is the shape of the truth. And he remained standing guard and could not move forward until Rabbi Akiva came and explained *Et* (the), including the wise disciples. This means that through adhering to wise disciples, it is possible to receive some support.

18 In Hebrew, *Ben* (son) has the same root as *Mevin* (understanding).

In other words, only a wise disciple can help him, and nothing else. Even if he is great in the Torah, he will still be called "a commoner," if he has not been rewarded with learning from the Creator's mouth.

Hence, one must surrender before a wise disciple and accept what the wise disciple places on him without any arguments, but by way of above reason.

"The measure thereof is longer than the earth." This means that the Torah begins after the earth. That is, if it is greater than the earth. And there is a rule that nothing can begin in the middle. Hence, if one wants to begin, the beginning is after the earth, meaning past earthliness. (And this is the meaning of "a high priest commoner." It means that even if one's work is in greatness, but if he has not yet been awarded the Light of the Torah, one is still in earthliness.)

Achieving *Lishma* (for Her Name) requires plenty of study in *Lo Lishma* (not for Her Name). This means that one should strain and exert in *Lo Lishma*, and then one can see the truth, that he has still not been awarded the *Lishma*. However, when one does not strain oneself with great efforts, one cannot see the truth.

On another occasion he said that man should study much Torah *Lishma* to be rewarded with seeing the truth–that one is working *Lo Lishma*. The work *Lishma* is considered reward and punishment, which is considered *Malchut*. And Torah *Lo Lishma* is considered ZA, considered private Providence.

This is why all of the kings of Israel, who had all been awarded private Providence, had nothing more to do, since they had nothing to add. This is why our sages said, "a king of Israel neither judges nor is he judged." Hence, they have no part in the next world, since they do not do anything, as they see that the Creator does everything.

This is the meaning of *Izevel* (Jezebel), Ahab's wife. They interpreted that his wife argued, *Ei Zevel* (where is refuse), meaning "Where is there refuse in the world?" She saw that it was all good. And *Ah Av* (Ahab) means that he was *Ah* (brother) to the *Av* (Father) in heaven. But the kings of David's house are judged because the kings of David's house had the power to unite the Creator and His *Shechina* (Divinity), although they are contradictory things, as Providence is opposite to the discernment of reward and punishment.

And this is the power of the great righteous, that they could unite the Creator and Divinity, meaning private Providence with reward and punishment. And precisely from the two of them emerges the complete and desirable perfection.

## 106. WHAT DO THE TWELVE CHALLAHS ON SHABBAT IMPLY

I heard on *Elul*, August, 1942

In the songs of Shabbat it is written, "will reveal to us the flavor of twelve challahs, which are a letter in His name, multiplied and faint."

We should interpret the words of the Holy Ari. It is known that two *Vavs* were made by the second *Tzimtzum* (restriction), meaning the right side and the left side. This is the meaning of the multiplication, from the word "multiply." And from this, from the power of the correction of the second *Tzimtzum* when there was the association of the quality of mercy with the judgment, the judgment became fainter than it was prior to the sweetening.

Afterwards the two *Vavs* shine in *Malchut*, which means "the gathering *Zayins*." The *Zayins* are *Malchut* called "seventh," who gathers the two *Vavs* within her.

The seventh day is considered *Gmar Tikkun* (the end of correction), discerned as the end of days. However, it also shines in the six thousand years. This is the meaning of the six days of action, discerned as "that God has created and performed." And Shabbat is called "resting" (as it is written, "and on the seventh day He ceased from work and rested").

This is considered Shabbat, which shines in the six thousand years, as then the Shabbat is considered resting, like a person who is carrying a load, and stands to rest in the middle of the way to regain his strength. Afterwards he should carry the weight once more. But on the Shabbat of *Gmar Tikkun* there is nothing more to add, hence there is no more work at all.

## 107. CONCERNING THE TWO ANGELS

I heard on *Tetzave*, February, 1943, Jerusalem

Concerning the two angels that accompany one on the eve of Shabbat, the good angel and the evil angel, a good angel is called "right," by which one comes closer to serving the Creator. This is called "the right brings closer." And the bad angel is considered left, pushing further. This means that it brings one alien thoughts, whether in mind or in heart.

And when one prevails over the evil and brings oneself closer to the Creator, it means that on each time, he overcomes the evil and attaches himself to the Creator. Thus, he has come closer to adhesion with the Creator through both of them. This means that both performed a single task–they have caused him to adhere to the Creator. In that state one says, **"Come in peace."**

And when one has completed all of one's work and has already admitted all the left into *Kedusha* (Sanctity), as it is written, "there is not a place to hide from Thee," the bad angel has nothing more to do, as the person has already prevailed all the difficulties that the evil presented. At that time the bad angel is idle, and the person tells it, **"Go in peace."**

## 108. IF YOU LEAVE ME ONE DAY, I WILL LEAVE YOU TWO

I heard in 1943, Jerusalem

Every person is remote from the Creator with the reception in him. But he is remote simply because of the will to receive in him. However, since that person does not crave spirituality, but worldly pleasures, his distance from the Creator is one day, meaning a distance of a day, which means that he is far from Him in only one aspect–in being immersed in the will to receive the desires of this world.

However, when a person brings himself closer to the Creator, and dismisses reception in this world, he is then considered close to the Creator. But if he later fails in the reception of the next world, he is then far from the Creator because he wants to receive the pleasures of the next world, and also falls into reception of pleasures of this world, too. It follows that now he has become remote from the Creator by two days: 1) by receiving pleasures in this world, to which he has fallen again, and 2) since he now has the desire to receive the crown of the next world. This is because by engaging in Torah and *Mitzvot* he forces the Creator to reward him for his work in Torah and *Mitzvot*.

It turns out that in the beginning he walked one day and drew closer to serving the Creator, and afterwards he walked two days backwards. Thus, now that person has become needy of two types of reception: 1) of this world; 2) of the next world. Thus, he has been walking in the opposite state.

The advice for it is to always go by the path of Torah, which is to bestow. And the order should be that first one must be cautious with the two rudiments: 1) the making of the *Mitzva*; 2) the sensation of pleasure from the *Mitzva*. One should believe that the Creator derives great pleasure when we keep His commandments.

It therefore follows that one should keep the *Mitzva* in actual fact, and believe that the Creator derives pleasure from the lower one keeping His *Mitzvot*. And here there is no difference between a big *Mitzva* and a small *Mitzva*. That is, the Creator derives pleasure even from the smallest act that is done for Him.

Afterwards there is a result, which is the main goal that one should see to. In other words, a person should feel delight and pleasure in causing contentment to his Maker. This is the main emphasis of the work, and this is called "serve the Lord with gladness." This should be the reward for one's work, to receive delight and pleasure in having been rewarded with delighting the Creator.

This is the meaning of, "The stranger that is in the midst of thee shall mount up above thee higher and higher; ... He shall lend to thee, and thou shalt not lend to him." The "stranger" is the will to receive (when beginning to serve the Creator, the will to receive is called "stranger." And before that, it is a complete gentile).

"He shall lend to thee." When it gives strength for work, it gives the strength by way of lending. This means that when a day in Torah and *Mitzvot* has passed, although it did not instantaneously receive the reward, it still believed him that afterwards, he would pay for the powers for the work that it has given him.

Hence, after the day's work it comes and asks for the debt that he had promised it, the reward for the powers that the body gave him to engage in Torah and *Mitzvot*. But he does not give it, so the stranger cries, "What is this work? Working without reward?" Hence, afterwards the stranger does not want to give Israel the strength to work.

"And thou shalt not lend to him." If you give it food and you ask that it will give you strength for work, then it tells you that it has no debt to pay you for the food that you are giving it. This is because "I gave you the strength for the work to begin with; and that was on condition that you would buy me possessions. Hence, what you are giving me now is all according to the previous condition. Therefore, now you come to me so I will give you more strength for the work, so that you will bring me new possessions."

So the will to receive has grown clever, and uses its cleverness to calculate the profitability of it. Sometimes it says that it settles for little, that the possessions it has are enough, and hence it does not wish to give him more powers for the work. And sometimes it says that the way you are going in now is dangerous, and perhaps your efforts will be in vain. And sometimes it says that the effort is greater than the reward; hence, I will not give you strength to work.

Then, when one asks it for strength to walk in the path of the Creator, in order to bestow, and that everything will be only to increase the glory of Heaven, it says, "What will I get out of it?" Then it comes with the famous arguments, such as "Who" and "What," that is, "Who is the Lord that I should obey His voice?" as Pharaoh's argument, or "What mean you by this service?" as the argument of the wicked.

All this is because it has a just argument, that this is what they had agreed between them. And this is called, "if thou wilt not hearken unto the voice of the Lord," then he complains because he does not keep the conditions.

But **when you hearken unto the voice of the Lord**, meaning right at the entrance (entrance is a constant thing because every time he has a descent he must begin anew. This is why it is called an "entrance." Naturally, there are many exits and many entrances) he tells his body: "Know that I want to enter the work of God. My intention is only to bestow and to not receive any reward. You should not hope that you will receive anything for your efforts, but it is all in order to bestow."

And if the body asks, "What benefit will you get out of this work?" meaning, "Who is it who receives this work, that I want to exert and toil?" Or it asks more simply: "For whom am I working so hard?"

The reply should be that I have faith in the sages who said that I should believe in abstract faith, above reason, that the Creator has so commanded us, to take upon ourselves faith, that He commanded us to keep Torah and *Mitzvot*. And we should also believe that the Creator derives pleasure when we keep the Torah and *Mitzvot* by way of faith above reason. And also, one should be glad at the Creator's pleasure from one's work.

Thus, there are four things here:

1. Believing in the sages, that what they said is true.
2. Believing that the Creator commanded to engage in Torah and *Mitzvot* only through faith above reason.
3. That there is joy when the creatures keep the Torah and *Mitzvot* on the basis of faith.
4. One should receive delight and pleasure and gladness from having been rewarded with pleasing the King. And the measure of the greatness and the importance of one's work is measured by the measure of gladness that one educes during one's work. And this depends on the measure of faith that a person believes in the above.

It follows that when you hear unto the voice of God, all the powers that he receives from the body are not considered receiving a loan from the body, which one should return, by way of, "if thou wilt not hearken unto the voice of the Lord." And if the body asks, "Why should I give you strength for the work when you promise me nothing in return?" he should answer, "Because this is what you were made for. What can I do if the Creator hates you, as it is written in the Holy *Zohar*, that the Creator hates the bodies."

Moreover, when the Holy *Zohar* says that the Creator hates the bodies, this refers specifically to the bodies of the servants of the Creator, since they want to be eternal receivers, as they want to receive the crown of the next world, too.

And this is considered, "and thou shalt not lend." This means that you do not have to give anything for the strength that the body gave you for the work. But if you lend it, if you give it any kind of pleasure, it is only as a loan, and it should give you strength for work in return, but not for free.

And it must always give you strength, meaning for free. You do not give it any pleasure and you always demand of it to have strength for the work, since "the borrower is servant to the lender." Thus, it will always be the servant and you will be the master.

## 109. TWO KINDS OF MEAT

I heard on *Heshvan* 20

We usually distinguish between two kinds of meat: beast meat and fish meat, and in both there are signs of impurity. The Torah gave us signs by which to know how to avoid them so as to not fall into the domain of impurity in them.

In fish, it gives us the signs of fins and scales. When one sees these signs in fish, one knows how to be cautious and not fall into the hands of impurity. ***Snapir*** **(fin)** implies ***Soneh-Peh-Ohr*** **(hating-mouth-Light)**. This refers to *Malchut*, called **"mouth,"** and all the Lights come from her, which is discerned as faith.

And when one sees that he is in the state of a taste of dust, at a time when one should believe, then one knows for certain that one should correct one's actions. And this is called "*Shechina* (Divinity) in the dust." One should pray to raise Divinity from the dust.

***Kaskeset*** **(scales)** means that at a time of *Snapir* one is unable to work at all. Rather, when one overcomes the *Snapir*, a question concerning Providence appears in one's thought. And this is called ***Kash*** **(straw)**. In that state one falls from one's work. Later, one prevails and begins to work above reason, and another doubt concerning Providence appears in one's mind.

It follows that one has two times ***Kash***, which are ***Kas-Keset*** **(scales)**. And every time one prevails above reason, he ascends and then he descends. Then one sees that he cannot prevail, due to the proliferation of the doubts. In that state, one has no other choice but to cry to the Creator, as it is written, "and the Children of Israel sighed by reason of the bondage, and their cry came up unto God, and He delivered them out of Egypt," meaning from all the troubles.

Our sages said a famous rule, that the Creator says, "He and I cannot dwell in the same abode," that is, because they are opposite from one another. This is so because there are two bodies in man—the inner body and the outer body. The spiritual sustenance dresses in the inner body, discerned as faith and bestowal, called "mind and heart." And the outer body has the corporeal sustenance, which is knowing and receiving.

And in the middle, between the inner body and the outer body, there is a middle body, which does not bear its own name. However, if one performs good deeds, the middle body clings to the inner body, and if one performs bad deeds, the middle body clings to the outer body. Thus, either one has corporeal sustenance or spiritual sustenance.

It follows that since there is oppositeness between the internal and the external, if the middle body clings to the inner body, it is considered the death of the outer body. And if it clings to the outer body, it is death to the inner body. This is so because in that state, the choice is in the middle body: to continue adhering to *Kedusha* (Sanctity), or to the contrary.

## 110. A FIELD WHICH THE LORD HAS BLESSED

I heard in 1943

"A field which the Lord hath blessed." The Holy *Shechina* (Divinity) is called "**a field**." And sometimes a ***Sadeh*** **(field)** is turned into ***Sheker*** **(a lie)**. The *Vav* within the *Hey* is the soul, and the ***Dalet*** is the Holy *Shechina* (Divinity). When the soul is dressed in it, it is called ***Hey***; and when one wants to add to the faith he extends the ***Vav*** below, and it becomes a ***Kof***.

At that time the ***Dalet*** becomes a ***Reish***, in the form of poor and meager, who wants to add. Then it becomes a ***Reish***, by way of "a poor was born in his kingdom," when the **meager** became **poor**. In other words, by inserting the evil eye into oneself, in both mind and heart, by way of "The boar out of the wood doth ravage it": the eye is hung, since it returns to the separation, that the *Sitra Achra* (other side) is destined to be a holy angel.

And this is the meaning of "May the glory of the Lord endure for ever." Because he has come to a state of the animal of the ***Yaar*** **(forest)**, from the word ***Iro*** **(his town)**, it means that all of his vitality has been poured out, and he is constantly strengthened. At that time he is awarded the state of "a field which the Lord hath blessed," when the evil eye is turned into a good eye.

And this is the meaning of "a hanging eye," meaning it hangs on a doubt, whether with a good eye or with a bad eye. And this is the meaning of returning to separation. And this is the meaning of "one opposite one," as our sages said, "There was no joy before Him as on the day when heaven and earth were created." This is so because at last, the "Lord will be One and His Name One," which is the purpose of creation.

But for the Creator, past and present are the same. Hence, the Creator watches over creation in its final shape, as it will be at *Gmar Tikkun* (the end of correction), when all the souls in their complete perfection are included in the world *Ein Sof*, as it will be at *Gmar Tikkun*. Their perfect form is already there, and nothing is missing.

But with the receivers it is apparent that they still need to complete what they must complete. This is, "which God has created and performed," meaning the deficiencies and the testiness. This is the meaning of what our sages said, "the angry yields only anger," and also, "all who are greedy, are angry."

This is the true form of the will to receive in its true form, as obscene as it is. And all the corrections are to turn it in order to bestow, which is the whole work of the lower ones. Before the world was created, it was in the form of "He is one and His Name One." This means that even though His name has already departed from the **He**, and became revealed, and it is already called **"His Name,"** still He was one. And this is the meaning of "one opposite one."

## 111. BREATH, SOUND, AND SPEECH

I heard on *Sivan* 29, July 2, 1943, Jerusalem

There is a discernment of Breath, Sound, and Speech, there is a discernment of Ice, and there is the discernment of Terrible. Breath means *Ohr Hozer* (Returning Light), which comes out of the *Masach* (screen). This is a limiting force. As long as it is not accumulated to the measure of "let them not turn back to folly," it is called "Breath."

When its measure is completed, this limitation, the *Masach* with the Returning Light, is called "Sound." Sound is like a warning that tells him not to breach the laws of the Torah. And if he should breach, as soon as he breaches he will stop tasting. Hence, when he knows for certain that if he breaches he will come to a halt, he retains the limitation.

And then he comes to a state of "Speech," which is *Malchut*. At that time there can be the *Zivug* (spiritual coupling) of the Creator and Divinity, and illumination of *Hochma* (Wisdom) will extend below.

It is known that there are two degrees: 1) Bestowal without any reception. 2) Reception in order to bestow.

Then, when he sees that he has already come to a degree where he can receive in order to bestow, why does he need the servitude, which is only in the form of bestowing in order to bestow? After all, the Creator senses more contentment from reception in order to bestow, since the Light of Wisdom, which enters the vessels of reception, is the Light of the purpose of creation. Hence, why should he engage in the work of bestowing in order to bestow, which is the Light of the correction of creation?

At that time he immediately stops tasting, and is then left bare and naked. This is because the Light of *Hassadim* (Mercy) is the Light that robes the Light of *Hochma*. And if the robe is missing, even though he has the Light of *Hochma*, he still has nothing with which to clothe the *Hochma*.

At that time he comes to the state called "the terrible ice." This is because *Yesod de Abba*, which gives *Hochma*, called "narrow of *Hassadim* and long of *Hochma*," is Ice. It is like water that has been crystallized: although there is water, it does not expand below.

And *Yesod de Ima* is called "terrible," considered short and wide. It is called "short" because there is blocking on the *Hochma*, because of the absence of *Hochma* there, due to the second *Tzimtzum*. And this is "terrible." Hence, it is precisely by both: the *Hochma* extends through *Yesod de Abba*, and *Hassadim* extends through *Yesod de Ima*.

## 112. THE THREE ANGELS

I heard on *Vayera*, October, 1942

Understand:

1. The matter of the three angels that came to visit Abraham during the circumcision.
2. The matter of the Creator coming to visit him and what He had told him during the visit.
3. That our sages said that the visitor takes the sixtieth part of the sickness.
4. The separation from Lot.
5. The destruction of Sodom and Gomorrah.
6. Abraham's request not to destroy Sodom.
7. The matter of Lot's wife looking back and becoming a pillar of salt.

8. The matter of Shimon and Levi's deceit of the people of Shechem concerning the circumcision, when they said, "for that were a reproach unto us."
9. The matter of the two separations that came out of Lot, which were erased in the days of David and Solomon, which are opposite to one another.

To understand the above, we should first say that we know that we discern *Olam* (world), *Shanna* (year), and *Nefesh* (soul) in everything. Hence, concerning the circumcision, too, which is the making of the covenant of the skin, applies the matter of *Olam*, *Shanna*, *Nefesh*. (There are four covenants: eyes, tongue, heart, and skin; and the skin includes them all.)

The skin, considered the foreskin, is the *Behina Dalet* (Phase Four), which should be removed to its place, meaning to the dust. This is considered *Malchut* in her place, that is, lowering *Malchut* to a state of dust. This follows the words, "*Abba* (father) gives the whiteness," meaning lowering *Malchut* from all thirty-two paths into its place. And you find that the *Sefirot* have been whitened from the *Aviut* of *Malchut* of the quality of judgment that was in them, since the breaking occurred because of this *Malchut*.

Afterwards, *Ima* (mother) gives the redness when she receives the *Malchut* that is sweetened in *Bina*, called "earth," and not "dust." This is so because we make two discernments in *Malchut*: 1) earth; 2) dust.

**Earth** is *Malchut* that is sweetened in *Bina*, called "*Malchut* that has risen to *Bina*." **Dust** is called "*Malchut* in the place of *Malchut*," which is *Midat ha Din* (the quality of judgment).

When Abraham had to beget Isaac, which is discerned as the whole of Israel, he had to purify himself with the circumcision, so that Israel would emerge pure. The circumcision, with respect to its ***Nefesh*** **(souls)**, is called "circumcision" and concerns the removal of the foreskin and throwing it to a place of dust.

The **Olam** (**world**) in the circumcision is called the destruction of Sodom and Gomorrah.

The integration of the souls in the world (a world means integration of many souls) is called "Lot," and the circumcision in the world is called "the destruction of Sodom." The healing of the circumcision-pain is called "the saving of Lot." Lot comes from the word "cursed land," called *Behina Dalet*.

We should know that when one has been awarded *Dvekut* (adhesion) with the Creator, when one has equivalence of form, and his only wish is to bestow and not receive anything for his own benefit, he comes to a state where he has no room to work. This is because that person does not need anything for himself; and for the Creator, one sees that the Creator has no deficiencies. Hence, he remains standing, without work. And this causes him the great pain of the circumcision, since the circumcision gave him room to work, as circumcision is the removal of the desire to receive for oneself.

It turns out that by removing the will to receive, when it no longer controls him, he has nothing more to add to his work. And there is a correction for that: even after one has been rewarded with circumcising oneself from the will to receive, there still remain sparks of *Behina Dalet* in him, and they, too, are awaiting correction. They are sweetened only by extending Lights of *Gadlut* (greatness), and thus one has room for work.

This is the meaning of Abraham the Patriarch's pains after the circumcision, and the Creator coming to visit him. And this is the meaning of the angel Raphael healing his pain (and we cannot say that since with the four angels, the order is that Michael is on the right, Gabriel is on the left, and Uriel is at the front, and behind, which is *Malchut*, implied in the west, it is Raphael. This is because he heals *Malchut* after the removal of the foreskin, so there will be more room for work).

And the second angel came to destroy Sodom. This means that when the removal of the foreskin in considered *Nefesh*, it is called "circumcision," and when it is discerned as *Olam*, it is called "the destruction of Sodom." And as they said, after the removal of the foreskin there remains pain, and then we need to heal that pain. Similarly, in the destruction of Sodom, the healing is called "Lot's salvation," due to two good separations that were about to unfold.

It is seemingly difficult to understand the matter of the good separation. If it is separation, how can it be good? Rather, following the removal of the foreskin, there is pain. This is because one has no room for work. And those separations, the sparks that remain of *Behina Dalet*, give one room for work, with his need to correct them.

They cannot be corrected prior to the removal of the foreskin, since first the 248 sparks must be elevated and corrected. Subsequently, the thirty-two sparks, called "the stony heart," are corrected. Hence, first the foreskin must be completely removed.

This is the meaning of the necessity of having a secret, that one should know ahead of time, that they should remain in the form of *Reshimo*. And this is the meaning of *Sod* (secret): through the correction of the circumcision, which is the disruption of the *Yesod* (foundation), meaning disrupting the *Yod* (the first letter in *Yesod*). Then, the *Sod* is turned into *Yesod*.

This is the meaning of the angel, Raphael, subsequently going to save Lot because of the "good separations." This is the meaning of Ruth and Naomi, considered mind and heart. Ruth comes from the word *Re'uia* (worthy), when the *Aleph* is unpronounced. And Naomi is from the word *Noam* (pleasantness), something that is pleasant to the heart, which were then sweetened in David and Solomon.

However, previously, the angel said, “look not behind thee,” since “Lot” is *Behina Dalet*, but she is still connected to Abraham. However, “behind thee,” past *Behina Dalet*, there is only raw *Behina Dalet*, without sweetening. This is the meaning of the great sea-monsters, of which our sages said that it is a Leviathan (whale) and his spouse, which killed the *Nukva* and salted her for the righteous in the future. The future means after all the corrections.

This is the meaning of Lot’s wife looking behind her, as it is written, “But his wife looked back from behind him, and she became a pillar of salt.” However, she first had to be killed, which is the destruction of Sodom. But Lot, who is considered the Leviathan (the connection between *Behina Dalet* and Abraham) had to be saved.

This explains a question the world asks, “How could the angel that healed Abraham save Lot? After all, there is a rule: one angle does not perform two missions.” However, this is a single issue, since there has to remain a *Reshimo* from *Behina Dalet*. But it must be a secret.

This means that before he circumcised himself, there was no need to know anything of it. Rather, she had to be put to death. And the Creator salted her for the righteous in the future, when the *Sod* was made into *Yesod*.

This is the meaning of the strife between the herdsmen of Abraham’s cattle and the herdsmen of Lot’s cattle (*Mikneh* (cattle) means spiritual *Kinyanim* (possessions)). This is because Abraham’s cattle was for the purpose of increasing the aspect of Abraham–faith. This means that in this manner he took for himself greater forces to go above reason, since he saw that specifically in this way of faith above reason, one is awarded all the possessions.

It follows that the reason he wanted the possessions was that these possessions would testify to the way, called "faith above reason," which is a true path. The evidence of that is that since he is given spiritual possessions from Above, through the possessions, he strains to go only by way of faith above reason. But he does not want the spiritual possessions because they are great degrees and attainments.

This means that it is not that he believes in the Creator in order to achieve great attainments through faith. Rather, he needs great attainments so as to know that he is treading a true path. Thus, after all the *Gadlut*, he wants specifically to walk in the path of faith, since through it he sees that he is doing something.

However, the only intention of the herdsmen of Lot's cattle was to achieve great possessions and attainments. This is called "increasing the discernment of Lot." Lot is called "the cursed land," which is one's will to receive, called *Behina Dalet*, whether in mind or in heart. This is why Abraham said, "separate thyself, I pray thee, from me," that is, that *Behina Dalet* would be separated from him, from the *Behina* of *Olam-Shanna-Nefesh.*

This is the meaning of the removal of the foreskin. The removal of the *Behina Dalet* in *Nefesh* is called "circumcision." In the *Behina* of *Olam*, the removal of the foreskin is called "the destruction of Sodom"; and from the *Behina* of *Shanna*, it is the *Hitkalelut* (integration) of many souls, and it is called *Shanna* (year). This is the *Behina* (discernment) of Lot, from the word "curse," called "the cursed land."

Hence, when Abraham said to Lot, "separate thyself, I pray thee, from me," still, Lot was still the son of Haran, referring to the second restriction, called "a river that flows out of Eden to water the garden." And there is the discernment of "beyond the River," being outside the river, meaning the first *Tzimtzum* (restriction), and there is a difference between the first *Tzimtzum* and the second *Tzimtzum*.

In the first *Tzimtzum*, the *Dinim* (judgments) stand below all the *Sefirot* of *Kedusha* (Sanctity), as they had come out in the beginning, by the order of the hanging down of the worlds. In the second *Tzimtzum*, however, they rose to the place of *Kedusha* and already have a hold of *Kedusha*. Hence, in this respect, they are worse than the first *Tzimtzum*; they have no further expansion.

The "land of Canaan" is from the second *Tzimtzum*, which are very bad because they have a hold of *Kedusha*. This is why it is written concerning them, "thou shalt save alive nothing that breathes." The *Behinat* Lot, however, *Behina Dalet*, should be salvaged. Hence, the three angels came as one: one for the blessing of the seed, considered the whole of Israel, which implies the multiplication in the Torah, too. This is the meaning of disclosing the secrets of Torah, called *Banim* (sons), from the word *Havanah* (understanding). And all this can only be attained after the correction of the circumcision.

This is the meaning of the Lord's words: "Shall I hide from Abraham that which I am doing?" Abraham was afraid of Sodom's destruction, lest he would lose all the vessels of reception. This is why he said, "Suppose there are fifty righteous within the city?" because a complete *Partzuf* is fifty degrees. And afterwards he asked, "Perhaps there are forty-five righteous?" meaning *Aviut* of *Behina Gimel*, which is forty, and the *Dalet de Hitlabshut* (clothing), which is *Vak*, half a degree, being five *Sefirot*, etc.. Finally, he asked, "Suppose there are ten righteous?" meaning the level of *Malchut*, only ten. Hence, when Abraham saw that even the level of *Malchut* could not emerge from there, he agreed to the destruction of Sodom.

It turns out that when the Creator came to visit him, he prayed for Sodom, as it is written, "according to the cry of it," meaning that they were all immersed in the will to receive. "**Altogether**... and if not, I will know." This means that there are discernments of bestowal in them, then we will know. This is the meaning of bonding, meaning He will bond them with the *Kedusha* (Sanctity). And since Abraham saw that no good would come from them, he agreed to the destruction of Sodom.

This is why after Lot's separation from Abraham, it is written, "and moved his tent as far as Sodom," the dwelling place of the will to receive, with respect to himself. And this is only in the land of Israel.

However, beyond the River, which is the first *Tzimtzum*, the domination of *Behina Dalet*, there is no room for work. This is because it rules and prevails in its own place. Only in the land of Israel, considered the second *Tzimtzum*. There is all the work. This is the meaning of Abraham's name *Be Hey Bera'am* (created them with the *Hey*). This means that the *Yod* that was there was divided into two *Heys*—the lower *Hey* and the Upper *Hey*—and Abraham took form the *Hitkalelut* of the lower *Hey* with the Upper *Hey*.

Now we can understand Simeon and Levi, who deceived the men of Shechem. Since Shechem wanted Dinah, since his whole intention was in the will to receive, they said that they had to be circumcised, meaning cancel the vessels of reception. And since their only aim was in the will to receive, they were killed by the circumcision, by losing the will to receive through the circumcision. For them, this was considered death.

It therefore follows that they themselves deceived, since their whole intention was in Dinah, their sister. They thought that they could receive Dinah in the vessels of reception. Hence, once they were circumcised, and then wanted to receive Dinah, they could only use the vessels of bestowal, and they had lost the vessels of reception by the circumcision. But since they lacked the spark of bestowal, since Shechem was the son of Hamor, who knows nothing but the vessels of reception, they could not receive Dinah in the vessels of bestowal, which is against their root. Their root is only Hamor, the will to receive, and hence they came out losing either way. This is considered that Simeon and Levi caused their death. But actually, it was their own fault, not Simeon's and Levi's.

This is the meaning of the words of our sages: "If you come across a villain, draw him to the seminary." We must understand what "If you come across" means. It means that the villain, meaning the will to receive, is not always found. Rather, it means that not every one consider their will to receive "a villain." But if there is someone who feels the will to receive as a villain and wants to be rid of it, as it is written, "Always will one move the good inclination over the evil inclination." If he prevails, good; and if not, he shall engage in the Torah; and if not, he shall read the *Shema* prayer; and if not, he shall remind him of the day of his death" (*Berachot*, p.5). In that state he has three counsels together, and one without the others is incomplete.

And now we can understand the question, which the *Gemarah* ends. If the first advice–"pull him to the seminary"–does not help, then "read the *Shema* prayer." And if that does not help, "remind him of the day of his death." Thus, if he is doubtful of their help, why does he need the first two counsels? Why should he not take the last advice right away, meaning reminding him of the day of his death? He answers that this does not mean that one counsel will help, but that it requires all three counsels together.

And this means:

1. Pull him to the seminary, meaning the Torah.
2. Read the *Shema* prayer, meaning the Creator and *Dvekut* (adhesion) with the Creator.
3. Reminding him of the day of his death, meaning devotion. This is considered Israel, who are likened

> unto a dove that stretches out its neck. In other words, all three discernments are one unity, called "the Torah and Israel and the Creator are one."

One can receive assistance from a Rav for the discernment of the Torah and the reading of *Shema*. However, for the discernment of Israel, which is the circumcision, which is devotion, one has to work alone. And even though there is help from Above for that, too, as our sages said, "and madest a covenant with him," meaning that the Creator helped him, still man must begin. This is the meaning of "remind him of the day of his death." We must always remember and never forget, since this is the essence of man's work.

And concerning the *Reshimot* that we must leave, by way of Lot's salvation, it is because of two good separations, which is the meaning of Haman and Mordecai. Mordecai wants only to bestow; he has no need to extend Lights of *Gadlut*. But through Haman, who wants to swallow all the Lights into his authority, through him, he is the cause that evokes man to draw the Lights of *Gadlut*.

Yet, after he has already extended the Lights, it is forbidden to receive them in Haman's vessels, called "vessels of reception," but only in the vessels of bestowal. This is the meaning of what is written, that the King told Haman, "and do so to Mordecai the Jew." This is considered the Lights of Haman shining in the vessels of Mordecai.

## 113. THE EIGHTEEN PRAYER

I heard on *Kislev* 15, Shabbat

In the *Shmone Esrei* (Eighteen) Prayer, "for You hear the prayer of every mouth in Your people, Israel, with mercy." This seems perplexing: first we say, "for You hear the prayer of every mouth," meaning even with an unworthy mouth—the Creator still hears. It is written, "every mouth," meaning even an unworthy one. Afterwards it says, "Your people, Israel, with mercy," meaning specifically a prayer that is in mercy. Otherwise it is not heard.

The thing is that we must know all the heaviness in the work of God is because of the oppositeness that is in every step. For example, there is a rule that man must be humble. But if we follow this end, although our sages said, "be very, very humble," still this end does not mean that it should be a rule. This is because it is known that one should go against the whole world, and not be cancelled by the proliferation of views that abound in the world, as it is written, "And his heart was lifted up in the ways of the Lord." Hence, this rule is not a rule that we can call complete.

And if we go by the other end, which is pride, that, too, is wrong, since "all who is proud," says the Creator, "he and I cannot dwell in the same abode." And we can also see oppositeness in the matter of suffering. That is, if the Creator sends suffering to some person, and we should believe that the Creator is benevolent, then the suffering He had sent are necessarily to that person's benefit. Thus, why do we pray that the Creator will remove the suffering from us?

And concerning suffering, we should know that sufferings only come to correct us to be qualified to receive the Light of the Creator. The role of the suffering is only to cleanse the body, as our sages said, "as salt sweetens meat, suffering cleanses the body." In the matter of prayer, they had made the correction that it would be instead of suffering. Thus, prayer, too, cleanses the body.

However, a prayer is called "the path of Torah." This is why the prayer is more effective in sweetening the body than suffering. Therefore, it is a *Mitzva* to pray for the suffering, since additional benefit stems from that to the individual and to the whole.

Because of that, the oppositeness causes one heaviness and cessations in the work of God, and one cannot continue the work, and feels bad. It seems to him that he is unworthy of assuming the burden of the Kingdom of Heaven "as an ox to the burden and as a donkey to the load." Thus, at that time he is called "unwanted."

However, one's sole intention is to extend faith, called *Malchut*, meaning to raise *Shechina* (Divinity) from the dust. One's aim is to glorify His Name in the world, meaning His greatness, so that the Holy *Shechina* will not take the form of meagerness and poverty. Thus, the Creator hears "the prayer of every mouth," even of one who is not so worthy, who feels that he is still remote from the work of God.

This is the meaning of "for You hear the prayer of every mouth." When does He hear every mouth? When the people of Israel pray with mercy, meaning simple mercy. When one prays to raise Divinity from the dust, to receive faith.

It is similar to one who has not eaten in three days. Then, when he asks of another to be given something to eat, he is not asking for any luxuries or extras; he is simply asking to be given something to revive his soul.

Similarly, in the work of God, when one finds oneself standing between heaven and earth, he is not asking for something redundant of the Creator, but only for the Light of faith, that the Creator will open his eyes so he can assume the discernment of faith. This is called "raising Divinity from the dust." And this prayer is accepted from "every mouth." That is, in any state a person is in, if one asks to revive one's soul with faith, this prayer is answered.

And this is called "with mercy," when one's prayer is only to be pitied from Above so he can sustain his vitality. And this is the meaning of what is written in *The Zohar*, that a prayer for the poor is immediately accepted. That is, when it is for the Holy *Shechina*, it is immediately accepted.

## 114. PRAYER

I heard in 1942

We must understand how a prayer, considered "mercy," is relevant. After all, there is a rule: "I labored and did not find, do not believe." The advice is that one should promise the Creator that he will give him the labor afterwards.

## 115. STILL, VEGETATIVE, ANIMATE, AND SPEAKING

I heard in 1940, Jerusalem

**Still** is something that does not have an authority of its own. Rather, it is under the authority of its Landlord and must satisfy every wish and desire of its Landlord. Hence, when the Creator created creation for His glory, as it is written, "everyone that is called by My Name and whom I have created for My glory," it means that the Creator created creation for His own needs. The nature of the Landlord is imprinted in the creatures, meaning all the creatures cannot work for another, but for themselves.

**Vegetative** is that which already has its own authority to some extent. It can already do something that is contrary to the opinion of the Landlord. This means that it can already do things not for itself but to bestow. This is already the opposite of what exists in the will of the Landlord, which He had imprinted in the lower ones to work only with the will to receive for themselves.

Yet, as we can see in corporeal flora, even though they are mobile and expand in width and length, still, all the plants have a single property. In other words, there is not a single plant that can go against the method of all the plants. Rather, they must adhere to the rules of the flora and are incapable of doing anything against the mind of their contemporaries.

Thus, they have no life of their own, but are parts of the life of all flora. This means that all the plants have a single form of life for all the plants. All the plants are like a single creature and the individual plants are specific organs of that animal.

Similarly, in spirituality there are people who have already acquired the force to overcome their will to receive to some degree, but are confined to the environment. They cannot do the opposite of the environment they live in, yet they do the opposite of what their will to receive wants. This means that they already work with the will to bestow.

**Animate:** We see that each animal has its own characteristic; they are not confined to the environment but each of them has its own sensation and characteristic. They can certainly operate against the will of the Landlord, meaning they can work in bestowal and are also not confined to the environment. Rather, they have their own lives, and their vitality does not depend on their friends' life. Yet, they cannot feel more than their own being. In other words, they have no sensation of the other. And naturally cannot care for the other.

**Speaking** has virtues: 1 – It acts against the will of the Landlord. 2 – It is not confined to its contemporaries like the vegetative, meaning it is independent from society. 3 – It also feels the other, and hence can care for them and complement them, by feeling and regretting with the public, and being able to rejoice in the solace of the public, and by the ability to receive from the past and from the future. Animals, however, feel only the present and only their own being.

## 116. WHY DID HE SAY THAT *MITZVOT* DO NOT REQUIRE INTENTION

I heard

"*Mitzvot* do not require intention," and "a *Mitzva's* reward is not in this world." This means that one who says that *Mitzvot* do not require intention believes that a *Mitzva's* reward is not in this world. An intention is the reason and the flavor in the *Mitzva*. And this is the real reward of the *Mitzva*.

If a person tastes the flavor of a *Mitzva*, and understands its reasoning, no greater reward is needed. Thus, if *Mitzvot* do not require intention, a *Mitzva's* reward is not in this world anyway, since one does not feel any taste or any reason in the *Mitzva*.

It follows that if one is in a state where he hasn't any intention, then one is in a state that the *Mitzva's* reward is not in this world. Because the reward for a *Mitzva* is the taste and the reason, if one does not have that, one certainly has no reward for a *Mitzva* in this world.

## 117. YOU LABORED AND DID NOT FIND, DO NOT BELIEVE

I heard

Necessity of the labor is a requirement. Since the Creator gives man a present, He wants man to feel the benefit in the present. Otherwise, that person would be like a fool, as our sages said,

"Who is a fool? He who loses what he is given." Because he does not appreciate the importance of the matter, he does not watch over the present closely.

There is a rule that one feels no importance in anything if one has no need for that thing. And as the measure of the need and the suffering if one does not attain it, so one senses gladness, pleasure, and joy at the fulfillment of the need. It is similar to one who is given all sorts of good beverages; but if one is not thirsty, he tastes nothing, as it is written, "As cold waters to a faint soul."

Hence, when meals are set, to please the people, there is a custom: as we prepare meat and fish and all sorts of good things, we take note to serve bitter and piquant things, such as mustard, hot peppers, sour, and salty foods. All of this is to evoke the suffering of hunger, since when the heart tastes a piquant and bitter flavor, it evokes hunger and deficiency, which one needs to satisfy with the meal of good things.

We should not ask, "Why do I need things to arouse hunger? After all, the host should only prepare fulfillment for the need, meaning the meal, and not prepare things that evoke the need for the fulfillment?" The obvious answer is that since the host wants the people to enjoy the meal, to the extent that they have a need for the food, to that very extent they will enjoy the meal. It follows that if he will give many good things, it will still not help them enjoy the meal, due to the above reason that there is no fulfillment without a need.

Hence, to be awarded the Light of God, there must also be a need. And the need for it is the labor: to the extent that one exerts and demands the Creator during the greatest concealment, to that extent one becomes needy of the Creator. This means that the Creator will open his eyes to walk by the path of the Creator. Then, when one has that *Kli* (vessel) of a deficiency, when the Creator gives him some help from Above, one will already know how to keep this present. It turns out that the labor is considered *Achoraim* (posterior). And when one receives the *Achoraim*, one has room in which to be awarded the *Panim* (face).

It is said about that, "a fool has no wish for wisdom." This means that he does not have a strong need to exert to obtain wisdom. Thus, he has no *Achoraim*, and he naturally cannot be awarded the discernment of *Panim*.

This is the meaning of "As is the sorrow, so is the reward." That is, the sorrow, called "effort," makes the *Kli*, so one can be awarded the reward. This means that to the extent that one regrets, to that extent one can later be rewarded with joy and pleasure.

## 118. TO UNDERSTAND THE MATTER OF THE KNEES WHICH HAVE BOWED UNTO BAAL

I heard

There is the discernment of a wife, and there is the discernment of a husband. A wife is considered that "she has nothing but what her husband gives her," and a husband is considered extending abundance into his own aspect. Knees are considered "bowing," as it is written, "unto Me every knee shall bow."

There are two discernments in bowing:

1. One who bows before one who is greater. And although he does not know his merit, but believes that he is great, he therefore bows before him.
2. When he knows his greatness and merit in utter clarity.

There are also two discernments considering the faith in the greatness of the Upper One:

1. He believes that he is great because he has no other choice, that is, he has no way of knowing his greatness.
2. He has a way to know his greatness in utter certainty, but he still chooses the path of faith because "It is the glory of God to conceal a thing." This means that although there are sparks in one's body that want specifically to know His greatness, and to not be as a beast, he still chooses faith, because of the above reason.

It follows that one who has no other choice, and chooses faith, is considered a woman, a female–"he grew as weak as female"–and she only receives from her husband. But one who has counsel, and struggles to go by the path of faith is called "a man of war." Hence, those who choose faith when they had the option of walking by the way of knowing, called *Baal* (husband), are called "which have not bowed unto Baal." This means that they did not surrender to the work of *Baal*, considered "knowing," but chose the path of faith.

## 119. THAT DISCIPLE WHO LEARNED IN SECRET

I heard on *Tishrei* 5, September 16, 1942

That disciple who learned in secret, Bruria struck him and said, "ordered in all things," if ordered in the 248, exists. **Secret** means *Katnut* (smallness), from the word **Chash-Mal**. **Chash** means *Kelim de Panim* (anterior vessels), and **Mal** means *Kelim de Achor* (posterior vessels), the *Kelim* below the *Chazeh* (chest), which induce *Gadlut* (greatness).

That disciple thought that if he had been awarded the state of **Chash**, a desire to bestow, and all his intentions are only to bestow, then he has been awarded everything. But the purpose of creating the worlds was to do good to His creations, to receive the most sublime pleasures so man would achieve the full stature, even below the *Chazeh*, meaning the whole 248. This is why Bruria told him the verse, **"ordered in all things,"** in all 248.

This means that he would extend below the *Chazeh*, too, meaning that he should extend *Gadlut*, too. This is *Mal*, speech, considered disclosure, to reveal the whole level. However, to avoid impairing, one must first receive the *Katnut*, called *Chash*, which is in secret, not yet revealed. Afterwards one needs to scrutinize the discernment of *Mal*, too, the *Gadlut*, and then the whole level will be revealed.

This is "ordered... and secure," when the *Katnut* is already secured in him and he can already extend the *Gadlut* without fear.

## 120. THE REASON FOR NOT EATING NUTS ON ROSH HASHANAH

I heard at the closing of Rosh Hashanah, 1942, Jerusalem

The reason for not eating nuts on *Rosh Hashanah* (the Jewish New Year) is that *Egoz* (nut), in *Gematria*, is *Het* (sin). And he asked, "But *Egoz*, in *Gematria*, is *Tov* (good)?" And he said that *Egoz* implies the tree of knowledge of good and evil.

And before one repents from love, the *Egoz* in him is still a sin. And one who has already been awarded repentance from love is permitted to eat nuts. Hence, his *Het* has become good, and then he is permitted to eat nuts. This is why we should take note that we eat only things that do not have any hint of a sin, which are considered the tree of life. However, things that have *Gematria* of *Het* imply the tree of knowledge of good and evil.

## 121. SHE IS LIKE MERCHANT-SHIPS

I heard

In the verse, "She is like the merchant-ships; she bringeth her bread from afar." When one demands and insists that "she is all mine," that all the desires will be dedicated to the Creator, the *Sitra Achra* awakens against him and claims, "She is all mine," too. And then there is a tradeoff. A tradeoff means that one wants to buy a certain object and the buyer and seller debate its worth, meaning each of them claims that he is right.

And here the body examines to whom it is worthwhile to listen: to the receiver or to the giving force. Both clearly argue, "She is all mine." And since one sees one's lowness, that in him, too, there are sparks that do not agree to observe the Torah and *Mitzvot* even as a dot on the iota, but that the whole body argues, "She is all mine," then, "she bringeth her bread from afar." This means that from the removals, when one sees how far one is from the Creator, and regrets, and asks of the Creator to bring him closer, "she bringeth her bread."

Bread means faith. In that state one is awarded permanent faith, since "God hath so made it that men should fear before Him." This means that all the removals that one feels were brought to him by the Creator, so he would have the need to assume the fear of heaven.

This is the meaning of "that man doth not live by bread only, but by everything that proceedeth out of the mouth of the Lord." This means that the life of *Kedusha* (Sanctity) within one does not come specifically from drawing closer, from entrances, that is, admissions into *Kedusha*, but also from the exits, from the removals. This is so because through the dressing of the *Sitra Achra* in one's body, and its claims, "She is all mine," with a just argument, one is awarded permanent faith by overcoming these states.

This means that one should unite everything with the Creator, that is, that even the exits stem from Him. And when he is rewarded, he sees that both the exits and the entrances were all from Him.

This forces one to be humble, since now he sees that the Creator does everything, the exits as well as the entrances. And this is the meaning of what is said about Moses, that he was humble and patient–that one must tolerate the lowness. Thus, in each degree one should hold on to the lowness. And the minute he loses the lowness, he immediately loses all the degrees of "Moses" that he had already achieved.

This is the meaning of patience. Lowliness exists in everyone; but not every person feels that lowliness is a good thing. Thus, one does not want to suffer. However, Moses tolerated the humility, which is why he was called "humble," since the lowness made him glad.

This is the rule: "Where there is no joy, *Shechina* (Divinity) does not dwell." Hence, during the purification period, there cannot be the *Shechina*. And although purification is a necessary thing (like the lavatory: although one must go there, one is still certain that this is not the King's Palace).

This is the meaning of *Beracha* (blessing) and *Bechora* (seniority), whose letters are the same (in Hebrew). Seniority is *Gar*, and the *Sitra Achra* wants the *Gar*, but not the blessings, since blessing is the clothing over the *Mochin*. And Esau wanted the seniority without the clothing, but it is forbidden to receive *Mochin* without clothing. This is the meaning of Esau's words: "Hast thou not reserved a blessing for me?" "A blessing" means the opposite of blessings, that is, a curse. It is said about that: "Yea, he loved cursing, and it came unto him; and he delighted not in blessing."

## 122. UNDERSTANDING WHAT IS WRITTEN IN *SHULCHAN ARUCH*

I heard on the eve of Shabbat, *Nitzavim*, *Elul* 22, September 4, 1942

Understand what is explained in *Shulchan Aruch* (*Set Table*–the Jewish code of Law): the rule is that one should repeatedly reflect upon the prayers of the Terrible Days so that when prayer time comes, he will be accustomed and used to praying.

The thing is that the prayer should be in the heart. This is the meaning of the work in the heart, that the heart will agree to what one says with one's mouth (otherwise, it is deceit, that is, one's mouth and heart are not the same). Hence, on the month of *Elul* one should accustom oneself to the great work.

And the most important thing is that one can say "write us to life." This means that when one says "write us to life," the heart, too, should agree (so it will not be as flattery) that one's mouth and heart will be the same, "for man looketh on the outward appearance, but the Lord looketh on the heart."

Accordingly, when one cries, "**write us to life**," "life" means adhesion with the Life of Lives, which is by that specifically, when one wants to work entirely in the form of bestowal, and that all of one's thoughts for self-gratification will be revoked. Then, when one feels what he is saying, his heart can fear lest his prayer will be accepted, that is, that he will have no desire whatsoever for himself.

And concerning self-gratification, there appears a state where it seems that one leaves all the pleasures of this world, all the people, friends, his kin, all his possessions, and retires to the desert where there is nothing but wild beasts, without anyone knowing of him and of his existence. It seems to him as though he loses his world all at once, and feels that he is losing a world filled with liveliness, and takes upon himself death from this world. He feels as though he is committing suicide, when he experiences this image.

Sometimes, the *Sitra Achra* helps him picture his state with all the dark colors. Then the body repels this prayer, and in such a state, one's prayer cannot be accepted, since he himself does not want his prayer to be accepted.

For this reason there must be preparation for the prayer, to accustom oneself to the prayer, as though his mouth and heart are equal. And the heart can come to agree through accustoming, so it would understand that reception means separation, and that the most important is the adhesion with the Life of Lives, which is bestowal.

One must always delve in the work of *Malchut*, called "writing," considered "ink" and *Shacharit* (blackness). This means that one should want one's work to be in the form of "Libni and Shimei,"[19] that only at the time of whiteness does he adhere to the Torah and *Mitzvot*, but unconditionally. Whether in white or in black, it will always be the same for him, and that come-what-may, he will always adhere to the commandments of the Torah and *Mitzvot*.

## 123. HIS DIVORCE AND HIS HAND COME AS ONE

I heard; memories of the ADMOR (Baal HaSulam)

In the matter of the Lower *Hey* in the *Eynaim* (eyes), it means that a *Masach* (screen) and a cover was placed over the eyes. Eyes mean seeing and Providence, when one sees hidden Providence.

Experimenting means that one cannot decide either way, that he cannot clarify the Creator's will and his Rav's intention. Although one can work devotedly, one cannot decide if this

19 Libni also means whiteness

work in devotion is in its place or, to the contrary, that this hard work will be against his Rav's view and the Creator's view.

And to determine, one chooses that which adds labor. This means that one should work according to the line that labor is all that is for one to do, and nothing else. Thus, one has no place to doubt one's actions and thoughts and words, but must always increase labor.

## 124. A SHABBAT OF GENESIS AND OF THE SIX THOUSAND YEARS

I heard

There are two discernments of Shabbat: 1) of *Beresheet* (Genesis/beginning); 2) of the six thousand years. And the difference between them is this: It is known that there is a stop, and there is rest. A stop is where there is nothing more to add. A rest, however, stems from the words "standing" and "resting," meaning that one is in the middle of one's work. And since one has no strength to continue with one's work, he stands and rests to revive himself, and afterwards continues with his work.

A Shabbat of *Beresheet* is a discernment of having nothing more to add. This is called "a stop." A Shabbat of the six thousand years is considered rest, by which one receives strength to continue one's work on the weekdays.

Now we can understand the words of our sages: "Shabbat said, 'You have given everyone a mate, but to me You did not.'" And the Creator replied, "Israel will be your partner." A partner means ZA. If there is a *Nukva*, there can be a *Zivug* (coupling), and from the *Zivug* come the offspring, meaning renewal and additions.

*Nukva* is a deficiency. If there is a deficiency in some place, there is room to correct the deficiency, and all the corrections are considered having been fulfilled by extending the Upper Light in the place of the lack. It follows that there was no deficiency here to begin with, but all the lack that they previously considered to be a deficiency, came in the form of correction to begin with, meaning that thus the Upper Light would flow from Above.

This is similar to one who delves in some matter, and exerts to understand it. And when he attains the meaning, then it is to the contrary, he does not feel that he was previously suffering when he did not understand the matter. Rather, he is glad because now he has joy. The joy is measured by the extent of the effort that he made prior to understanding the matter.

Thus, the delving time is called *Nukva*, a deficiency. And when one unites with the deficiency, he produces the offspring, the renewal. This is what the Shabbat argued, "Since there is no work on Shabbat, there will be no offspring and renewals."

## 125. WHO DELIGHTS THE SHABBAT

I heard on *Sivan* 8, June 15, 1949

"One who delights the Shabbat is given an unbounded domain, as it is said, 'Then shalt thou delight thyself in the Lord, and I will make thee to ride upon the high places of the earth, and I will feed thee with the heritage of Jacob thy father,' etc.. Unlike Abraham, about whom it is written, 'Arise, walk through the land in the length of it,' etc.. And not as Isaac, as it is written, 'for unto thee and unto thy seed I will give all these lands,' but as Jacob, about whom it is written, 'and thou shalt spread abroad to the west, and to the east, and to the north, and to the south'" (Shabbat, 118).

It is difficult to understand this *Gemarah* as it is. Should every one of Israel be given the whole world, an unbounded domain?

We should begin with the words of our sages: "In the future, the Creator will take the sun out of its sheath and will darken. The wicked are judged by it, and the righteous are healed by it, as it is written, 'For behold, the day cometh, it burneth as a furnace; and all the proud, and all that work wickedness, shall be stubble; and the day that cometh shall set them ablaze, saith the Lord of hosts, that it shall leave them neither root nor branch,' neither a root in this world nor a branch in the next world." The righteous are healed by it, as it is written, "'But unto you that fear My Name shall the sun of righteousness arise with healing in its wings.' And moreover, they are refined by it" (*Avoda Zarah (Idolatry)*, 3b).

And we need to understand the riddle of the sages, what is a sun and what is a sheath, and whence does this oppositeness come. Also, what is "neither a root in this world nor a branch in the next world"? And what is "moreover, they are refined by it"? He should have said, "healed and refined by it"; but what is the "moreover" that he said?

Now we can understand the words of our sages: "Israel count by the moon and the nations of the world, by the sun" (*Sukkah* 29). Thus, the sunlight is an epithet to the clearest knowledge, as it is written, "clear as the sun." And the nations of the world, who did not receive the Torah and *Mitzvot*, as it is written that the Creator brought it to every nation and tongue, since they did not want to delight in the Light of the Torah, considered "the moon," which receives from His Light, being the light of the sun, that is, the common Light. Yet, they do have craving and desire to study in the Name and to know Him, Himself.

But Israel count by the moon, which are the Torah and *Mitzvot*, where the sunlight is clothed within them. Hence, the Torah is the sheath of the Creator.

It is written in *The Zohar* that "the Torah and the Creator are one." This means that the Light of the Creator is clothed in the Torah and *Mitzvot*, and He and His sheath are one. Hence,

Israel count by the moon, to complement themselves in Torah and *Mitzvot*. Therefore ,they are naturally awarded the Creator, too. Yet, since the nations of the world do not keep the Torah and *Mitzvot*, meaning the sheath, they do not have even the Light of the sun.

This is the meaning of "in the future, He brings the sun out of its sheath." And they said, "*Shechina* (Divinity) in the lower ones; a sublime need." This means that the Creator craves it and yearns for it.

This is the meaning of the six days of action, meaning the work in Torah and *Mitzvot*, since "The Lord hath made every thing for His own purpose." And even the work on the six days is still the work of God, as it is written, "He created it not a waste, He formed it to be inhabited." This is why it is called "a sheath."

And the Shabbat is the light of the sun, the day of rest in the eternal life. That is, He has prepared the world in two degrees: 1) that His Divinity would be revealed through the Torah and *Mitzvot* in the six days of action; 2) that He will be revealed in the world without the Torah and *Mitzvot*.

And this is the meaning of "in its time; I will hasten it." Rewarded–I will hasten it, meaning through Torah and *Mitzvot*. Not rewarded–in its time. This is because the evolution of creation through the increase of the suffering brings the end and the redemption to humanity, until the Lord places His Divinity in the lower ones. And this is called "in its time," evolution over time.

## 126. A SAGE COMES TO TOWN

I heard during the *Shavuot meal*, May 1947, Tel-Aviv

"A sage comes to town." The Creator is called "Sage." He comes to town, because on *Shavuot* (Pentecost) He shows Himself to the world.

"The sluggard saith: 'There is a lion on the way'; perhaps the sage is not at his home? Perhaps the door is locked?" Our sages said that the thing is, "if you labored and did not find, do not believe." Hence, if he sees that he has not found the nearness of the Creator, then he is told that he must have not labored sufficiently. This is why the verse calls him, "sluggard."

And what is the reason that he did not labor? If he is seeking the nearness of the Creator, why does he not want to make an effort? After all, even if you want to obtain a corporeal thing, you still cannot obtain it without labor. In truth, he does want to labor, and it is not that he says, "There is a lion on the way," meaning the *Sitra Achra*, as it is written, "as a lion in secret places." This means that one who begins the path of the Creator encounters the lion on the way. And those who fail in it cannot recover.

This is why he is afraid to start, for who can defeat it? Then he is told, "There is no lion on the way," meaning "There is none else besides Him," it is written. This is because there is no other force but Him, by way of "and God hath so made it, that men should fear before Him."

And then he finds another excuse: "Perhaps the Sage is not at home?" His home is *Nukva*, the Holy *Shechina* (Divinity). Then he cannot know for certain if he is walking on the path of *Kedusha* (Sanctity) or not.

This is why he says that perhaps the Sage, meaning the Creator, is not at His home. That is to say, this is not His home, not of the *Kedusha*. So how can he know that he is advancing in *Kedusha*? Then he is told: "The Sage is at His home," meaning "One's soul shall teach him," and at last he will know that he is advancing in *Kedusha*.

Then he says, "Perhaps the door is locked, and it is impossible to get in, as it says, 'not all who wish to take the Creator will come and take'?" Then he is told, "The door is not locked." After all, we can see that many people have been rewarded with admission into the King's palace.

And then he replies, "Either way, I will not go." This means that if he is sluggard and does not want to exert, he becomes argumentative and shrewd, and thinks that they are only making the work heavier on him.

But in truth, one who wishes to exert sees the opposite. He sees that many have succeeded. And those who do not want to exert see that there are people who did not succeed. And even though they did not succeed, it is because they discovered that they did not want to exert. But since he is sluggard and only wants to justify his actions, he preaches like a wise one. In truth, the burden of Torah and *Mitzvot* should be accepted without any arguments and complaints, and then he will succeed.

## 127. THE DIFFERENCE BETWEEN KERNEL, ESSENCE, AND ADDED ABUNDANCE

*Sukkot* Inter 4, September 30, 1942

It is known that the departure of the *Mochin* and the cessation of the *Zivug* occur only to the additions of the *Mochin*, and the core of the degree in *ZON* is *Vav* and a *Nekuda* (point). This means that, at its essence, *Malchut* has no more than a point, a black point that has no whiteness in it.

And if one accepts that point as the core, and not as something superfluous that one wishes to be rid of, but moreover, accepts it as adornment, it is called "a handsome abode in one's heart." This is because he does not condemn this servitude, but makes it essential to him. This is called "raising Divinity from the dust." And when one sustains the basis as essential, one can never fall from one's degree, since there is no departure in the essence.

And when one takes upon himself to work as a black point, where even in the greatest darkness in the world, the Holy Divinity says, "there is no place to hide from you." Hence, "I am tied to Him in one knot," "and it will never be detached." Because of that, one has no cessation of *Dvekut* (adhesion).

And if some illumination, called "addition," comes to him from Above, he accepts it by way of "unavoidable and unintended," since it comes from the Emanator, without the lower one's awakening. And this is the meaning of "I am black, but comely," because if you can accept the blackness, you will see that I am comely.

And this is the meaning of "Whoso is thoughtless, let him turn in hither." When he turns from all his dealings and wants to work only to benefit the Creator, and works by way of "I was as a beast before Thee," he is then rewarded with seeing the final perfection. This is the meaning of "a heartless one, she saith to him." This means that since he was heartless, he had to be thoughtless; otherwise he would not be able to approach.

But sometimes we encounter a state of Divinity in exile, when the point descends to the separated *BYA*. Then it is called "As a lily among thorns," since it has the shape of thorns and thistles. In that state, it cannot be accepted, since it is the domination of the *Klipot*.

And this comes through man's actions, as man's actions below affect the root of one's soul Above, in the Holy Divinity. This means that if a person below is enslaved to the will to receive, he thus makes the *Klipa* reign over the *Kedusha* Above.

This is the meaning of *Tikkun Hatzot* (midnight correction). We pray to raise Divinity from the dust, meaning to elevate it, to be important, as Above and below are calculations of importance. And then it is considered a black point.

In the *Tikkun Hatzot* he prevails and says that he wants to keep the verse of "Libni and Shimei." Libni means *Lavan* (white), and not black, and Shimei means *Shmi'a* (hearing), meaning reasonability, which means that assuming the burden of the kingdom of Heaven is a reasonable and acceptable matter for him. And the *Tikkun Hatzot* is the *Tikkun* of the *Mehitza* (partition), the correction of separating the *Kedusha* from the *Klipa*, meaning to correct the bad feeling within the will to receive, and connect to the desire to bestow.

*Golah* (exile) has the letters of *Ge'ulah* (redemption), with the difference being the *Aleph*. This means that we must extend the *Aluf* (Champion) of the world into the *Golah*, and then we immediately feel the *Ge'ulah*. This is the meaning of "He who could guard the harmful, must compensate the harmed with the best kind that one has." And this is the meaning of "where there is judgment below, there is no judgment Above."

## 128. DEW DRIPS FROM THAT *GALGALTA* TO *ZEIR ANPIN*

I heard on *Mishpatim* 3, February 27, 1943

Dew drips from that *Galgalta* to *Zeir Anpin*. And concerning the pale hair, there is a dent under each hair, and this is the meaning of "He that would break me with a tempest." And this is the meaning of, "Then the Lord answered Job out of the whirlwind." And this is the meaning of "This they shall give, every one that passeth among them that are numbered, half a shekel after the shekel of the sanctuary." And this is the meaning of, "a beka (dent) a head," "to make atonement for your souls."

To understand the issue of the hair, it is the black and the ink. This means that when one feels remoteness from the

Creator, because one has alien thoughts, this is called "hair." And "pale" means whiteness. This means that when the Light of God pours onto him it brings him closer to the Creator, and both of them together are called "Light and *Kli* (vessel)."

And the order of the work is that when one awakens to the work of God, it is by being given paleness. At that time one feels vitality and liveliness in the work of God. And afterwards comes an alien thought, by which one falls from one's degree and drifts away from the work. The alien thought is called *Se'ara* (storm and hair). And there is a dent under the hair, which is dent and a deficiency in the skull.

Before the alien thoughts came to him, he had a complete *Rosh* (head) and he was close to the Creator, and through the alien thoughts he drew far from the Creator. And this is considered having a deficiency. And by the sorrow, that he regrets it, he extends a flowing of water. Thus, the hair becomes a hose for the transference of abundance, by which it is considered that he has been awarded whiteness.

And afterwards the alien thoughts come to him again, and he thus becomes remote from the Creator once more. This creates a dent again, a hole and a deficiency in the skull, and through the sorrow, that he regrets it, he extends a flowing of water once again, and the hair becomes a hose to transfer the abundance.

And this order continues repeatedly, by way of ups and downs, until the hairs are accumulated into the complete measure. This means that each time he corrects, he extends abundance. This abundance is called "dew," as in "my head is filled with dew." This is because the abundance comes intermittently, and each time it is as though he receives a drop. And when one's work is complete, and he achieves the full amount, until "but let them not turn back to folly," it is considered that from that dew, the dead will be revived.

And this is the meaning of the dent, meaning the alien thoughts that make holes in the head.

And also, concerning the matter of the half-shekel, meaning that he is half worthy, half unworthy. But we must understand that the halves are not at the same time. Rather, at each time there must be a complete thing. This is because if he has broken one *Mitzva* and did not keep it, he is no longer considered half, but a complete wicked.

However, it is in two times. At one time he is righteous, adhered to the Creator, and then he is completely worthy. And when he is in descent, he is wicked. This is the meaning of "the world was not created but either for the complete righteous or for the complete wicked." And this is why it is called "half," having two times.

And this is "to make atonement for your souls." Through the dent, when one feels that one's head is incomplete, because when an alien thought comes, his mind is not wholly with the Creator. And when he regrets it, it makes him make atonement for his soul. This is so because if he repents every time, then he extends abundance until the abundance is filled by way of "my head is filled with dew."

## 129. DIVINITY IN THE DUST

I heard

"You are fond of suffering. Then he said, 'neither they nor their reward,' about this beauty, which wears off in the dust." Suffering is primarily in a place that is above reason. And the measure of the suffering depends on the extent to which it contradicts the reason. This is considered faith above reason, and this work gives contentment to the Creator. It follows that the reward is that by this work there is contentment to one's Maker.

However, in between, before one can prevail and justify His guidance, Divinity is in the dust. This means that the work by way of faith, called the Holy Divinity, is in exile, canceled in the dust. And he said about that: "neither they nor their reward." This means that he cannot tolerate the period in between. And this is the meaning of his reply to him, "I am crying for this and for that."

## 130. TIBERIAS OF OUR SAGES, GOOD IS THY SIGHT

I heard on *Adar* 1, February 21, 1947, on a trip to Tiberias

Tiberias of our sages, good is thy sight. Seeing means wisdom. Good means that he can be awarded wisdom there. And Rabbi Shimon Bar-Yochai was purifying the markets of Tiberias. The impurity of the dead, that is, of the will to receive, means, "the wicked, in their lives, are called 'dead.'" And all impurities belong only to *Hochma* (wisdom); hence, in Tiberias, where there is the quality of *Hochma*, the market had to be purified.

## 131. WHO COMES TO BE PURIFIED

I heard in 1947

"He who comes to be purified is aided." This means that one should always be in a state of "coming." And then, in any case, if he feels that he has already been purified, he no longer needs to aid him, since He has purified and left. And if he feels that he is in a state of coming and going, then he is certainly assisted, since there is no prevention before the desire, as he is seeking the truth.

"For thy love is better than wine." This means that wine can intoxicate, and a drunk, the whole world is his, since he has no deficiencies, even in the six thousand years.

## 132. IN THE SWEAT OF THY FACE SHALT THOU EAT BREAD

I heard on *Adar* 14, March 6, 1947, Tel-Aviv

"In the sweat of thy face shalt thou eat bread." Bread means Torah, which is "Go, fight with My bread." The study of Torah should be with fear, tremor, and sweat, by which the sin of the tree of knowledge is sweetened.

## 133. THE LIGHTS OF SHABBAT

I heard in 1947

The Lights of Shabbat come to the discernment of the *Guf* (body). Hence, on Shabbat we say, "A Psalm of David. Bless the Lord, O my soul; and all that is within me," meaning the *Guf*. A new head, however, is considered a *Neshama* (soul), which comes only to the discernment of the *Neshama* and not to the *Guf*. This is why we only say, "Bless the Lord, O my soul," and not "and all that is within me," since they do not reach the *Guf* (see *Zohar* 1,97).

## 134. INTOXICATING WINE

I heard in 1947

It is impossible to be awarded the Torah in its entirety. And through intoxication in the wine of Torah, when one feels that the whole world is his, even though he still does not have the whole of the wisdom, he will think and feel that he has everything in perfection.

## 135. CLEAN AND RIGHTEOUS SLAY THOU NOT

I heard on *Nisan* 2, March 23, 1947, Tel Aviv

"The clean and righteous slay thou not." A righteous is one who justifies the Creator: whatever he feels, whether good or bad, he takes above reason. This is considered "right." Clean refers to the cleanness of the matter, the state as he sees it. This is so because "a judge has only what his eyes see." And if one does not understand the matter, or cannot attain the matter, one should not blur the forms as they seem to one's eyes. This is considered "left," and he should nurture both.

## 136. THE DIFFERENCE BETWEEN THE FIRST LETTERS AND THE LAST LETTERS

I heard on *Purim* 1947

The difference between the first letters and the last letters is only in the copy of the writing, meaning the content of the writing that was given off the King's house. And the King's authors expand the content to make it understandable for all.

The content was merely "that they should be ready against that day." And the authors interpreted it as applying to the nations, that they are destined to avenge the Jews. And that force was so that Haman would think, "Whom would the king delight to honor besides myself?" Hence, in the last letters he specifically wrote, straight from the King, "that the Jews should be ready." Conversely, in the first letters he did not specifically write "the Jews." This is why they had the strength to complain.

The thing is that this force was given because one should not justify any desire for reception of Lights, to extend the

Upper Lights below, as the whole work was to bestow. Hence, he cannot extend something from below. Hence, by giving strength to Haman, he specifically wants the greater Lights, as his name testifies, Haman the Agagite, the *Gag* (roof) of the degree, which is *Gar*.

## 137. ZELOPHEHAD WAS GATHERING WOOD

I heard in 1947

Zelophehad was gathering wood. *The Zohar* interprets that he was measuring which tree was bigger: the tree of life or the tree of knowledge. A righteous is called "the tree of life," who is entirely to bestow. And in that, there is no hold to the external ones. However, wholeness lies in the tree of knowledge, the extension of *Hochma* (wisdom) below. This is the meaning of doing good to His creations. And they must not be measured; they should be, "that they may become one in thy hand."

This means that one without the other is incomplete. And Mordecai was from the discernment of the tree of life, not wanting to extend anything below, since he had no deficiencies. Hence, He had to increase the Haman, so he would draw the Lights below. And afterwards, when he disclosed his deficiency, Mordecai would receive them in the form of reception in order to bestow.

Now we can see why later, when Mordecai said good things about the King, when he saved Him from death, the King promoted Haman, who was his enemy. It is as our sages said, "according to every man's wish," according to the will of Haman and Mordecai, who were hateful of each other.

## 138. ABOUT FEAR THAT SOMETIMES COMES UPON A PERSON

I heard in 1942

When fear comes upon a person, one should know that there is none else but Him. And even witchcraft. And if one sees that fear overcomes him, he should say that there is no such thing as chance, but God has given him an opportunity from Above, and he must contemplate and study the end to which one has been sent this fear. It appears that it is so that he will prevail and say, "there is none else besides Him."

But if after all that, the fear has not departed from him, one should take it as an example and say that one's servitude of the Creator should be in the same measure of the fear, meaning that the fear of God, which is a merit, should be in the same manner of fear that he now has. That is, that the body is impressed by this superficial fear, and exactly in the same way that the body is impressed, the fear of God should be.

## 139. THE DIFFERENCE BETWEEN THE SIX DAYS OF ACTION AND THE SHABBAT

I heard

The six days of action are considered ZA, and Shabbat is considered *Malchut*. And he asked, but ZA is a higher degree than *Malchut*, so why is Shabbat more important than the weekdays? And moreover, why are they called *Yemey Hol*[20] (weekdays)?

The thing is that the world is nourished only through *Malchut*. This is why *Malchut* is called "the assembly of Israel,"

---

20 *Yemey*—days; *Hol* comes from the word *Hulin*—secular, not holy.

since all the good influence to the whole of Israel comes from there. Therefore, although the six days imply ZA, there is no unification between ZA and *Malchut*. This is why it is called *Hol*, since no abundance extends from ZA to *Malchut*.

And when no *Kedusha* (Sanctity) extends from *Malchut*, it is therefore called *Yemey Hol*. However, on Shabbat there is a unification of ZA and *Malchut*, and then *Kedusha* extends from *Malchut*. This is why it is called "Shabbat."

## 140. HOW I LOVE THY LAW

I heard at thc conclusion of Passover 7, 1943

"O how I love Thy law! It is my meditation all the day." He said that even though King David had already been awarded perfection, he still craved the Torah, because the Torah is greater and more important than any perfection in the world.

## 141. THE HOLIDAY OF PASSOVER

I heard

The holiday of Passover is on *Mochin de Haya*, and the count is on *Mochin de Haya*. Hence, during the count there is departure of the *Mochin*, since the count is considered raising MAN. It is known that when raising *MAN* there is departure of Lights; but after the count, the *Mochin* returns to its place. This is so because the *Katnut* (smallness) during the count is *Katnut* of *Yechida*, but along with it there is the *Mochin* of the weekdays, which is *YESHSUT*. And *Mochin* of Shabbat, which are *Mochin* of *AVI*.

## 142. THE ESSENCE OF THE WAR

I heard

The essence of the war should be in a place of permission. However, with *Mitzva* and sin, the loss is near and the reward is far. Hence, there he should observe without any considerations.

However, waging war and keeping the *Mitzva* of choice should be made in a place of permission, since the act is only a matter of permission. Hence, even if one fails, the sin will not be so great. This is why it is considered near to the reward, since if he wins the war, he will bring a new authority under the *Kedusha*.

## 143. ONLY GOOD TO ISRAEL

I heard from my Father, Master and Teacher.

"Only good to Israel, God is to the pure in heart." It is known that "only" and "just" are diminutives. This means that in every place the Torah writes "only" and "just," it comes to diminish.

Therefore, in work matters we should interpret it as when one diminishes oneself and lowers himself. Lowness applies when one wants to be proud, meaning wants to be in *Gadlut* (greatness). This means that one wants to understand every single thing, that his soul craves seeing and hearing in everything, but he still lowers himself and agrees to go with his eyes shut and keep Torah and *Mitzvot* in utter simplicity. This is "good to Israel." The word *Ysar-El* (Israel) is the letters of *Li Rosh* (the head (mind) is mine).

This means that he believes he has a mind of *Kedusha* (Sanctity) although he is only discerned as "just," meaning that he is in a state of diminution and lowness. And he says about this "just" that it is absolute good. Then the verse, "God is to the pure in heart," exists in him, meaning that he is awarded a pure heart. And this is the meaning of "and I will take away the stony heart out of your flesh, and I will give you a heart of flesh." The heart of flesh is *Mochin de Vak*, called *Mochin* of clothing, which comes from the Upper One. *Mochin de Gar*, however, should come from the lower one, through the scrutinies of the lower one.

The issue of *Vak de Mochin* and *Gar de Mochin* requires explanation: there are many discernments of *Vak* and *Gar* in each degree. And perhaps he is referring to what he wrote in several places, that the *Katnut*, called "*GE* of the lower one," rise to *MAN* through the *Kli* that raises *MAN*, called "*AHP* of the Upper One." It therefore follows that the Upper One elevates the lower one. And then, to receive the *Gar* of the Lights and the *AHP* of the *Kelim*, the lower one should rise by itself.

## 144. THERE IS A CERTAIN PEOPLE

I heard on the night of *Purim*,
after reading the *Megillah*, 1950

"There is a certain people scattered abroad and dispersed among the peoples." Haman said that in his view, we will succeed in destroying the Jews because they are separated from one another; hence, our force against them will certainly prevail, as it causes separation between man and God. And the Creator will not help them anyway, since they are separated from Him. This is why Mordecai went to correct that flaw, as it is explained in the verse, **"the Jews gathered,"** etc., **"to gather themselves together, and to stand for their life."** This means that they had saved themselves by uniting.

## 145. WHAT IS WILL GIVE WISDOM SPECIFICALLY TO THE WISE

I heard on *Truma* 5, February 11, 1943

"Will give wisdom to the wise." He asked, "But it should have said, 'Will give wisdom to the fools?'"

And he said, "It is known that there is no coercion in spirituality." Rather, everyone is given according to one's own will. The reason is that spirituality is the source of life and pleasure. So how can there be coercion in a good thing? Hence, if we see that when we engage in Torah and *Mitzvot* coercively, we have to overcome the body, since it does not agree. This is because it does not feel pleasure in this work. And this must be because it does not feel the spirituality in them, as we have said, that spirituality is the source of life and pleasure, as it is written in the Holy *Zohar*, "Where there is labor, there is *Sitra Achra*."

This is the reason that only wise can be given wisdom, since fools have no need for wisdom. Rather, only wise can be given wisdom because of their nature. This means that one who is wise loves wisdom, and this is his **only wish!** And following the rule, "there are no preventions before a desire," he makes every effort to obtain wisdom. Hence, at last he will be awarded wisdom. Therefore, one who loves wisdom can be called "wise," after his end.

But it is written of fools, "A fool hath no delight in understanding." The verse, "will give wisdom to the wise" comes to tell us that one who loves wisdom will not be impressed by not having obtained wisdom despite the great efforts he has made. Rather, he will continue with his work and he will certainly achieve wisdom, since he loves wisdom. This is why they say, "Go by this path and you are certain to succeed."

However, we must understand, what can one do if by nature, "a wild ass's colt is born a man"? Whence will he take the desire to crave wisdom?

For this, we are given the advice to work by way of "that fulfill His word," and the adornment, "hearkening unto the voice of His word." This means that one does things to obtain the thing which one wants. Hence, here, when he has no desire for wisdom, it means that the thing he lacks is the desire for wisdom. For this reason he begins to exert and take actions to obtain the desire for wisdom, as this is the only thing that he needs.

And the order is that one should exert in the Torah and the work although he has no desire for it. This is called "labor." This means that one does things even though he has no desire for the thing he does. It is as our sages said, "whatsoever thy hand attaineth to do by thy strength, that do." And by the virtue of exerting, a desire and craving for wisdom will be made within him.

And then the verse, "will give wisdom to the wise" will become true for him, and he will be rewarded with "hearkening unto the voice of His word." Thus, that which was previously by way of doing, an act without a will, he has been awarded a desire for it.

Therefore, if we want to know who loves wisdom, we need to look at those who strain for wisdom, even though they have not yet been rewarded with being among those who love wisdom. The reason is, as we have said, that through the effort, they will be awarded being among those who love wisdom.

And afterwards, after they have a desire for wisdom, they will be awarded wisdom. Thus, the desire for the wisdom is the *Kli*, and the wisdom is the Light. And this the meaning of "there is no coercion in spirituality."

The Light of Wisdom means the Light of life. Wisdom is not perceived by us as an intellectual concept, but as the actual life, the essence of life, to the extent that without it, one is considered dead. (Hence, we can say that for this reason wisdom is called *Haya* (alive).)

## 146. A COMMENTARY ON *THE ZOHAR*

I heard in the year 1938

In *The Zohar*: "When one is born, he is given a soul from the side of the pure beast." And he interprets that his animate soul, too, agrees to be a servant of the Creator. "If he is further rewarded, he is given a soul of the Holy Wheels." This means that he has a soul that always longs, and it rolls from place to place. Like an ever turning wheel, it turns and rolls to cling to the *Kedusha* (Sanctity).

## 147. THE WORK OF RECEPTION AND BESTOWAL

I heard on *Adar* 21, March 8, 1953

The matter of work in reception and bestowal depends on the heart. This is considered *Vak*. However, work in faith and knowledge is considered *Gar*. And although they are one discernment, meaning that faith is accepted by him according to the value of the work in reception and bestowal, they are still two distinct discernments.

This is so because even if one can work in bestowal, he still wants to see to whom he is bestowing, and who accepts his work. Hence, he needs to work in the form of *Mocha* (mind), meaning believe that there is a Guide who accepts the work of the lower ones.

## 148. THE SCRUTINY OF BITTER AND SWEET, TRUE AND FALSE

I heard

There is a discernment of "bitter and sweet," and there is a discernment of "true and false." The discernment of "true and false" is in the mind, and the discernment of "bitter and sweet" is in the heart. This is why we must pay attention to the work in the heart, to be in the form of bestowal and not in the form of reception.

By nature, only reception is sweet to man, and bestowal is bitter. And the work—to turn reception into bestowal—is called "the work in the heart."

In the mind, the work is of "true and false." And for this, we need to work in faith, meaning believe in faith in the sages. This is so because the worker cannot clarify the matter of "true and false" to himself.

## 149. WHY WE NEED TO EXTEND *HOCHMA*

I heard on *Adar* 22, March 9, 1953, Tel-Aviv

He asked, "Why do we need to extend the discernment of *Hochma* (wisdom), which is knowing, if all our work is by way of faith above reason?"

And he answered, "If the righteous of the generation were not in the form of knowing, the whole of Israel would not be able to work in the form of faith above reason. Rather, precisely when the righteous of the generation extends illumination of *Hochma*, his mind shines in the whole of Israel."

For example, if one's mind knows and understands what one wants, the organs perform their action, and do not need any intellect. Rather, the hand and the leg and the rest of the organs do what they must. And no sane person would think of asking or saying that if the hand and the leg had brains, their work would be better.

Thus, the mind does not change the organs, but the organs are set according to the greatness of the mind. This means that if the brain has a great mind, all the organs are named after it; they are called "great organs."

Similarly, if the collective is adhered to a true righteous, who has already been awarded knowing, the collective can do things with faith. They have complete satisfaction, and have no need for any discernment of knowledge.

## 150. PRUNE UNTO THE LORD, FOR HE HATH DONE PRIDE

I heard on *Shevat* 14

In the verse, "Prune[21] unto the Lord; for He hath done pride," it seems that "prune" is like "my strength and pruning." This means that we should always prune and cut the thorns off of the Creator's vineyard. And even when one feels that one is whole, and thinks that he has already removed the thorns, the verse concludes, "for He hath done pride."

This means that He has seemingly created pride in this world, that man likes to be honest and true in one's own eyes. And when one feels about himself that he has already removed the thorns and that he is a whole man, it is a kind of pride.

Rather, one should always examine one's actions, and check them with ten kinds of examinations, and not rely on one's

21 *Zamru*, in Hebrew means both sing and prune. In this case it is referring to the latter.

temporary sensation, for this is only a kind of pride. It is as the verse says in the name of the righteous: "Ye are idle, ye are idle; therefore ye say: 'Let us go and sacrifice to the Lord our God.'"

This means that He said to the children of Israel, "when you say, 'Let us go and sacrifice to the Lord,' and you feel that you are already willing to go and sacrifice yourselves on the altar before the Lord, it is like idleness and weakness, that you no longer want to work and constantly examine yourselves, to make you ready for this great work. This is why you think that you are already perfect in this servitude, as they interpret at the end of the verse, 'for He hath done pride.'"

## 151. AND ISRAEL SAW THE EGYPTIANS

I heard on *Beshalach*

In the verse, "and Israel saw the Egyptians dead upon the seashore," "...and the people feared the Lord; and they believed in the Lord and in His servant Moses," we must understand how is "they believed" relevant here? Obviously, the miracle of the exodus from Egypt and the division of the sea brought Israel to greater faith than they had had before. After all, our sages said about the verse, "this is my God, and I will glorify Him," that a maid at the sea saw more than did Ezekiel the prophet.

Hence, this means that the exodus from Egypt was a case of open miracles, which brings to knowledge of the Lord, which is the opposite of the meaning of "faith," since it does not mean above reason. And when seeing open miracles, it is very hard to be in faith, since, moreover, it is a time of expansion of the reason. Therefore, what is the meaning of the text, "and they believed in the Lord"?

However, we should interpret according to the commentary that "All believe that He is a God of faith." The verse narrates

Israel's praise, who, even after seeing the revealed miracles, their servitude of the Creator was not reduced in them, by way of faith above reason. And it is great work to hold on to the path of faith and not slight it at all once you are awarded and can serve the Creator within reason.

## 152. FOR A BRIBE DOTH BLIND THE EYES OF THE WISE

I heard on *Tevet* 24, January 6, 1948

"For a bribe doth blind the eyes of the wise." When one begins to criticize the work and its conditions, one is faced with the possibility that it will be impossible to receive the work, for two reasons:

1. The reward for the work is not one hundred percent guaranteed. He does not see those who have already been rewarded, and when he visits people who have given their toil to suffer the weight of the work, he does not see if they have already been rewarded for their work. And if he asks himself, "why have they not received?" if he succeeds in giving the highest answer, it is because they did not follow all the conditions of the work to the letter. But those who follow the orders to the letter receive their reward from the Whole.

And then comes a second question: He knows that he is better capable to the conditions of the work than his friend, to be able to cope with all its terms. Hence, he is one hundred percent certain that there is no one who can criticize him for evading, but he is one hundred percent right.

2. Therefore, the question arises: One who begins the work has certainly experienced all the calculations, and yet, took the work upon himself. Thus, how did he answer all the questions to himself? The thing is that to see the truth, we need to look with

open eyes. Otherwise, we only think that we see who was right, the righteous or the world. But in truth, we do not see the justice. And to have open eyes, we must be wary of bribery, "for a bribe doth blind the eyes of the wise, and pervert the words of the righteous."

And the essence of the bribe is in the will to receive. Hence, one has no other counsel but to first accept the work with all its terms, without any knowledge, but only in the form of faith above reason. Afterwards, when one is cleaned from the will to receive, when he criticizes, he can hope to see the truth of the matter. This is why those who only look with reason, certainly cannot ask a thing, since in truth, he is right, and he will always win the argument, since he will not be able to see the truth.

## 153. A THOUGHT IS AN UPSHOT OF THE DESIRE

I heard on *Shevat* 7, January 18, 1948

A thought is an upshot of the desire. A person thinks of what he wants, and does not think of what he does not want. For example, a person never thinks of his dying day. On the contrary, he will always contemplate his eternity, since this is what he wants. Thus, one always thinks of what is desirable for him.

However, there is a special role to the thought: it intensifies the desire. The desire remains in its place; it does not have the strength to expand and perform its action. Yet, because one thinks and contemplates on a matter, and the desire asks of the thought to provide some counsel and advice to carry out the desire, the desire thus grows, expands and performs its actual work.

It turns out that the thought serves the desire, and the desire is the "self" of the person. Now, there is a great self or a small self. A great self dominates the small selves.

He who is a small self and has no dominion whatsoever, the advice to magnify the self is through the persisting with the thought of the desire, since the thought grows to the extent that one thinks of it.

And so, "in His law doth he meditate day and night," for by persisting in it, it grows into a great self until it becomes the actual ruler.

## 154. THERE CANNOT BE AN EMPTY SPACE IN THE WORLD

I heard on *Shevat* 7, January 18, 1948, Tel Aviv

There cannot be an empty space in the world. And because man's core is the desire, as this is the core of creation, this is where one's greatness and smallness are measured. It follows that one must have some desire—either for corporeality or for spirituality. One who is devoid of any desires is considered dead, since the whole of creation is only the desire, considered existence from absence. And because he lacks this substance, the substance of the whole of creation, it is naturally considered that he is regarded as aborted who cannot last.

Thus, one should try to have a desire, as this is the whole substance of creation. But the desire must be clarified, as it is natural that each animal feels what is harmful to it. Similarly, we must take note that the desire will be for some thing.

## 155. THE CLEANNESS OF THE BODY

I heard during a Shabbat meal, *Shevat* 13

The cleanness of the body indicates to the cleanness of the mind. The cleanness of the mind is called "truth," where no falsehood is involved. And not everyone is equal in that: some are partially meticulous. But the cleanness of the body is not so important to preserve, since the dirt that we so loathe is because the dirt is considered harmful, and we should keep it from harm.

Hence, with the body, it is not so important to be meticulous, since it will finally be canceled, even if we watch over it with all kinds of cares. But with the soul, which is an eternal thing, it is worthwhile to be meticulous with all kinds of cares, to avoid any kind of dirt, since any dirt is considered harmful.

## 156. LEST HE TAKE OF THE TREE OF LIFE

I heard on *Shevat* 15

"Lest he put forth his hand, and take also of the tree of life, and eat, and live forever." Baal HaSulam interpreted that perhaps he would take from the covered *Hassadim* (mercy), considered from the *Chazeh* (chest) upwards. This is because in that, there is complete sufficiency, and thus he would not be corrected by the sin of the tree of knowledge, considered from the *Chazeh* down. It follows that the tree of life is called "from the *Chazeh* upwards," where there are covered *Hassadim*. And I think that we should accordingly interpret what we say, "a life that has the fear of heaven and a life that has the fear of sin."

The difference between them, as Baal HaSulam interprets, is that what he takes from life is for fear of sinning, meaning that he has no other choice. But fear of heaven means that he has other choices. That is, even if he does not take this discernment, he will still not sin; but still he chooses it due to fear of the Creator.

But, accordingly, we cannot say that covered *Hassadim* is considered *Katnut*. This is precisely when he has no other choice. But when he achieves the revealed *Hassadim* from the discernment of Rachel, then the discernment of Leah, which is covered *Hassadim*, is called *Gar* and *Gadlut* (greatness).

And this is called "fear of heaven," that he has revealed *Hassadim*, but he nevertheless chooses covered *Hassadim*. Thus, there are two kinds of covered *Hassadim*: 1) when he does not have the discernment of Rachel, when he is called *Vak*; 2) when he does have the discernment of Rachel, called "Leah," *Gar*.

## 157. I AM ASLEEP BUT MY HEART IS AWAKE

I heard on *Nisan* 9, April 18, 1948

In *The Zohar*, (Parashat Amor, 95a): "The assembly of Israel said, 'I sleep in exile in Egypt, where my children were in harsh enslavement.'" The *Mochin* were in the state of sleep, as it is written about the verse, "there is," their God is sleeping.

"But my heart is awake to guard those who will not be extinguished in exile." This means that when they receive the *Mochin* of the *Achoraim*, they are guarded by them, even though they still do not shine in her, and they are still in exile. However, it is still considered awake, by way of "does not reveal from heart to mouth."

The heart is *Vak*, since there is *Vak de Hochma* there. Thus, even at the time of the *Gadlut*, there is no other *Hochma* there, but only from what she received here.

"My Beloved knocketh." This is the beating, the *Masach* (screen) *de Hirik* (of the *Hirik*—a punctuation mark) in ZA. "And I have remembered My covenant." This is the circumcision, which is *Dinim* (judgments) of *Nukva*, which cancel the *Dinim* of *Dechura* (male). *Dinim* are a discernment that cancels the *Gar*, and this is considered "cutting."

And there are other corrections, called "payment." "Open for Me an opening as the point of a needle, and I will open for you the Upper Gates." The meaning of this slight opening is the tiny lights, as without *Hassadim*, *Hochma* shines very diminutively.

Only afterwards, when *Hassadim* are drawn, the *Hochma* is integrated with the *Hassadim*, *Vak*, great convoys. And the meaning of the Upper Gates concerns the *Hassadim* from the perspective of *AVI*, called "pure air." This is because only once he has *Hochma*, but draws *Hassadim*, these *Hassadim* are called "pure air," since he prefers *Hassadim* to *Hochma*.

However, when he has *Hassadim* without *Hochma*, it is considered *Katnut*. "Open for Me," that ZA and his sister *Malchut*, in the form of *Hochma*, she would draw *Hochma*. The door to enter Me is within you." Thus, only when you have *Hochma* will I have a vent, to enter in the form of *Hassadim*, which I have from *AVI*, called "pure air."

"Come and see: When the Creator was slaying the firstborn of Egypt, and lowered the degrees from Above downward," Egypt is the left line. However, they are in the form of *Klipa*, without any integration of the right. And when Israel were in Egypt, they were under their dominion, and they, too, had to receive the left.

And the plague of the firstborn, meaning the revoking of the domination of the *Gar* of the left, this is "and lowered the degrees from Above downward. At that time Israel came into the covenant of the holy sign."

Circumcision concerns the *Dinim de Nukva*, which is a *Masach* of *Hirik*, which cancels the *Dinim de Dechura*. In doing so, she cancels the *Gar* of the left, and only the *Vak* shine. It follows that by the Creator striking their firstborn, they had the strength to keep the covenant, "as the blood that was shown on the door."

"And they were two bloods: one of Passover and one of circumcision." The Passover blood is the correction of the integration of the left line; and the circumcision blood is the correction of the *Dinim de Nukva*, which is the *Hirik*. And the Passover blood...

## 158. THE REASON FOR NOT EATING AT EACH OTHER'S HOME ON PASSOVER

I heard during a *Shacharit* (morning) meal on Passover, 1948

He explains why it is a custom to not eat at each other's home for reasons of *Kashrut*. And why it is not so all year long. Also, even if there is one of whom it is known that there it is completely *Kosher*, even better than in one's own home, still the custom is to not eat. This is so because the prohibition on *Hametz* (leavened bread) is on *anything*, and it is impossible to guard oneself from anything. Rather, the Creator can watch over for him, that he will not transgress even with anything.

This is why it is written that with leavened bread, you should be careful with anything. One is commanded to caution, and he should seek advice how not to come to "anything" leavened.

However, one cannot guard oneself. Hence, only the Creator guards. And certainly, the guard is in such a way that not everyone is equal. Some are better guarded by the Creator, and some are less guarded, depending on one's need. This is so because there are people who know that they need great care, so they draw greater care, and there are people who feel that they do not need such guarding from Above. Also, this cannot be said, as it depends on the sensation: some feel themselves deficient, and need greater care.

## 159. AND IT CAME TO PASS IN THE COURSE OF THOSE MANY DAYS

I heard

"And it came to pass in the course of those many days that the king of Egypt died; and the children of Israel sighed by reason of the bondage, and they cried, and their cry came up unto God by reason of the bondage. And God heard their groaning" (Exodus 2:23-4). This means that they suffered so much that they could not bear it any longer. And they so pleaded with prayer, that "their cry came up unto God."

But we can see that they were saying, "Would that we had... when we sat by the flesh-pots, when we did eat bread to the full." And they also said, "We remember the fish, which we were wont to eat in Egypt for naught; the cucumbers, and the melons, and the leeks, and the onions, and the garlic."

The thing is that, indeed, they were very fond of the work in Egypt. This is the meaning of "But mingled themselves with the nations, and learned their works." It means that if Israel are under the dominion of a certain nation, that nation controls them and they cannot retire from their dominion. Thus, they tasted sufficient flavor in that work and could not be redeemed.

So what did the Creator do? "The king of Egypt died," meaning they had lost this servitude. Thus they could no longer work; they understood that if there is no perfection of the *Mochin*, the servitude is also incomplete. Hence, "and the children of Israel sighed by reason of the bondage." The work means that they did not suffice for the work, that they had no liveliness in the work.

This is the meaning of "the king of Egypt died," that all the dominations of the king of Egypt, which he was providing for and nourishing, had died. This is why they had room for prayer. And they were immediately salvaged. And afterwards, when they walked in the desert and came to a state of *Katnut* (smallness), they craved the servitude that they had had prior to the death of the king of Egypt.

## 160. THE REASON FOR CONCEALING THE *MATZOT*

I heard

He explains why it is customary that the *Matzot* (unleavened bread) are always placed in concealment, on a matzo-plate or on some other covered thing. It is written, "And the people took their dough before it was leavened, their kneading-troughs being bound up in their clothes upon their shoulders." The hint is in "bound up in their clothes."

The thing is that on Passover, the *Kelim* were not yet properly corrected. This is why there is the matter of the count, to correct the *Kelim*. This is the meaning of her words, "I saw the image of a drop of a rose." It means that on Passover night there was a miracle that although there could have been a grip, there still wasn't, since it was covered and nothing was showing on the outside. And this is the intimation, "bound up in their clothes."

## 161. THE MATTER OF THE GIVING OF THE TORAH

I heard during a *Shavuot* meal

Concerning the giving of the Torah on Mount Sinai: it does not mean that the Torah was given then, and that now it is not. Rather, the giving of the Torah is an eternal thing–the Creator always gives. However, we are unfit to receive. But then, on Mount Sinai, we were the receivers of the Torah. And the only merit that we had then was that we were as "one man in one heart." This means that we all had but one thought–the reception of the Torah.

However, from the Creator's perspective, He always gives, as it is written in the name of the Ribash, "Man must hear the ten commandments on Mount Sinai every day."

The Torah is called "the potion of life" and "the potion of death." We should ask, "How can two opposites be in one subject?" Everything we see with our eyes is nothing more than sensations, but reality itself does not interest us. Hence, when one studies Torah and the Torah removes him from the love of God, this Torah is certainly called "the potion of death." And if the Torah brings him closer to the Creator, it is certainly called "the potion of life."

But the Torah itself, meaning reality in itself, is not taken into account. Rather, the sensations determine the reality here below. And the Torah itself, without the receivers, it seems we should interpret the Torah in and of itself as Light without a *Kli*, where we have no attainment. This is considered "essence without matter." And we have no attainment in the essence, even in a corporeal essence; all the more so with a spiritual one.

And when one works for oneself, it is considered *Lo Lishma* (not for Her Name), and from *Lo Lishma* we come to *Lishma* (for Her Name). Hence, if one has not been awarded the reception of the Torah, he hopes that he will receive it next year. And when he receives the complete *Lishma*, he has nothing more to do in this world.

This is why each year there is a time of reception of the Torah, since the time is ripe for an awakening from below, since then it is the awakening of the time when the Light of the giving of the Torah is revealed in the lower ones.

This is why there is always an awakening from Above, so the lower ones can act as they did then, at that time. Thus, if one continues on the path that the *Lo Lishma* will bring him *Lishma*, he is progressing correctly and hopes that he will eventually be rewarded with the reception of the Torah *Lishma*.

But if the goal is not always before his eyes, he is moving in an opposite line from the Torah, called "the tree of life," which is why it is considered "the potion of death," as he is constantly drifting away from the line of life.

"I labored and did not find, do not believe." We must understand the meaning of "I found." What is there to find? Find concerns finding grace in the eyes of the Creator.

"I did not labor and found, do not believe." We must understand; after all, he is not lying; this is not about the person himself, as an individual. Rather, it is the same rule with the whole. And if one sees that he is favored by the Creator, why "not believe"? The thing is that sometimes a person is favored by the Creator as it is in prayer. It is because this is the power of the prayer–it can act like labor. (We also see in corporeality that there are some who provide by exertion, and some who provide for themselves through prayer. And by asking for provision, one is allowed to provide for himself.)

But in spirituality, although he is rewarded with being favored, he must still pay the full price later–the measure of the labor that everyone gives. If not, he will lose the *Kli*. This is why he said, "I did not labor and found, do not believe," since he will lose everything. Thus, one should subsequently repay one's full labor.

## 162. CONCERNING THE *HAZAK* WE SAY AFTER COMPLETING THE SERIES

I heard during a *Shacharit* (morning) meal on Shabbat, *Av* 2, Tel-Aviv

The *Hazak*[22] we say after completing the series means that the completion should give us strength to complete all the degrees. As the body has 248 organs and 365 tendons, the soul, too,

22 *Hazak* means strong; it's a blessing said after finishing each book from the Five Books of Moses (the Pentateuch).

has 613, which are the channels of the soul by which the bounty extends. And these channels are opened through the Torah. As long as not all of them have been opened, even if a deficiency appears in a particular degree, the particular degree is included in the whole.

Thus, if an element is missing from the whole, that same discernment is missing from the individuals, too, and they gradually incarnate by the order of degrees. And when they are all completed, this will be the end of correction. Prior to that, they will emerge and become corrected one by one.

Now we can understand what our sages said, "the Torah preceded the world." This means that before the limitation of the world appeared, the Torah had already been there.

And how could it then shine within the world, which is a boundary? Rather, the Torah shines by way of one after the other. And when all the discernments are completed, one must leave this world, since he has harvested all the discernments of the Torah. Therefore, each ending should give us strengthening to continue further. And the five books of Torah correspond to the seven *Sefirot*, which are essentially five, since *Yesod* and *Malchut* are not the essence, only included.

## 163. WHAT THE AUTHORS OF *THE ZOHAR* SAID

I heard after Shabbat, *Parashat Masa'ei*,
August 7, 1948, Tel Aviv

About the authors of *The Zohar* saying their words as a morals, it did not have to be in this way. They could have revealed their secrets by other means, too. However, they wanted to clothe their secrets as morals so that the reader would clearly understand that the important thing was not the wisdom in the Torah but the giver of the Torah, that the essence of the Torah and *Mitzvot* is only to cleave to the Giver of the Torah.

Hence, since the clothing of morals is the most reminiscent of it, they set it up in this dressing. And the many times they give it a clothing of wisdom is so that they would not err and say that there is nothing more than morals, that no wisdom is hidden there, but that it is simple morals. This is why they wrote in two dresses, that one points to the other.

## 164. THERE IS A DIFFERENCE BETWEEN CORPOREALITY AND SPIRITUALITY

I heard on *Av* 3, August 8, 1948

There is a difference between corporeality and spirituality: in corporeality, the force precedes the act, as it is written, "before they call, I will answer," arranged according to the end of correction, where nothing is done before they have the strength to do it. In spirituality, however, where it is still not arranged according to the end of correction, but by the order of scrutinies, the work must begin before the attainment of the strength, as it is written, "that fulfill His word, hearkening unto the voice of His word."

## 165. AN EXPLANATION TO ELISHA'S REQUEST OF ELIJAH

I heard

Elijah asked him: "what I shall do for thee?" And he replied, "a double portion of thy spirit." And he replied, "Thou hast asked a hard thing."

The thing is that there is the scrutiny of the 248, and there is the stony heart, which cannot be scrutinized. However, when scrutinizing the 248, the stony heart, too, is thus scrutinized, though it is forbidden to touch in itself. And one who scrutinizes these 248, in doing so he scrutinizes the stony heart, as well.

## 166. TWO DISCERNMENTS IN ATTAINMENT

I heard

There are two discernments: 1) the cascading of the worlds from Above downward; 2) from below upward.

First discernment: "that God has created and performed." This means that the Creator has prepared for us a place for work.

Second discernment: when we begin to engage and clothe from below upward. However, before we achieve the completion of the degree, we cannot know anything for certain. This is called "learning first, understanding next."

A little one, who is beginning to eat bread, still has no knowledge, but only of the bread. And when beginning to grow, he begins to understand that there is a reason for the bread, which causes the shape of the bread, that shapes it as it appears to our eyes: white, soft, tasty, etc..

Then he attains the shape of the bread, after it has been taken out of the oven: the bread is too soft and very hot, until it is not fit for eating. There is an act missing–the cooling and drying over time, when the air makes the bread fit, giving it the shape of the bread as it appears when it comes to the table.

But then he begins to research further, and sees yet another shape–before it is placed in the oven. Although it has a similar shape, there are great differences. Thus, the heat of the oven makes the bread larger and more solid, and crusts its face.

Previously, it was white, and now it is a different color. And when he begins to research he sees that the bread acquired its shape and weight even before it was placed in the oven.

Thus he continues until he comes to the state when the wheat is taken and sowed in the ground. Until then, he can only receive from the bread, meaning reduce the bread that exists in the world. But afterwards he already knows how to add.

Similarly, in spirituality, first one needs to receive from below upward, and can only receive and not add. But afterwards, in the second state, one can add, as well.

## 167. THE REASON WHY IT IS CALLED *SHABBAT TESHUVAH*

I heard on *Shabbat Teshuvah*, October 9, 1948, Tel-Aviv

The reason why it is called "Shabbat *Teshuvah*" (Shabbat of repentance) is that (at the end of the ten penitential days, on the Day of Atonement) we say **"for a sin."** And anyone who examines the "for a sin" does not find his place there, at least in sixty percent, and forty percent can be explained and excused, perhaps there is a doubt that he does not feel there. But in sixty percent he certainly does not find himself.

This is why there is the virtue of the Shabbat: the Light of the Shabbat can shine and show, so one can find oneself in all one hundred percent of the "for a sin," that this was given only for him, and not for others. But without the Light, we do not feel.

This is why it is called "Shabbat *Teshuvah*." The Shabbat is good for *Teshuvah* (repentance), so one can feel the sin. This is because first we must confess to the sin, and then ask for forgiveness. But if we say "for a sin" without feeling the sin, what kind of confession is this? After all, he is saying in his heart that he did not sin. And what he says in his mouth when his heart is not with him, such a confession is certainly worthless.

## 168. THE CUSTOMS OF ISRAEL

I heard

The customs of Israel are so important, that it is safe to say that they give more spirituality to a person than the *Mitzvot* themselves. This is so although breaking a custom does not yield punishment, and breaking a judgment does yield punishment. Still, concerning the benefit, meaning producing fear of heaven, the customs yield more spirituality, since the great ones who established the customs arranged it so that spirituality would shine through them.

This is why he said that he who avoids the custom of eating meat and fish on Shabbat denies spirituality of himself. However, this concerns a person who has not achieved perfection, meaning seeing what he does. This means that he has still not been rewarded with the flavors of the *Mitzvot*, so he needs to observe the customs.

It is like an apple that is spoiled before it rots, but when it is spoiled, rotting is certain. Similarly, when a person becomes free, he rejects the customs, and following the rejection either he becomes free or his sons become free.

## 169. CONCERNING A COMPLETE RIGHTEOUS

I heard

In the matter of "complete righteous" who did not sin. It is written, "For there is not a righteous man on earth that does good and sins not." He replied that in each degree there is a discernment of "complete righteous," where there is no sin. And in that degree he has never sinned. This is the discernment of from the *Chazeh* (chest) upwards in each degree, considered "the tree of life" and "covered *Hassadim* (mercy)."

And in the discernment of the *Chazeh* and below, there is sin and repentance. And when this is corrected we arrive at a higher degree. And there, too, begins this order, meaning "complete righteous," and "For there is not a righteous man on earth that does good and sins not."

## 170. THOU SHALT NOT HAVE IN THY POCKET A LARGE STONE

I heard

"Thou shalt not have in thy pocket a large stone and a small stone." *Even* (stone) is called "faith" (stones to weigh with). This is considered small, above reason. But at the same time, you should say that you have a "large stone," meaning that you have reason. This means that what you do is not like the rest of the world, but that you have a solid basis, which is *Gadlut* (greatness) and not *Katnut* (smallness), meaning without basis and a complete *Even*.

There must be a "small stone" but it must be "complete," meaning sufficient to keep the whole of the Torah and *Mitzvot* based on the "small stone," and only then is it called "complete."

But if it is "small," and makes you do only small things, it is not considered "a complete stone." And a large measure and a small measure? If you have a small basis, it is considered small. But when you have a "large stone," a large basis, you consider yourself great, meaning that you are great. And a "complete stone" is when he is awarded private Providence.

## 171. ZOHAR, AMOR

I heard on Passover Inter 4, April 18, 1949

In *The Zohar*, Parashat Amor: "The assembly of Israel said, 'I sleep in the exile in Egypt'" (*Zohar*, Amor, p.43).

The departure of the *Mochin* is called "sleep." "And my heart is awake." Heart is considered the thirty-two paths of wisdom. This means that *Hochma* (wisdom) was shining in them, but without the clothing of *Hassadim* (mercy), and this is called "the exile in Egypt." For this reason it is called "sleep." But at the same time they were worthy of receiving *Mochin de Hochma*, but in the form of *Achoraim* (posterior).

"Hark! my beloved knocketh," meaning the voice of ZA, who is considered *Hassadim*. And this is what the Creator said, "Open for Me an opening like the tip of a needle." This means that during the redemption, He had told them to draw the discernment of *Hochma* once more. And when it is without *Hassadim*, its opening was called "the tip of a needle," since she does not shine without *Hassadim*.

"And I will open for you the Upper Gates," meaning bestowing upon her the discernment of *Hassadim*, and then she will have abundance, *Hochma* and *Hassadim*.

"Open for Me... for the opening to enter Me is in you, for My children will not enter in Me, but in you." This means that He cannot give to the children, who need *Mochin de Hochma*, as His discernment is only *Hassadim*. However, when she draws *Hochma*, it will be possible for the children to receive *Hochma*, too. This is why it is considered that only she can open this opening, whereas "I am closed so they will not find Me," meaning "that they will not find Me in completeness."

When ZA has only *Hassadim*, he has only *Vak*, and he is called "just air." However, when he has *Hochma*, too, even though he then receives only *Hassadim*, his *Hassadim* are called "pure

Air." This is because then his *Hassadim* are better than *Hochma*, although without *Hochma*, he will not be found complete.

This is the meaning of the words: "To mate with You and to always be in peace with You. Come and see, when the Creator killed the firstborn of Egypt, all those that He killed at midnight and lowered the degrees from Above downward." This is done through the correction of the *Masach de Hirik*, which causes two discernments: the departure of the *Gar*, and the extension of *Hassadim*, where by this *Hitkalelut* (integration), there is ability for the expansion of *Mochin* from Above downward.

"At the time when Israel came into the covenant of the holy sign, they were circumcised." The "plague of the firstborn," the "Passover blood," and the "circumcision blood" are all one discernment. It is a known secret that the God of Egypt was a lamb. This means that the Passover sacrifice was aimed at their God.

The *Klipa* of Egypt was that they wanted to extend from the end of correction, like the sin of the tree of knowledge, that they wanted to extend the Light of *Gar* from Above downward. And through the Passover slaughter, they slaughtered the *Gar de Hochma*, by which there was the plague of the firstborn.

The firstborn is considered *Gar*; and they canceled the *Gar*. This occurred using the *Masach de Hirik*, which is considered raising the lock, which causes the cancellation of the *Gar*.

***Dam*** **(blood)** comes from the word ***Dmamah*** **(silence)**, which puts the *Gar* to death. This is the meaning of the circumcision blood. The chisel is the *Dinim de Nukva*, and the *Dinim* revoke the *Dinim de Dechura*, as it is written, "they were two bloods: the Passover blood and the circumcision blood." By throwing the Passover blood, the *Gar* was cancelled and there was the *Hitkalelut* in the *Tikkun* of the lines. This is the meaning of the lintel and the two *Mezuzahs*.

"And on the fourth ... and Israel departed from the other authority, and they were united with a *Matzoh* holy knot." The leavened bread is the *Mochin* that expand from the *Chazeh* down, at which time they shine from Above downward. And the *Matzoh* is the *Mochin* that shine from the *Chazeh* upwards, a discernment in which there is no hold for the outer ones. And the reason is that the lock that appeared on Passover night, by which there was the Passover slaughtering and the plague of the firstborn, operates only from itself downward. This means that it was revealed at the *Chazeh*.

It follows that everything above it does not work with the judgment in it. However, it is not so from the *Chazeh* down, since the whole expansion is below its own discernment. This is why the judgment in it is felt, and this is why Israel were cautious on Passover night to eat *Matzoh* and not leavened bread.

There is a merit to the *Matzoh* which is not in the leavened bread, and a merit to the leavened bread which is not in the *Matzoh*. The merit in the *Matzoh* is that they are complete *Mochin*, *Gar de Hochma*, which are still considered "the two great Lights." However, they are in the form of *Achoraim*, since they cannot shine because of the lack of *Hassadim*.

And there is a merit to the leavened bread: although it is only *Vak*, it is already clothed in *Hassadim*. At the Temple, where there was *Mochin de Hochma*, they were also in the form of from the *Chazeh* upwards, considered a *Matzoh*. This is why it is said, "for ye shall make no leaven, nor any honey, smoke as an offering."

## 172. THE MATTER OF PREVENTIONS AND DELAYS

I heard on Passover 7, April 20, 1949, Tel Aviv

All the preventions and delays that appear before our eyes are but a form of nearing–the Creator wants to bring us closer. And all these preventions bring us only nearing, since without them we would have no possibility of coming closer to Him. This is so because, by nature, there is no greater distance, as we are made of pure matter, and the Creator is higher than high. And only when one begins to approach does one begin to feel the distance between us. And any prevention that one overcomes brings the way closer for that person.

(This is so because one grows accustomed to moving on a line of growing farther. Hence, whenever one feels that one is distant, it does not induce any change in the process, since he knows in advance that he is moving on a line of growing farther. It is so because this is the truth: there are not enough words to describe the distance between us and the Creator. Hence, every time one feels that distance to a greater extent than one thought, it causes him no contention.)

## 173. WHY DO WE SAY *L'CHAIM*

I heard during a Shabbat meal, *Parashat Acharei-Kedoshim*, *Omer* Count 23, May 7, 1949

He said about saying *L'Chaim* (to life–cheers (when toasting a drink)) when drinking wine, that it is as our sages said, "Wine and life according to the sages and their disciples." This is perplexing: why specifically according to our sages? Why not according to the uneducated?

The thing is that saying *L'Chaim* implies Higher Life. When we drink wine, we should remember that wine implies "the wine of Torah," a reminder that we should extend the Light of Torah, called "life." The corporeal life, however, is called by our sages, "The wicked, in their lives, are called 'dead.'"

Hence, it is specifically our sages who can say, "wine and life." This means that only they are qualified to extend spiritual life. Uneducated people, however, have no tools for it, with which to extend. (And perhaps, "according to our sages" means according to the view of our sages. This means that life, what they call "life," refers to spiritual life.)

## 174. CONCEALMENT

I heard

Concerning the concealment, which is a correction, had it not been for that, man would have been unable to attain any perfection, since he would not be worthy of attaining the importance of the matter. However, when there is concealment, the thing becomes important to him. Even though one cannot appreciate the importance as it truly is, the concealment grants it merit. This is because to the extent that one senses the concealment, so a bedding of importance is made within him.

It is like rungs. He climbs rung-by-rung until he comes to his designated place. This means that he achieves a certain measure of importance with which he can at least endure, though His true importance and sublimity are immeasurable, but nonetheless a measure that will suffice him to persist.

However, concealment in itself is not considered concealment. Concealment is measured by the demand. The greater the demand for something, the more the concealment is evident. And now we can understand the meaning of "the whole earth is full of His glory." Although we believe it, the concealment still fills the whole earth.

It is written about the future: "For I, ... will be unto her a wall of fire round about, and I will be the glory in the midst of her." Fire means concealment. But still, glory is in the midst of her, meaning that then the glory will be revealed. This is because then the demand will be so great, even though there will be concealment then, too. And the difference is that at this time there is concealment, but no demand. Hence, this is considered "exile." Then, however, although there will be concealment, there will also be demand, and this is what is important–only the demand.

## 175. AND IF THE WAY BE TOO LONG FOR THEE

I heard during a *Shevat* meal, *Parashat Behar-Bechukotai*, *Iyar* 22, May 21, 1949

"And if the way be too far for thee, so that thou art not able to carry it."

He interpreted, why is the way so far? Because "thou art not able to carry it." This is because he cannot carry the burden of Torah and *Mitzvot*, and hence he regards the way as far. The counsel for it, as the verse says, "bind up the money in thy hand." *Kesef* (money) is *Kisufin* (longing), that he will draw longing in the work. Thus, through the desire, the craving for the Creator, he will be able to carry the burden of Torah and *Mitzvot*. *Kesef* also concerns shame. This is because one is created for the goal of glorifying heaven, as it is written, "Blessed is... who created us in His honor."

In general, Torah and *Mitzvot* are things that one does in order to be favored by Him. This is because it is the slave's nature to want to be liked by his master, since then his master's heart is for him. So it is here: the many actions and meticulousness that one becomes proficient in are but a means by which to be favored in His eyes, and then he will have the desired goal of Him.

And a person observes Torah and *Mitzvot* to be favored in the eyes of people. And he turns the needs of heaven into a means. Meaning, through them he will obtain favor in the eyes of people. And as long as one has not been awarded the Torah *Lishma* (for Her Name), he works for people.

And although one has no other choice but to work for people, he should still be ashamed of such servitude. Then, through this *Kesef*, he will be awarded the *Kesef* of *Kedusha* (Sanctity), meaning to want *Kedusha*.

"And bind up the money in thy hand." This means that even though the craving is not up to man, if he has no desire for it, he cannot do a thing. Nevertheless, he should show the desire for the *Kisufin*, thc dcsirc to want (and perhaps *VeTzarta* (bind) comes from the word *Ratzita* (wanted)). One needs to show a desire for it, to show the desire and the craving to want the Creator, meaning to want to increase the glory of heaven, to bestow contentment upon Him, to be favored by Him.

There is a discernment of *Zahav* (gold), and there is a discernment of *Kesef* (silver/money). *Kesef* means having *Kisufin* (longing) in general; and *Zahav* (gold, made of the words "give this") means that he wants only one thing, and all the longing and the craving that he had for several things are cancelled in this desire. And he says "give this" only, meaning he does not want anything except to raise Divinity from the dust. This is all that he wants.

It follows that even though one sees that he has not the proper desire, he should still see and exert in deeds and thoughts to obtain the desire. And this is called "And bind up the money in thy hand." One should not think that if it is in the hands of man, it is a small thing. Rather, "for oxen (with grace), or for sheep," etc., for only by this will he be rewarded with the most sublime Lights.

## 176. WHEN DRINKING BRANDY AFTER THE *HAVDALA*

I heard after *Yom Kippur*, September 21, 1950

"And he would make a good day when he came out of holiness." Holiness is considered wisdom, and the left line, where there is fear of the *Dinim* (judgments). Hence, there is no place for a good day there. But rather, "when he came out of holiness," called "wisdom" and "left line," he would make a good day, considered Light of *Hassadim*.

## 177. ATONEMENTS

I heard

"Atonement of sins" is done through manifestation of the Light of *Hochma* (wisdom). The confession is the drawing of *Hochma*. The more one confesses, the more the *Hochma* appears on him. It is said about that: "and in that time, ... the iniquity of Jacob shall be sought for, and there shall be none." This is because for all the sin, when it is forgiven, it is not forgiven until *Hochma* is extended upon it. This is why they were looking for iniquities, to draw upon him the Light of Wisdom.

"The embrace of the left" means the extension of the left line. On each of the ten penitential days, one discernment of the ten *Sefirot* of *Mochin de Hochma*, called "left line," is extended. And on *Yom Kippur* (Day of Atonement) is the *Zivug* (coupling).

The embrace of the right is the drawing of *Hochma* below the *Chazeh* (chest), the place of the manifestation, where it is already sweetened in *Hassadim* (mercy). It is primarily considered extending of *Hassadim*. The building of the *Nukva* itself continues until the eighth day of *Sukkot*, and on the eighth day is the *Zivug*.

## 178. THREE PARTNERS IN MAN

I heard during a meal celebrating the completion of Part Nine of *The Zohar*, *Iyar* 3, May 9, 1951

Concerning the three partners in man: the Creator, father, and mother.

And he said that there is a fourth partner: the earth. If one does not take nourishment from the earth, one cannot persist. Earth is considered *Malchut*, which is generally considered having four discernments, called *HB TM*. And the nourishment one takes off the earth is the scrutinies, whereby the nourishment, the food, is separated from the *Klipa* (shell).

There are two discernments in *Malchut*: 1) *Kedusha* (Sanctity); 2) The Evil Lilith. Hence, when a person eats and makes the first and last blessings, the food is thus brought out of the dominion of the *Sitra Achra*. And since the food becomes blood, and blood is considered *Nefesh*, his *Nefesh* is now secular, and not of the *Sitra Achra*.

However, when one eats of a *Mitzva* meal, when the food is considered *Kedusha*, if he eats it with intention, the food becomes blood, and the blood becomes *Nefesh*. And then he comes to a state of *Nefesh de Kedusha*. This is why the evil inclination always comes to a person and makes him understand that it is not worthwhile to eat at a *Mitzva* meal for several reasons. Its primary intention is to not eat at a *Mitzva* meal for the above reason, since it is a part of *Kedusha*.

## 179. THREE LINES

I heard on Passover Inter 2, *Omer* Count 2, April 23, 1951

There is the matter of the three lines, and the matter of Israel holding to the body of the King. There is the matter of the exile in Egypt, when the people of Israel had to descend to Egypt, and the matter of the exodus from Egypt. And there is the matter of "he who is about to sanctify a woman will bring along an uneducated man." And there is the matter of Abraham's question: "How shall I know that I will inherit it?" and the Creator's reply: "Know of a surety that your seed will be a stranger in a land that is not theirs, and they shall afflict them four hundred years, and afterward shall they come out with great substance." There is the matter of *Gar*, the matter of *Vak*, and the matter of *Vak de Gar*.

The Thought of Creation was to delight His creatures, and the *Tzimtzum* (restriction) and the *Masach* (screen) were only to avoid the bread of shame. What extended from that is the place of work, and from that extended the three lines. The first line is considered right, regarded as *Vak* without a *Rosh* (head), considered "faith." The second line is considered left, attainment. And then they are in dispute, since faith contradicts attainment, and attainment contradicts faith.

Then there is the discernment of the middle line, considered *Vak de Gar*, or *Hochma* and *Hassadim*, or the right and left lines, integrated in one another. This means that he receives attainment to the extent that he has faith. Thus, to the extent that he has faith, he receives the same measure of attainment. And where he has no faith, he does not draw attainment to complement it, but always stands and weighs the lines, so one will not overpower the other.

And *Gar* (that appears before him) is called "attainment without faith." And this is called "the work of the gentiles." And the work of Israel is considered faith, where attainment is included. This is called "the King's body," meaning faith and attainment.

Abraham is called "the patriarch of faith," meaning *Hassadim*. Then he will know that anyone who wants to come near Him, must first assume the discernment of "right," meaning faith.

But faith contradicts attainment. Thus, how can they draw attainment when they haven't the tools for it? This is why He told him that "your seed will be a stranger in a land that is not theirs." And this is the meaning of "mingled themselves with the nations, and learned their works," that is, that they were dominated by the nations, that they, too, were under their dominion, and would draw *Gar de Hochma*.

And this is the meaning of the exile in Egypt, that Israel, too, extended *Gar de Hochma*. And this is their exile, when a discernment of darkness was extended.

The exodus from Egypt was through the plague of the firstborn. The firstborn means *Gar de Hochma*, that the Lord struck the firstborn of Egypt. This is the meaning of the Passover blood, and the circumcision blood, and this is what is written in *The Zohar* (*Amor*, 43): "When the Creator was slaying the firstborn of Egypt, at that time Israel went into the covenant of the holy sign, they were circumcised and bonded in the assembly of Israel."

The left line is called "foreskin," as it blocks the Lights. Hence, when He killed the firstborn, meaning cancelled the *Gar*, Israel below were circumcised, meaning cut off their foreskins. This is called *Dinim de Dechura* (male judgments), which block the Lights. Thus, through circumcision with a chisel, which is iron, called *Dinim de Nukva* (female judgments), the *Dinim de Dechura* are canceled. And then *Vak de Hochma* extends to them.

This means that in the beginning, there must be drawing of perfection, meaning *Gar de Hochma*. It is impossible to draw half a degree. And this must be specifically through the Egyptians, and this is called "exile," when the Jews, too, must be under their rule. Afterwards, through the exodus from Egypt, meaning correction of the *Masach de Hirik*, they exit their rule, meaning the Egyptians themselves shout, "Rise up, get you forth."

And this is, "Me and not a messenger." "Me" means *Malchut*, the lock, which cancels the *Gar*, by which there is the mingling of the left in the right and the right in the left.

And this is “He who wishes to sanctify a woman,” meaning *Hochma*, called “left.” “Will bring an uneducated man with him,” because he is in a state of “right,” which is faith. But he wants attainment. Thus, specifically through the uneducated man can he draw *Hochma*, since he has repentance, but for attainment, not for faith.

“I rose up to open to my beloved; and my hands dropped with myrrh, and my fingers with flowing myrrh, upon the handles of the bar.” Myrrh means “yet shall not thy Teacher hide Himself any more, but thine eyes shall see thy Teacher.” And “my hands” means attainment. And “fingers” mean seeing, as in, “each one pointing with his finger, saying, ‘this is our God.’” “On the bar” refers to the lock.

## 180. IN *THE ZOHAR*, AMOR

I heard on Passover Inter 2, April 23, 1951, Tel-Aviv

In *The Zohar* (*Amor*, 43): “Rabbi Hiyah opened, ‘I sleep, but my heart waketh,’ etc.. The assembly of Israel said: ‘I sleep in the exile in Egypt, where my children were in harsh enslavement, and my heart is awake to guard them from perishing in the exile. Hark! my beloved knocketh,’ this is the Creator, who said, ‘and I shall remember my covenant.’”

We must understand the issue of sleep. When Israel were in Egypt, they were under their dominion, and they, too, extended *Gar de Hochma*. And since *Hochma* does not shine without *Hassadim*, it is called “sleep.” And this is called “the harsh enslavement in Egypt,” meaning hard work, called *Dinim de Dechura*.

“And in all manner of service in the field,” which is considered *Dinim de Nukva*.

**"But my heart waketh"** means that even though she is asleep from the perspective of the left line, at which time *Malchut* is considered "the two great Lights," at that time *Malchut* is called "the fourth leg." She is regarded as *Tifferet*, above the *Chazeh*. "But my heart waketh" means that the lock-point is already there, which causes the determining of the middle line, the return to the point that is considered *Panim*, by which they will not perish in exile.

This is the meaning of "Open for Me an opening like the point of a needle." This means that ZA tells *Malchut* to draw *Hochma*. And even though *Hochma* cannot shine without *Hassadim*, for which it is only called "like the point of a needle," "and I will open for you the Higher Gates." That is, afterwards he will give her the *Hassadim*, and thus she will be given abundance. However, if she does not draw *Hochma*, meaning there will be no drawing of *Hochma* but of *Hesed*, this is called "Open to me, my sister." Thus, from the perspective of *Hochma*, *Malchut* is called "sister."

## 181. HONOR

I heard on *Nisan* 25, May 1, 1951

Honor is something that stops the body, and to that extent, it harms the soul. Hence, all the righteous that became famous and respected, it was a punishment. But the great righteous, when the Creator does not want them to lose by being famous as righteous, the Creator guards them from being honored, so as to not harm their souls.

Hence, to the extent that they are honored on the one hand, on the other hand they are disputed. These righteous are degraded with all kinds of degradations. To give an equal weight to the honor given to a righteous, the other side gives disgraces to that very measure.

## 182. MOSES AND SOLOMON

I heard on *Iyar* 3, May 10, 1951

Moses and Solomon are considered *Panim* (anterior, face) and *Achoraim* (posterior). It is written about Moses: "and thou shalt see My back." Solomon, however, is considered *Panim*. And only Solomon used the *Achoraim* of Moses, which is why the letters of *Shlomo* (Solomon) are the same letters as in *LeMoshe* (to Moses).

## 183. THE DISCERNMENT OF THE MESSIAH

I heard

There is a discernment of the Messiah Son of Josef, and the Messiah Son of David, and both must unite. And then there will be true wholeness in them.

## 184. THE DIFFERENCE BETWEEN FAITH AND MIND

I heard on *Shevat* 15, February 14, 1949

The difference between faith and the mind. There is an advantage to faith because it affects the body more than the mind, as it is closer to the body. Faith is considered *Malchut*, and the body is related to *Malchut*; hence it affects it.

The mind, however, is attributed to the Upper Nine, and hence cannot effectively influence the body. Yet, there is an advantage to the mind, as it is considered spiritual compared to faith, which is attributed to the body.

There is a rule in spirituality: "there is no absence in spirituality," and "each coin is accumulated to a great amount."

But faith is considered corporeality, which is considered separation. There is no adding in corporeality, and what is gone, is gone. What happened in the past does not join the present and the future.

Hence, although faith in something affects him during the act one hundred percent more than the effect of the mind, it only works for a time. The mind, however, although it is effective by only one percent, still, that percent remains constant and existing. Hence, after one hundred times, it is added to the amount that faith could affect in a single time. When he works with faith one hundred times, he will remain in the same state. But with the mind, it will remain perpetually existing in him.

It is as we study something with the intellect. Although we forget, the records remain in the brain. This means that the more one learns knowledge, accordingly is one's evolution of the brain. With corporeal things, however, extended over time and place, a place in the east will never come to the west, or the past hour into the present hour. But in spirituality, everything can be at one time.

## 185. THE UNEDUCATED, THE FEAR OF SHABBAT IS UPON HIM

I heard

Our sages said, "An uneducated man, the fear of Shabbat is upon him." A wise disciple is considered Shabbat, and Shabbat is considered *Gmar Tikkun* (the end of correction). Thus, as in *Gmar Tikkun*, the *Kelim* (vessels) will be corrected and fit to dress the Upper Light. Also, Shabbat is considered "end." This means that the Upper Light can appear and clothe in the lower ones, but this is only considered an awakening from below.

## 186. MAKE YOUR SHABBAT A WEEKDAY, AND DO NOT NEED PEOPLE

I heard

On Shabbat, it is forbidden to do works, meaning an awakening from below. And a wise disciple, one who has been rewarded with being the disciple of the Creator, called "Wise," is also considered an awakening from Above, meaning by revealing the secrets of the Torah.

Therefore, when an awakening from Above comes, that, too, is called "Shabbat." At that time, the uneducated, meaning the body, has fear, and then there is no room for work in any case.

## 187. CHOOSING LABOR

I heard

The issue of the lower *Hey* in the *Eynaim* (eyes) means that there was a *Masach* (screen) and a cover over the eyes. The eyes mean guidance, when one sees hidden guidance.

A trial means that a person cannot decide either way. It is when one cannot determine the Creator's will, and the will of his teacher. Although one can work devotedly, one is unable to determine if this devoted work is appropriate or not, that this hard work would be against his teacher's view, and the view of the Creator.

To determine, one chooses that which adds more labor. This means that one should act according to one's teacher. Only labor is for man to do, and nothing else. Hence, there is no place for doubt in one's words and actions. Instead, one should always increase labor.

## 188. ALL THE WORK IS ONLY WHERE THERE ARE TWO WAYS

I heard after Shabbat *Beshalach*, *Shevat* 14, January 25, 1948

All the work is only where there are two ways, as we have found, "and he shall live in them, and he shall not die in them." And the meaning of "shall be killed but shall not breach" applies only to three *Mitzvot*. And yet, we also find that the first *Hassadim* gave their lives on actions.

But in truth, this is the whole work. When one should keep the Torah, this is the time of the heavy load. And when the Torah keeps the person, it is not at all difficult, by way of "one's soul shall teach one." And this is considered that the Torah keeps a person.

## 189. THE ACT AFFECTS THE THOUGHT

I heard on *Tishrei* 27

Understand the reason for the sharpness, the excitement, and the shrewdness, when all the organs work in coordination at full speed, when one thinks of corporeal possessions. But with matters concerning the soul, the person, the body, and all the senses work heavily with any thing that concerns the needs of the soul.

The thing is that man's mind and thought are but projections of man's actions. They are reflected as if in a mirror. Hence, if most of one's actions are of corporeal needs, it is reflected in the mirror of the mind. This means that they are sufficiently perceived in the mind, and then one can use the mind for whatever one wishes, as the mind receives its sustenance from corporeal things.

Thus, the mind serves that place from which it receives sustenance. And because there are not many *Reshimot* (records) in the brain to suffice for reception of sustenance and impression, the mind is therefore unwilling to serve it for the needs of the soul.

For this reason one must prevail and do many things, until they are recorded in the mind. And then the knowledge will certainly increase, and the mind will serve him with shrewdness and speed, even more than for corporeal needs, since the mind is a close dressing for the soul.

## 190. EVERY ACT LEAVES AN IMPRINT

I heard during a meal, Passover 1, April 15, 1949

He asked if the redemption of our land from the oppressors is affecting us. We have been rewarded with liberation from the burden of the nations, and have become like all the nations, where one is not enslaved to another. And if that freedom has acted upon us so that we would have some sensation of the servitude of the Creator, and he said that we should not think that it does not affect us, that no change appears in this servitude from that freedom.

This is impossible, since the Creator does not act in vain. Rather, everything He does affects us, for better or for worse. This means that additional power is extended to us from every act that He performs, positive or negative, Light or dark. From this act we can also come to ascend, since there is not always permission and strength in spirituality, as we must continue under this force.

Hence, one cannot say that the freedom one has achieved induced no change in him. Yet, if we do not feel any change for the better, then we must say that this is a change for the worse, even though we do not feel.

And he explained it after the good day, after the *Havdala* (end of holiday blessing). It is like a meal of Shabbat or a good day, where the corporeal pleasures awaken spiritual pleasures by way of root and branch. It is a kind of "next world." And certainly, tasting from the next world requires great preparations during the six days of action. To the extent that one has prepared, so is one's sensation.

But without any proper preparation to extend the spiritual taste of Shabbat, it is to the contrary: he grows worse due to the corporeal pleasures. This is so because after corporeal meals one is only drawn to sleep, and nothing more, since after eating comes sleep. Thus, his eating brought him lower.

But it requires great exertions to come to spirituality through corporeal pleasures, since this was the King's will. Although they are in contrast, as spirituality is positioned under the line of bestowal, and corporeality under reception, and since this was the King's will, hence spirituality is attracted to corporeal pleasures, placed under His *Mitzvot*, which are the pleasures of Shabbat and a good day.

We should also see that even with this freedom that we have been granted, we need great preparation and intention, to extend the spiritual freedom, called "freedom from the angel of death." Then we would be rewarded with "the whole earth is full of His glory," called *Mochin de AVI*. This means that we would not see a time or a place where the Creator could not be dressed, that we would not be able to say that "He cannot be dressed" at that time or at that place, but rather, "the whole earth is full of His glory."

But before that, there is a difference "between Light and darkness, and between Israel and the nations": in the lit place the Creator is present, and it is not so in a place of darkness.

Also, in Israel, there is a place for the Godly Light of Israel to be. This is not so in the nations of the world: the Creator does not dress in them. "And between the seventh day and the six days of action." Yet, when we are awarded *Mochin de AVI*, we are rewarded with "the whole earth is full of His glory." At that time there is no difference between the times, and His Light is present at all the places and at all the times.

And this is the meaning of Passover, when Israel were awarded freedom, meaning *Mochin de AVI*, considered "the whole earth is full of His glory." Naturally, there is no place for the evil inclination since it is not distanced by its actions from the work of God. Quite the contrary, we see how it has brought man to His work, although it was only by way of an awakening from Above.

This is why they said that the Holy Divinity says, "I saw the image of a drop of a red rose." It means that he saw that there was a place that still needed correction, that He could not shine in this place. This is why they needed to count the seven weeks of the *Omer* count, to correct those places, so we would see that "the whole earth is full of His glory."

It is similar to a king who has a tower filled with goodly matters, but no guests. Hence, He created the people, so they would come and receive His abundance.

But we do not see the tower filled with goodly matters. On the contrary: the whole world is filled with suffering. And the excuse is that "and royal wine in abundance," that from *Malchut's* perspective, there is no need for the wine, for the pleasures that are comparable to the wine.

Rather, the deficiency is only from the perspective of the *Kelim* (vessels), that we do not have the appropriate vessels to receive the abundance, as it is specifically in the vessels of bestowal that we can receive.

The measure of the greatness of the abundance is according to the value of the greatness of the *Kelim*. Hence, all the changes are only in the vessels, not in the Lights. This is what the text tells us: "vessels of gold–the vessels being diverse from one another–and royal wine in abundance," as it was in the Thought of Creation, to do good to His creations, according to His ability.

## 191. THE TIME OF DESCENT

I heard on *Sivan* 14, June, 1938

It is hard to depict the time of descent, when all the works and the efforts made from the beginning of the work until the time of descent are lost. To one who has never tasted the taste of servitude to God, it seems as though this is outside of him, meaning that this happens to those of high degrees. But ordinary people have no connection to serving God, only to crave the corporeal will to receive, present in the flow of the world, washing the whole world with this desire.

However, we must understand why they have come to such a state. After all, with or without one's consent, there is no change in the Creator of heaven and earth; He behaves in the form of the Good who does good. Thus, what is the outcome of this state?

We should say that it comes to announce His greatness. One does not need to act as though one does not want Her. Rather, one should behave in the form of fearing the majesty, to know the merit and the distance between himself and the Creator. It is difficult to understand it with a superficial mind, or have any possibility of connection between Creator and creation.

And at the time of descent he feels that it is impossible that he will have connection or belonging to the Creator by way of

*Dvekut* (adhesion). This is so because he feels that servitude is a foreign thing to the whole world.

In truth, this is actually so, but "In the place where you find His greatness, there you find His humbleness." This means that it is a matter that is above nature, that the Creator gave this gift to creation, to allow them to be connected and adhered to Him.

Hence, when one becomes reconnected, he should always remember his time of descent so as to know and appreciate and value the time of *Dvekut*. So he will know that now he has salvation above the natural way.

## 192. THE LOTS

I heard in the year 1949, Tel-Aviv

The lots mean that they are both equal, and that it is impossible to examine which is more important with the intellect. This is why a lot is required. In *The Zohar*, *Amor*, it asks, "how can a goat for the Lord and a goat for *Azazel* be equal?"

The thing is that a goat for the Lord is considered "right," and a goat for *Azazel* is considered "left," where there is *Gar de Hochma*. It is said about that, "rewarded–good; not rewarded–bad." This means that *Malchut* of the quality of *Din* (judgment) appeared. This is considered a lock and a blockage on the Lights. The lock is at the place of the *Chazeh* in each *Partzuf*, hence *Hochma* can shine up to the place of the lock, but stops at the place of the *Chazeh*, since any restriction affects only from itself downward and not upward.

And the goat for the Lord is integrated with the left of the goat for *Azazel*, meaning with the *Hochma*. However, it is not like the left of *Azazel*, where it is from Above downward. This is why the Light stops, since the lock takes effect, though only from below upward, at which time the lock is concealed and the key is revealed.

It follows that concerning *Hochma*, the goat for *Azazel* has *Hochma* from the *Gar*, whereas the goat for the Lord is considered *Vak*. However, *Vak* can shine, while *Gar* must be stopped, hence the goat for *Azazel*, so the devil will not complain.

He complains because his only wish is to extend *Hochma*, which belongs to *Behina Dalet*, since it is not completed by any other degree, as its source is *Behina Dalet*. Therefore, if it does not receive into its own degree, it is not completed.

This is why it always entices man to extend into *Behina Dalet*, and if man is unwilling, it has all kinds of ploys to force man to extend. Hence, when it is given a portion of the discernment of *Hochma* it does not complain about Israel, since it is afraid that the abundance that it already has would be stopped.

Yet, when it extends *Gar de Hochma*, at that time Israel extends the *Vak de Hochma*. This Light of Wisdom is called "the Light of absolution," by which one is awarded repentance out of love, and sins become as virtues. This is the meaning of the goat for *Azazel* carrying the sins of the children of Israel upon it, meaning that all the sins of Israel have now become virtues.

There is the parable that *The Zohar* tells of a King's fool. When he is given wine and told of everything that he had done, even the bad deeds that he did, he says about those deeds that they are good deeds, and that there is none other like him in the whole world. In other words, the devil is called "the fool." When it is given wine, meaning wisdom, when it draws it, it is the Light of absolution, and thus all the sins become as virtues.

It follows that it says about all the bad deeds that they are good, since the sins have become as virtues. And since the devil wishes to be given its share, it does not complain about Israel.

This is the meaning of the complaints that were in Egypt: it asked, "How are those different from those? Either Israel die like the Egyptians, or Israel will return to Egypt." The thing is that Egypt is the source for extension of wisdom, but there it is a wisdom in the form of *Gar*, and when Israel were in Egypt they were under their control.

## 193. ONE WALL SERVES BOTH

The issue of the *Achoraim* (posterior) concerns primarily the absence of Light of Wisdom, which is the essence of the vitality, called "Direct Light." And this Light was restricted so as to not come to disparity of form. This is why *ZON* have no *Gar* when they are not corrected, so the *Sitra Achra* would not draw.

Yet, since there is a lack of *Gar*, there is fear that the external ones will have a grip. This is because they enjoy wherever there is a deficiency in the *Kedusha* (Sanctity), since they come and ask the "where" question, and it is unrealistic to answer this question before there is *Hochma* (wisdom). Hence, there is a correction to *ZON*: they rise and become integrated in *Bina*, considered, "for he delights in mercy," and rejects *Hochma*, while *Bina* herself has no need for *Hochma*, since she herself is essentially *Hochma*.

This is called following their Rav's view in everything, that their whole foundation is their root, meaning their Rav's view. And the question, "Where is His honor?" is irrelevant there.

And they are in *Bina* until they are corrected by raising MAN of efforts and labors, until they are purified from reception for themselves. Then they are qualified to receive *Hochma*, and only then are they permitted to disclose their own discernment, as they are deficient, since they do not have *Hochma*, and to accept the answer, to extend the Light of *Hochma* to shine in them by way of illumination of *Hochma*. In that state they are in their own authority, and not in the authority of *Bina*. This is because they have the Light of Wisdom, and Light clears and expels the external ones. And perhaps this is the meaning of, "Know what to answer an Epicurean."

This is called "one wall," meaning the *Achoraim* of *Bina*, which is enough for both, and which is a shield from the *Sitra Achra*. In other words, by relying oneself on the view of one's Rav, by being one with one's Rav, it means that the wall that his Rav has, being "delighting in mercy," is sufficient for him, too. However, afterwards they are separated, when he extends illumination of *Hochma* and can be on his own by being able to answer all of the *Sitra Achra's* questions.

## 194. THE COMPLETE SEVEN

Copied from the writings of my father, Lord and teacher

In the matter of the seven full ones of the Sanctification of the New Moon, it is customary to wait for seven full ones, and the end of Shabbat, too. It is not like the custom that if the end of Shabbat occurs in the middle of the seven days, we sanctify the moon, or when the seven days have been completed from the time to the time, they do not wait for the end of Shabbat. This is not so, as we should wait the full seven, and specifically on the end of Shabbat.

The thing is that the moon is considered *Malchut*, called "seventh," which is "He is in me." This means that when the Shabbat is filled by the six days of action, called "He," the Shabbat says, "He is in me." "He" is the sun, and "me" is the moon, which receives all of its light from the sun, and has nothing of its own.

However, there are two *Behinot* (discernments) in it, called "Shabbat" and "Month," since *Malchut* itself is regarded as the four known discernments *HB* and *TM*. The first three *Behinot*

(*Hochma*, *Bina*, and *Tifferet*) are the Shabbat. These are the three meals, called and implied in the Holy Torah in the three times "this day." Indeed, the *Behina Dalet* in her is the end of Shabbat or month, and it is not included in the "this day," as she is night, and not day.

And we could ask, "the first meal of Shabbat is night, too, so why does the holy Torah call it 'this day'"? However, the eve of Shabbat is "And there shall be one day which shall be known as the Lord's, neither day, nor night; but it shall come to pass that there shall be light at evening time."

However, the night of the end of Shabbat is still dark, and not light. Hence, our sages instructed us in the oral Torah to set up a table on the end of Shabbat, too, so as to correct this darkness and night, too, which are still uncorrected. This is called "*Melaveh Malkah*" (Escorting the Queen), sustaining and complementing that Luz Bone, which is *Behina Dalet*, which does not receive anything from the three meals of Shabbat, as we've explained. Yet, this *Behina Dalet* is gradually completed by way of "the month, the day." This is the meaning of the sanctification of the month, that Israel sanctify the times, meaning that residue of Israel that is not nourished by the meal of Shabbat.

Hence, even the greatest among the priests, of which there is none higher, is therefore warned to caution not to defile any dead from among his relatives. The writing warns him: "except for his kin, ... for her may he defile himself." From all the above, you can understand that any Higher *Kedusha* (Sanctity) comes from Shabbat. And since that Luz Bone, meaning *Behina Dalet*, called "his kin," does not receive from the Shabbat meal, the great priest is not exempted from being defiled by it.

Indeed, the meaning of the correction in the sanctification of the month extends from the Shabbat and its illuminations. This is the meaning of "Moses was perplexed, until the Creator showed him the similitude of a coin of fire and told him, 'Thus behold and sanctify.'" This means that Moses was very confused because he could not sanctify it, since the whole power of Moses is the Shabbat, since the Torah was given on Shabbat.

Hence, he could not find a correction to this residue in all the Lights of the Holy Torah, since this residue is not fed by all that. And this is why Moses was perplexed.

And what did the Creator do? He took it, and molded a shape within a shape within it, like a coin of fire, where the shape imprinted in its one side is not like the shape on the other side. This is reminiscent of our sages, who said about the coin of Abraham that an old man and an old woman were on its one side, representing *Behina Bet*, the quality of mercy, and a young man and a virgin on the other side, which are *Behina Dalet*, the harsh quality of judgment, from the words, "neither had any man known her."

And these two forms collaborated in such a way that when the Creator wanted to extend a correction of the Lights of Shabbat there, through the work of the righteous, the Creator showed the righteous that shape that extended from the first three discernments of *Malchut*. We call it *Behina Bet*, and the righteous can sanctify it with the Lights of Shabbat. This is the meaning of...

## 195. REWARDED–I WILL HASTEN IT

I heard in the year 1938

"Rewarded–I will hasten it," meaning the path of Torah; "not rewarded–through suffering," an evolutionary path that will finally lead everything to utter perfection. And concerning the path of Torah, that an ordinary person is given virtues by which he can make for himself vessels that are ready for it. And the vessels are made through the expansion of the Light and its departure.

A *Kli* (vessel) is specifically called "the will to receive." This means that he is deficient of some thing. And "there is no Light without a *Kli*"; the Light must be caught in some *Kli*, so it would have a hold.

But an ordinary person cannot have desires for sublime things, since it is impossible to have a need before there is fulfillment, as it is written, "the expansion of the Light, etc.." For example, when a person has a thousand pounds, he is rich and content. However, if he subsequently earns more, up to five thousand pounds, and then loses until he is left with two thousand, he is then deficient. Now he has *Kelim* (vessels) for three thousand pounds, since he had already had it. Thus, he has actually been cancelled.

And there is a path of Torah for it. When one is accustomed to the path of Torah, to regret the scantiness of attainment, and every time he has some illuminations, and they are divided, they cause him to have more sorrow and more *Kelim*.

This is the meaning of every *Kli* needing Light, that it is not filled, that its Light is missing. Thus, every deficient place becomes a place for faith. Yet, were it filled, there would be no existence of a *Kli*, existence of a place for faith.

## 196. A GRIP FOR THE EXTERNALS

I heard in the year 1938

We should know that the *Klipot* can only get hold in a place of deficiency. But in a place where there is wholeness, they flee and cannot touch.

Now we can understand the issue of the breaking: it is written in several places that it concerns the separation of the Light of Wisdom from the Light of Mercy. In other words, since a *Parsa* (division/partition) was made between *Atzilut* and *BYA*, the Light of Wisdom can no longer come down. Only the Light of *Hassadim*, which previously contained Light of Wisdom, has now been separated from the Light of Wisdom and came down. Thus, they still have the powers they had had before, and this is called "lowering *Kedusha* (Sanctity) into the *Klipa* (shell)."

## 197. BOOK, AUTHOR, STORY

I heard in the year 1938

Book, author, story. A book is considered prior to creation. An author is the owner of the book. An author is the unification of the author and the book, which should assume the form of a story, that is, the Torah along with the Giver of the Torah.

## 198. FREEDOM

I heard in the year 1938

*Harut* (engraved), do not pronounce it *Harut* but *Herut* (freedom). This means that it is written, "write them upon the table of thy heart." Writing is with ink, which is considered darkness. And each time a person writes, it means that one makes decisions about how to behave, and then reverts to his evil ways, since the writing has been erased. Thus, one should constantly write, but it must be in the form of *Harut*, so it will be *Harut* in his heart so he cannot erase.

And then he is immediately awarded *Herut*. Thus, the *Kli* for *Herut* is the extent to which it is written in his heart. To the extent of the engraving, so is the salvation. This is because the essence of the *Kli* is the hollow, as it is written, "my heart is slain[23] within me." And then he is awarded freedom from the angel of death, since the lowliness is the SAM itself, and he must know it to the fullest, and overcome it until the Creator helps him.

## 199. TO EVERY MAN OF ISRAEL

I heard Inter 3

Every man of Israel has an internal point in the heart, which is considered simple faith. This is an inheritance from our fathers, who stood at Mount Sinai. However, it is covered by many *Klipot* (shells), which are all kinds of dresses of *Lo Lishma* (not for Her Name), and the shells should be removed. Then his basis will be called "faith alone," without any support and outside help.

## 200. THE PURIFICATION OF THE MASACH

I heard in Tiberias, *Kislev* 1, Shabbat

The *Hizdakchut* (purification) of the *Masach* (screen), which occurs in the *Partzuf*, causes the departure of the Light, too. And the reason is that after the *Tzimtzum* (restriction), the Light is captured only in the *Kli* of the *Masach*, the rejecting force. And this is the essence of the *Kli*.

And when that *Kli* leaves, the Light leaves, too. This means that a *Kli* is considered faith above reason. And then the Light

23 In Hebrew, the word *Halal* means both slain and hollow.

appears. And when the Light appears, its nature is to purify the *Kli*, to cancel the *Kli* of faith. Because this is so, meaning that it comes into a form of knowing in him, the Light immediately leaves him. Thus, he should see to increasing the *Kli* of faith, meaning the *Masach* over the knowing, and then the abundance will not stop from him.

And this is the meaning of each *Kli* being deficient of Light, that it is not filled by the Light that it lacks. It follows that every place of dearth becomes a place for faith. Were it filled, there would be no possibility for a *Kli*, a place for faith.

## 201. SPIRITUALITY AND CORPOREALITY

I heard on *Hanukah* 1, December 18, 1938

Why do we see that there are many people who work so diligently for corporeality, even in life-threatening places, but in spirituality, each and every one examines one's soul very carefully? Moreover, one can exert in corporeality even when one is not given a great reward for one's work. But in spirituality, one cannot agree to work unless one knows for certain that he will receive a good reward for his work.

The thing is that it is known that the body has no value. After all, everyone sees that it is passing and leaves without a trace, so it is easy to abandon it, as it is worthless anyway.

However, in spirituality there is a discernment of *Klipot* (shells), which guard the body and sustain it. This is why it is hard to let go of it. This is why we see that it is easier for secular people to abandon their body, that they do not find heaviness in their body.

But this is not so in spirituality; it is the *Achoraim* (posterior) of *Kedusha* (Sanctity), called "devotion." It is specifically through that that one is awarded the Light. And before one is completely devoted, one cannot achieve any degree.

## 202. IN THE SWEAT OF THY FACE SHALT THOU EAT BREAD

I heard

Diminishing the Light is its correction. This means that nothing is achieved without effort. And because it is impossible to achieve the complete Light in utter clarity, the advice is to diminish the Light. In this way it is possible to attain it with the little effort that the lower one can give.

This is similar to one who wishes to move a large building; of course this is impossible. So what does he do? He takes the building apart into small bricks, and he can move each piece. So it is here: through diminishing the Light, one can make a little effort.

## 203. MAN'S PRIDE SHALL BRING HIM LOW

I heard on *Sukkot* Inter 2, October 12, 1938

"Man's pride shall bring him low." It is known that a man is born in utter lowness. However, if the low one knows one's place, one does not suffer for being low, as this is one's place. The legs, for example, are not at all degraded because they are always walking in the litter, and must carry the full weight of the body, whereas the head is always above. This is so because they know their place; hence, the legs are not at all degraded, and do not suffer for being in a low degree.

Yet, if they had wanted to be above, but were forced to be below, they would feel the suffering. And this is the meaning of "Man's pride shall bring him low." If one had wanted to remain in one's lowliness, no lowliness would have been felt, no suffering for being "a wild ass's colt is born a man." But when they want to be proud they feel the lowliness, and then they suffer.

Suffering and lowliness go hand in hand. If one feels no suffering, it is considered that one has no lowliness. It is precisely according to the measure of one's pride, or that he wants to have but doesn't. Thus, he feels lowliness. And this lowliness later becomes a vessel for pride, as it is written, "The Lord reigneth; He is clothed in pride." If you cleave to the Creator, you have a clothing of pride, as it is written, "Pride and glory are to the Creator." Those who cleave to the Creator have great pride. And to the extent that he feels the lowliness, and according to the measure of one's suffering, so one is rewarded with the clothing of the Creator.

## 204. THE PURPOSE OF THE WORK

I heard in the year 1938

During the preparation period, the whole work is in the no's, that is, in the no, as it is written, "and they shall be afflicted in a land that is not." However, with matters of the tongue, which is considered "me," one must first be awarded the discernment of love.

Yet, during the preparation, there is only work in the form of no's, by way of "thou shalt not have," and by the profusion of no's we come to the point of God[24] of *Hesed* (mercy). But prior to that, there are many no's, which is another God, many no's. This is so because from *Lo Lishma* one comes to *Lishma*.

And since the *Sitra Achra* provides support, hence, even afterwards, when we work and extend *Kedusha* (Sanctity), still, when she takes the support, we fall from the degree, and then she takes all the abundance that they extended. Thus, the *Sitra Achra* has the power to dominate a person, so one is compelled

24 In Hebrew, the word God (*El*) and 'no' are written with the same letters but in the opposite order

to fulfill her wish. And he has no other counsel but to raise himself to a higher degree.

Then the sequence begins anew, as before, with the forty-nine gates of impurity. This means that one walks in the degrees of *Kedusha* until the forty-nine gates. But there she has control to take all the vitality and bounty, until a person falls each time into a higher gate of impurity, since "God hath made even the one opposite the other."

And when one comes into the 49th gate, one can no longer raise oneself, until the Creator comes and redeems him. And then "He hath swallowed down riches, and he shall vomit them up again; God shall cast them out of his belly." This means that now one takes all the bounty and vitality that the *Klipa* (shell) was taking from all of the forty-nine gates of *Kedusha*. This is the meaning of "the looting of the sea."

Yet, it is impossible to be redeemed before the exile is felt. And when one walks on the forty-nine, one feels the exile, and the Creator redeems on the 50th gate. And the only difference between *Galut* (exile) and *Ge'ula* (redemption) is in the *Aleph*, which Is *Alupho Shel Olam* (Champion of the world). Hence, if one does not properly attain the exile, too, he is deficient in the degree.

## 205. WISDOM CRIETH ALOUD IN THE STREETS

I heard in the year 1938

"Wisdom crieth aloud in the streets, she uttereth her voice in the broad places. Whoso is thoughtless, let him turn in hither; as for him that lacketh understanding, she saith to him." This means that when one is awarded adhesion with the Creator, the Holy *Shechina* (Divinity) tells him that the fact that he first had to be a fool was not because he really is so. The reason was that he was heartless. This is why we say, "And all believe that He is a God of faith."

This means that later, when we are rewarded with true *Dvekut* (adhesion), it is not considered being a fool, that I should say that it is above reason. Moreover, one must work and believe that one's work is above reason even though one's senses tell him that his work is within reason. It is to the contrary: he previously saw that the reason did not obligate the servitude, and then he had to work above reason and say that there is real reason in it. This means that he believes that the servitude is the actual reality.

And afterwards it is the opposite: his whole work compels him, his reason. In other words, the *Dvekut* impels him to work. However, he believes that everything he sees within reason is all above reason. And this was not so before, when everything that is in the form of above reason is within reason.

## 206. FAITH AND PLEASURE

I heard in the year 1938

One will never ask about pleasure, "What is the purpose of this pleasure?" If even the smallest thought about its purpose appears in one's mind, it is a sign that this is not a true pleasure. This is because pleasure fills all the empty places, and then of course there is no vacant place in the mind to ask about its purpose. And if one does ask about its purpose, it is a sign that the pleasure is incomplete, since it has not filled all the places.

And so it is with faith. Faith should fill all the places of knowing. Hence, we should picture what it would be like, had we had knowledge, and to that very extent there should be faith.

## 207. RECEIVING IN ORDER TO BESTOW

I heard on Shabbat, *Tevet* 13

The people of the world walk on two feet, called "pleasure and pain." They always chase after the place of pleasure, and always flee the place of suffering. Hence, when one is rewarded with tasting the flavor of Torah and *Mitzvot*, as it is written, "taste and see that the Lord is good," then he is chasing the servitude of the Creator. The result of that is that one is always awarded degrees of Torah and *Mitzvot*, as it is written, "and in His law doth he meditate day and night."

But how can one restrict one's mind to one thing? Rather, love and pleasure always tie one's thoughts so that one's mind and body are attached to the love and the pleasure, as we see with corporeal love. This is so precisely when one has already been awarded the expansion of the mind, which yields love. And this discernment is called "within reason." But one should always remember to work by way of above reason, since this is called "faith and bestowal."

This is not so within reason. At that time, all the organs agree with one's work because they, too, receive delight and pleasure, and this is why it is called "within reason."

At such a time one is in a difficult position: it is forbidden to spoil the discernment, as it is a Godly illumination within him, as this is abundance from Above. Instead, one should correct both, meaning the faith and the reason.

And then he needs to arrange it so that everything he has achieved so far, meaning the Torah that he has now achieved and the bounty that he now has, what has this got to do with this? This is only because he had had prior preparation, by assuming the above reason.

This means that through engagement in *Dvekut* (adhesion), he attached himself at the root, and has thus been awarded reason. This means that the reason he has obtained by way of faith was a true revelation. It follows that he appreciates primarily the above reason, and he also appreciates the reason, that he has now been rewarded with the revelation of His names to extend abundance.

This is why he should now strengthen further through reason, and assume the greatest above reason, as *Dvekut* in the root occurs primarily through faith, and this is his whole purpose. And this is called "reception," the reason he extended in order to bestow, by which he can assume faith above reason in the greatest measure, in quantity and quality.

## 208. LABOR

I heard

The efforts that one makes are but preparations for achieving devotion. Hence, one should grow accustomed in devotion, since no degree can be achieved without devotion, as this is the only tool that qualifies one to be rewarded with all the degrees.

## 209. THREE CONDITIONS IN PRAYER

I heard

There are three conditions in prayer:

1. Believing that He can save him, although he has the worst conditions of all his contemporaries, still, "Is the Lord's hand waxed short" from saving him? If not, then "the Landlord cannot save His vessels."

2. He no longer has any counsel, that he has already done all that he could, but saw no cure to his plight.
3. If He does not help him, he will be better off dead than alive. Prayer is the lost[25] in the heart. The more he is lost, so is the measure of his prayer. Clearly, one who lacks luxuries is not like one who has been sentenced to death, and only the execution is missing, and he is already tied with iron chains, and he stands and begs for his life. He will certainly not rest or sleep or be distracted for even a moment from praying for his life.

## 210. A HANDSOME FLAW IN YOU

I heard

It the Talmud: "He who had said to her, to his wife, 'until you see a handsome flaw in you.' Rabbi Ishmael, son of Rabbi Yosi said that the Creator says that she cannot cleave to him, until you see a handsome flaw in you" (*Nedarim* 66b). The first interpretation of the *Tosfot* means that she is forbidden to enjoy until she can find a handsome thing.

This means that if one can say that he, too, has nice things with which he had helped the Creator, so they can cleave to one another, so why has He not helped another? This must be since he has good things in him, that he has good faith or good qualities, since he has a good heart, that he can pray.

And this is the meaning of his commentary: "He said unto them, 'perhaps like a handsome woman?'" This means that

25 In the manuscript, this word is written with what seems like two initial letters. With one, it means "lost" and with the other it means "work." It would seem that the "proper" meaning would be to write "work" since it is a part of the phrase "prayer is the work in the heart," but he apparently deliberately switches the letters to mean "lost," as this is the word he is relating to through the rest of the article.

there is an external mind, better than all his contemporaries. Or "perhaps her hair is handsome?" This means that he is as meticulous with himself as a hair's breadth. Or "perhaps her eyes are fair?" This means that he has more grace of holiness than all the people of his generation. Or "perhaps his ears are handsome?" This means that he cannot hear any slander.

## 211. AS THOUGH STANDING BEFORE A KING

I heard on *Elul* 1, August 28, 1938

One who is sitting at one's home is not like one who is standing before a King. This means that faith should be that he will feel as though he is standing before the King all day long. Then his love and fear will certainly be complete. And as long as he has not achieved this kind of faith, he should not rest, "for that is our lives, and the length of our days," and we will accept no recompense.

And the lack of faith should be woven in his limbs until the habit becomes a second nature, to the extent that "when I remember Him, He does not let me sleep." But all the corporeal matters quench this desire, since he sees that anything that gives him pleasure, the pleasure cancels the deficiency and the pain.

However, one must want no consolation, and should be careful with any corporeal thing that one receives, so it will not quench his desire. This is done by regretting that by this pleasure, the sparks and powers of the vessels of *Kedusha* (Sanctity) are missing in him, meaning desires for *Kedusha*. And through the sorrow, he can keep from losing the vessels of *Kedusha*.

## 212. EMBRACE OF THE RIGHT, EMBRACE OF THE LEFT

I heard on *Kislev* 8, November 28, 1941

There is the embrace of the right and there is the embrace of the left. And both have to be eternal. This means that when one is in the state of "right," one should think that there is no such discernment as "left" in the world. And also, when one is in the left, he should think that there is no such discernment as "right" in the world.

"Right" means private Providence, and "left" means Guidance of reward and punishment. And although there is reason, which says that there is no such thing as right and left together, he needs to work above reason, meaning that reason will not stop him.

The most important is the above reason. This means that one's whole work is measured by his work above reason. And although he later comes into within, it is nothing, since his basis is the above reason, and so he always sucks from his root.

However, if, when he comes into within reason, he wants specifically to be fed within reason, at that time the Light immediately leaves. And if he wants to extend, he must begin with above reason, as this is his whole root. And afterwards he comes to the reason of *Kedusha* (Sanctity).

## 213. ACKNOWLEDGING THE DESIRE

I heard

The basic, primary principle is to increase the need, for that is the basis upon which the whole structure is built. And the strength of the building is measured by the strength of its foundation.

Many things compel one to labor, but they do not aim at the cause. Therefore the foundation impairs the whole of the building. Although from not for His Name one comes to for His Name, it still lengthens the time before one returns to the goal.

Therefore, one must see that the goal is always before one's eyes, as it is written in *Shulchan Aruch (Set Table)*: "I see the Lord before me always." And one who stays home is not like the one who stands before the king. He who believes in the reality of the Creator, that the whole earth is full of His glory, he is filled with fear and love, and needs no preparations or observation, only to nullify oneself before the king from his actual nature.

Just as we see in corporeality, that he who truly loves his friend, thinks only of the best of his friend, and avoids anything that isn't beneficial to his friend. All that is done without any calculation, and it does not require a great mind, since it is as natural as a mother's love for her child, who only wants to benefit her child. She needs no prior preparations and thought to love her son, since a natural thing does not require an intellect that will necessitate it, but it is done by the senses themselves. The senses themselves are devoted, since this is how it is in nature, as due to the love for some thing, they give their heart and soul, until they achieve the goal. And as long as they do not obtain, their life is not a life.

Thus whoever feels, as it is written in *Shulchan Aruch*, that for him it is similar, etc., he is certainly in completeness, meaning that he has faith. And as long as one does not feel one stands before the king, then one is the opposite.

Hence, one should first and foremost regard slavery, and one must regret not having sufficient faith, as the lack of faith is one's foundation, and one should pray for labor and desire to feel that want, for if one hasn't this desire, one hasn't the vessel to receive the filling. One must believe that the Creator hears our every prayer and that one, too, will be salvaged in complete faith.

## 214. KNOWN IN THE GATES

I Heard on *Shavuot* (Pentecost), 1939, Jerusalem

"I am the Lord thy God" (Exodus 20:2). Also, in *The Zohar*, "known in the gates" (Proverbs 31:23). Question: Why did our sages change from the written word of calling the holiday of Pentecost by the name "the giving of our Torah"? In the Torah, it is specified by the name "offering of first-fruits," as it is written, "Also in the day of the first-fruits" (Numbers 28:26). Our sages came and named it "the giving of our Torah."

The thing is that our sages did not change a thing, only interpreted the issue of the offering of the first-fruit. It is written, "Let the field exult, and all that is therein; Then shall the trees of the forest sing for joy" (Psalms 96:12). The difference between a field and a wood is that the field bears fruit and woods are infertile trees, which do not bear fruit.

This means that a field is discerned as *Malchut*, which is discerned as acceptance of the burden of the Kingdom of Heaven, which is faith above reason.

But how much is the measure of the faith? This has a measurement, meaning it should be filled to the very same extent of the knowledge. Then, it will be called "a field which the Lord hath blessed" (Genesis 27:27), meaning bearing fruit. This is the only way by which it is possible to cleave to Him, because it places no limits on him, since it is above reason.

Knowledge, however, is limited. The measure of the greatness is according to the measure of the knowledge. And this is called "another God is sterile and does not bear." This is why it is called "a wood." However, in any case, both are called "edges." Rather, there should be a discernment of the middle line, meaning he needs knowledge, too. But this is on condition that he does not spoil the faith above reason.

Yet, if he works with knowledge a little better than with faith, he immediately loses everything. Instead, he should have it without any difference. Then, "the field will exult etc., the trees of the wood sing for joy," for then there will be correction even for "another God," discerned as the "wood," because he will be strengthened by faith.

This is the meaning of what is written about Abraham, "walk before Me, and be thou wholehearted" (Genesis 17:1). Rashi interprets that he does not need support. And about Noah, it is written, "Noah walked with God" (Genesis 6:9), meaning he needed support, though in any case it is support from the Creator. However, the worst that can even be is needing the support of people.

There are two issues concerning that:

1. A gift;
2. A loan.

The gift that one takes from people is the taking of the support. And he doesn't want to give it back, but wants to use it for the rest of his life.

And a loan is when he takes for the time being, meaning as long as he hasn't strength and power of his own, but he hopes that by work and labor in Sanctity and purity he will obtain his own strength. At that time, he gives back the support that he took. Yet, this, too, is not good, because if he is not rewarded with obtainment he falls anyway.

And let us return to the issue that the "giving of the Torah" and not the "receiving of the Torah" was because then they were rewarded with the Giver of the Torah, as it is written, "we wish to see our King." Hence, the importance is that they were rewarded with the "Giver of the Torah." And then it is called "a field which the Lord hath blessed," meaning a field that bears fruit.

This is the meaning of the first-fruit, meaning the first fruit of the field. It is a sign of being rewarded with the "Giver of the Torah" and complete awareness. This is why he says, "A wandering Aramean was my father" (Deuteronomy 26:5). Previously, he had descents and craftiness; but now it is a sustainable connection. This is why our sages interpret the issue of the first-fruit, that the "giving of the Torah" is to be rewarded with "the Giver of the Torah."

## 215. FAITH

I heard

Faith, specifically, is pure work. This is because the will to receive does not participate in this work. Moreover, the will to receive objects to it. The nature of that desire is only to work in a place that it sees and knows. But above reason is not so. Hence, in this manner the *Dvekut* (adhesion) can be complete, since there is the element of equivalence here, meaning it is actually to bestow.

Therefore, when this basis is fixed and solid, even when receiving favorable things, he considers it "a place," which, in *Gematria*, is Torah. And there should be fear with this Torah. Meaning, he should see that he does not receive any support and assistance from the Torah, but from faith. And even when he already considers it superfluous because he is already receiving from the pleasant land, he should still believe that this is the truth. And this is the meaning of "and all believe that He is a God of faith," since specifically through faith can he sustain the degree.

## 216. RIGHT AND LEFT

I heard on *Tevet* 6

There is the discernment of "right" and there is "left." On the "right" there are *Hochma*, *Hesed*, *Netzah*, and on the "left" there are *Bina*, *Gevura*, and *Hod*. Right is considered "Private Providence," and left is considered "reward and punishment."

When engaging in the right, we should say that all is in Private Providence, and then one naturally does nothing. Thus, one has no sins. However, the *Mitzvot* that one performs are also not one's own, but are a gift from Above, so one should be thankful for them, as well as for the corporeal benefits that He has done to him.

And this is called *Netzah*, when one *Nitzah* (defeated) the *Sitra Achra*. And from this extends *Hesed* (mercy), which is love, and thus he comes to *Hochma*, called *Risha de Lo Etyada* (The Unknown Head). Afterwards, one should go to the left line, considered *Hod*.

## 217. IF I AM NOT FOR ME, WHO IS FOR ME

I heard on *Adar Aleph* 27

"If I'm not for me who is for me, and when I am for me, what am I?" This is a paradox. The thing is that one should do all of one's work by way of "If I'm not for me who is for me," that there is no one who can save him, but "in thy mouth, and in thy heart, that thou mayest do it," that is, in the form of reward and punishment. However, to oneself, in private, one should know that "when I am for me, what am I?" This means that everything is in Private Providence and there is no one who can do anything.

And if you say that if everything is in Private Providence, why is there the issue of working in the form of "If I'm not for me who is for me?" Yet, through working in the form of "If I'm not for me who is for me," one is awarded Private Providence, that is, attains it. Thus, everything follows the path of correction. And the division of the duty and the Torah, called "children of the Creator," is not revealed unless it is preceded by work in the form of "If I'm not for me who is for me."

## 218. THE TORAH AND THE CREATOR ARE ONE

I heard

"The Torah and the Creator are one." Certainly, during the work they are two things. And moreover, they contradict one another. This is because the discernment of the Creator is *Dvekut* (adhesion), and *Dvekut* means equivalence, being cancelled from reality. (And one should always picture how there was a time when one had little *Dvekut*, how he was filled with liveliness and pleasure. Always crave to be in *Dvekut*, since a spiritual matter is not divided in half. Moreover, if this is a fulfilling matter, he should always have the good thing. And one should picture the time that he had, since the body does not feel the negative, but the existing, that is, states he had already had. And the body can take these states as examples.)

And the Torah is called "the Light" in it. This means that during the study, when you feel the Light, and want to give to the Creator with this Light, as it is written, "One who knows the Master's commandment will serve Him." Hence, he feels that he exists, that he wants to bestow upon the Creator, and this is the sensation of one's self.

However, when one is awarded the discernment of "the Torah and the Creator are one," one finds that all is one. At that time one feels the Creator in the Torah. One should always crave the Light in it; and we can the Light with what is learned, although it is easier to find the Light in matters of reception.

And during the work, they are two ends. One is drawn to the discernment of the Creator, at which time he cannot study the Torah, and he yearns after the books of *Hassidim*. And there is one who craves the Torah, to know the ways of God, the worlds, their processes, and matters of Guidance. These are the two ends. But in the future, "and shall smite through the corners of Moab," that is, they are both included in the tree.

## 219. DEVOTION

I heard

The work should be with love and fear. With love, it is irrelevant to say that we must be devoted to it, since it is natural, as love is as fierce as death, as it is written, "for love is as strong as death." Rather, devotion should primarily be concerning fear, that is, when one still does not feel the taste of love in the servitude, and the servitude is coercive for him.

There is a rule that the body does not feel a thing that is coercive, as it is built by way of correction. And the correction is that the servitude, too, should be in the form of love, as this is the purpose of the *Dvekut*, as it is written, "in a place where there is labor, there is the *Sitra Achra*."

The servitude that should primarily be in devotion is on the discernment of fear. At that time, the whole body disagrees with one's work, since it does not feel any taste in the servitude. And with each thing that the body does, the body calculates that this servitude is not in wholeness. Thus, what will you get out of working?

Then, because there is no validity and taste in this servitude, overcoming is only through devotion. This means that the servitude feels bitter, and each act causes him horrendous suffering, since the body is not accustomed to work in vain: either the work should benefit oneself, or others.

But during the *Katnut* (smallness), one does not feel any benefit for oneself, since one does not presently feel any pleasure in the servitude. And also, one does not believe that there will be benefit to others, since it is not important to himself, so what pleasure would others have of it? Then the suffering is harsh. And the more he works, the suffering increases proportionally. Finally, the suffering and the labor accumulate to a certain amount until the Creator has mercy on him and gives him the taste in the servitude of the Creator, as it is written, "Until the spirit be poured upon us from on high."

## 220. SUFFERING

I heard

The harsh suffering that one feels is only because of the absence of vitality. However, what can one do? It is not within one's power to take vitality. At such a time, one comes into a state of boredom. And it is specifically at such a time that one needs great strengthening, but you are not taking.

## 221. MULTIPLE AUTHORITIES

I heard

A *Kli* (vessel) does not leave its own authority, unless it is filled with something else. But it cannot remain empty. Hence, because it is in the authority of the *Sitra Achra*, of course it must be brought out. Therefore, we must try to fill it with other things. This is why it must be filled with love. It is written, "and then he will be taken after her for love of self."

## 222. THE PART GIVEN TO THE *SITRA ACHRA* TO SEPARATE IT FROM THE *KEDUSHA*

I heard

"In the beginning, He created the world with the quality of *Din* (judgment). Saw that the world did not persist." Interpretation: the quality of *Din* is *Malchut*, the place of the *Tzimtzum* (restriction). From there down is the place where the external ones stand.

However, in the Upper Nine, there can be reception of the abundance without any fear, but the world did not persist, meaning *Behina Dalet*. The world cannot be corrected because this is her place, and it is impossible to change, meaning revoke the vessels of reception, since this is nature, and cannot be changed. Nature means Upper Force, that this was His will, that the will to receive would be in completeness, and impossible to cancel.

Also, in man below, it is impossible to change nature. And the advice for that was to associate it with the quality of mercy, meaning to make the boundary that exists in *Malchut* in the place of *Bina*. This means that He made it as though there is a prohibition on reception, and then it is possible to work there, that is, to receive in order to bestow. This is because this is not the place of *Behina Dalet*, and it can therefore be revoked.

It follows that *Behina Dalet* is actually corrected, that is, by lowering the *Behina Dalet*. This means that she discovers that this is not her place. And this is done through *Mitzvot* and good deeds. When he discovers, he scrutinizes *Behina Dalet* in *Behina Bet*, which shows that her place is below.

And then the *Zivug* (coupling) rises and the *Mochin* (Light) extends below. At that time the lower *Hey* rises to the *Eynaim* (eyes) and the work on turning the vessels of reception begins anew.

And the essence of the correction is because it gives a portion to the *Sitra Achra*. That is, previously there was room for her suction only from *Behina Dalet*, as only there is the quality of *Din*, which is not so in *Bina*. Now, however, *Bina*, too, takes the discernment of diminution, since the quality of *Din* has been mingled with her, too. It follows that the place of the quality of *Din* has grown. Yet, it is through this part that there is room for work, the ability to reject, since this is not her real place. And then, after being accustomed to rejecting it from where it is possible, it results in the ability to reject her from where it was previously impossible.

And this is "He hath swallowed down riches, and he shall vomit them up again." Thus, by stretching her boundary, she swallows up great riches, and thus she herself is made completely corrected. And this is the meaning of "a goat for *Azazel*": she is given a part, by which she is subsequently separated from *Kedusha* (Sanctity), when she is corrected in the place He gives her, which is not her place.

## 223. CLOTHING, BAG, LIE, ALMOND

I heard

"None might enter within the king's gate clothed with sackcloth." This means that when one awakens oneself to how one is remote from the Creator and filled with transgressions, sins, and crimes, one cannot be attached to the Creator or receive any salvation from the Creator. This is because he has a clothing of a sackcloth and cannot enter the King's palace.

Hence, it is necessary that one will see one's true state, as it is, without covering. On the contrary, the whole purpose of the *Klipot* (shells) is to cover, but if one has been rewarded from Above, one can discover and see one's true state. However, one should know that this is not perfection, but necessity. And a time of bitterness is called *Dalet* (the Hebrew letter). When it is added by a *Sack* (the Hebrew and English words are the same here), they form *Shaked* (almond), which rushes salvation.

Yet, when one makes the bitterness in the work by himself, that is, when one can make the self-scrutiny, one is glad that at least he sees the truth. This is considered making this the *Rosh* (head), that is, important. And this is called *Reish* (the Hebrew letter), and joined with the *Sack* it creates *Sheker* (lie). However, this work should be with tremor and fear, and he should immediately strengthen himself with complete faith that everything will be corrected.

## 224. *YESOD DE NUKVA* AND *YESOD DE DECHURA*

I heard

The matter of the ascent of *Malchut* to the place of the *Eynaim* (eyes) is called *Yesod de Nukva*. This is because *Nukva* means deficiency, where diminution is considered a lack. Because it is in the *Eynaim*, which is *Hochma*, it is nevertheless called *Behina Aleph* of the four *Behinot*. However, when the lower *Hey* is in *Keter*, and *Keter* is a desire to bestow, no diminution applies there, since there is no limitation on the will to bestow. This is why it is called *Yesod de Dechura*.

## 225. RAISING ONESELF

I heard

One cannot raise oneself above one's circle. Hence, one must suck from one's environment. And one has no other counsel, except through much work and Torah. Therefore, if one chooses for oneself a good environment, one saves time and efforts, since one is drawn according to one's environment.

## 226. WRITTEN TORAH AND ORAL TORAH

I heard on *Mishpatim* 3, February 2, 1943, Tel-Aviv

The written Torah is considered an awakening from Above, and the oral Torah is considered an awakening from below, and together they are considered, "six years he shall serve; and in the seventh he shall go out free." The issue of work is relevant precisely where there is resistance, and it is called *Alma* (Aramaic: world) from the word *He'elem* (Hebrew: concealment). Then, during the concealment, there is resistance, and then there is room for work. This is the meaning of the words of our sages: "6,000 years the world exists, and one will be destroyed," meaning that the concealment will be ruined, and then there will be no more work. Instead, the Creator makes wings for him, which are covers, so we would have work.

## 227. THE REWARD FOR A *MITZVA*—A *MITZVA*

I heard

One should crave being awarded the reward of a *Mitzva* (commandment/good deed). This means that through keeping the *Mitzvot* (plural for *Mitzva*) he will be rewarded with adherence to the *Metzaveh* (Commander).

## 228. FISH BEFORE MEAT

I heard on *Adar* 1, February 21, 1947, Tiberias

The reason we eat fish first in a meal is that fish are given free, without preparation. This is why they are eaten first, as they do not require preparation, as it is written, "We remember the fish, which we were wont to eat in Egypt for nothing." And *The Zohar* interprets "for nothing" as without *Mitzvot*, meaning without preparation.

And why don't fish require preparation? The thing is that we see that a fish is only considered *Rosh* (head); it has no hands or legs. A fish is discerned as "Josef wanted a fish and found a *Margalit* (gemstone) in its flesh."

*Margalit* means *Meragel* (spy), and a fish means that there is no negotiation there. This is the meaning of the absence of hands and legs. And "halved" means that through the rise of *Malchut* to *Bina*, each degree has been halved, and by this division, a place was made for the *Meragelim*. Thus, the whole negotiation was only over the *Meragelim*, as the whole Torah extends from here. And this is the meaning of the *Margalit* hanging on his neck, and that all who were sick would look at it and heal immediately.

However, there is no reward in the discernment of the fish alone, except that it is free, as it is written, "which we were wont to eat in Egypt for nothing." "An open eye, which never sleeps, needs no guarding," since the issue of the fish is considered *Hochma* (wisdom) and Shabbat, which precede the Torah.

And the Torah means negotiation. This is the meaning of "I could not find my hands and legs at the seminary," meaning that there was no negotiation. "For nothing" means without negotiation, and "Torah" is called "the next world," discerned as "satiated and delighted," and that the satiation does not quench the pleasure, as it is the pleasure of the soul. However, in the discernment of "the Shabbat that precedes the Torah," considered *Hochma*, it comes to a state of *Guf* (body), and the *Guf* is a boundary, where the satiation quenches the pleasure.

## 229. HAMAN POCKETS

I heard on Purim Night, after reading the *Megillah*, March 3, 1950

Concerning the eating of the *Haman Tashim*, meaning Haman's Pockets,[26] he said that since "man must be intoxicated on Purim until he cannot tell between the evil Haman and the blessed Mordecai," we eat Haman Pockets. This is so that we will remember that Haman did not give us more than pockets, vessels, and not the interior. This means that it is only possible to receive Haman's *Kelim* (vessels), and not the Lights, called "internality." This is so because the vessels of reception are in Haman's domain, and this is what we must take away from him.

However, it is impossible to extend Lights with the *Kelim* of Haman. This occurs specifically through the *Kelim* of Mordecai, which are vessels of bestowal. But the vessels of reception were restricted. And this is explained in the verse: "Now Haman said in his heart: 'Whom would the king delight to honor besides myself?'"

This is called "a real will to receive." This is why he said "let royal apparel be brought which the king uses to wear, and the horse that the king rides upon," etc.. But in truth, Haman's vessels, called "vessels of reception," do not receive anything because of the *Tzimtzum* (restriction). All he has is a desire and a deficiency, meaning he knows what to ask. This is why it is written, "Then the king said to Haman: 'Make haste, and take

26 Haman's Pockets are better known as "Haman's Ears," a traditional Purim pastry.

the apparel and the horse, as thou hast said, and do even so to Mordecai the Jew.'"

This is called "the Lights of Haman in the vessels of Mordecai," in the vessels of bestowal.

## 230. THE LORD IS HIGH AND THE LOW WILL SEE

I heard on Shabbat *Teruma*, March 5, 1949, Tel-Aviv

"The Lord is high and the low will see." How can there be equivalence with the Lord, when man is the receiver and the Lord is the Giver? The verse says to that: "The Lord is high and the low will see." If one revokes oneself, then no authority separates one from the Creator, and then he will "see," meaning he will be awarded *Mochin* (Lights) of *Hochma* (wisdom).

"And the haughty He knoweth from afar." But one who is proud, who has his own authority, he is remote, since he lacks the equivalence.

And lowliness does not imply lowering oneself before others; this is humbleness, and one feels wholeness in this work. Lowliness means that the world despises him. It is precisely when people despise him that it is considered lowliness, and then one does not feel any wholeness, since it is a law—what people think, affect a person. Hence, if people value him, he feels whole, and those whom people despise consider themselves low.

## 231. THE PURITY OF THE VESSELS OF RECEPTION

I heard on *Tevet*, January 1928, Givat Shaul (Jerusalem)

We should be cautious with anything the body enjoys. One should regret this, since through reception, one becomes removed from the Creator. This is because the Creator is the Giver, and if he will now be a receiver, he thus comes into oppositeness of form. In spirituality, disparity of form is remoteness, and then he does not have adhesion with the Creator.

This is the meaning of "and to cleave onto Him." Through the sorrow that one feels upon reception of pleasure, the sorrow revokes the pleasure. It is like a person who suffers form scabbiness in his head. He must scratch his head and it gives him pleasure. However, at the same time he knows that this will only worsen his scabbiness, and his plight will spread and he will not be able to heal. Thus, during the pleasure he has no real delight, even though he cannot stop receiving the pleasure of scratching.

He should also see that when he feels pleasure from some thing, he should extend sorrow over the pleasure, since thus he becomes remote from the Creator to such an extent as to feel that the pleasure is not worthwhile compared to the loss that this pleasure will subsequently bring him. And this is the work in the heart.

*Kedusha* (Sanctity): that which brings one closer to the work of God is called *Kedusha*.

*Tuma'a* (impurity): that which removes one from the work of God is called *Tuma'a*.

## 232. COMPLETING THE LABOR

I heard

"I labored and did not find, do not believe." We must understand the meaning "I found." What is there to find? Finding concerns finding grace in the eyes of the Creator. "I did not labor and found, do not believe."

We must ask; after all, he is not lying; this is not about a person concerning oneself as an individual. Rather, it is the same rule with the whole. And if one sees that he is favored by

Him, why "not believe"? The thing is that sometimes, a person is being favored through prayer. This is because so is the power of the prayer—it can act like labor. (We also see in corporeality that there are some who provide by exertion, and some who provide through prayer. And by asking for provision, one is allowed to provide for himself.)

But in spirituality, although he is awarded being favored, he must still pay the full price later on—the measure of the labor that everyone gives. If not, he will lose the *Kli*. This is why he said, "I did not labor and found, do not believe," since he will lose everything. Thus, one should subsequently pay one's full labor.

## 233. PARDON, FORGIVENESS, AND ATONEMENT

I heard

***Mechila*** **(pardon)**, as in from ruin to praise. This means that sins have become to him as merits through repentance from love. Thus, he turns the sins into a praise, to merits.

***Slicha*** **(forgiveness)** comes from *VeShalach Et Be'iro* ("and shall let his beast loose," exchanging the *Samech* with a *Shin*). This means that he sends the sins away from him and says that from now on he will do only merits. This is considered repentance from fear, when sins become as mistakes to him.

***Kapara*** **(atonement)** comes from *VeKipper Et HaMizbe'ach* ("and he shall make atonement for the altar"), from "wishes to atone his hands in this man." Hence, when one knows that he is dirty, he has not the audacity and impudence to enter the King's palace. Therefore, when one sees and remembers one's bad deeds, which are against the King's will, it is difficult for him to engage in Torah and *Mitzvot*; all the more so to ask of the King to cleave onto Him and unite with Him.

This is why he needs atonement, so he will not see his poor state, that he is in utter lowness, and so he will not remember his state, so he will have room to receive gladness by being able to engage in the Torah and the work. And then, when he has gladness, he will have room to ask for bonding with the King, since "Divinity dwells only in a place of joy." Hence, first we need repentance, and then, when we repent from fear, we are awarded forgiveness. And then repentance from love, we are awarded pardon.

We should believe that everything that happens in our world is guided, that there are no coincidences. We should also know that everything that is written as admonition, meaning the curses, in "if ye will not hearken," are terrible torments, and not as everyone thinks. Some say that they are blessings and not curses. They bring the Sayer of Kuznitz as evidence to their words. He would always make *Aliya la Torah* (ritual reading of the Torah during service) on *Parashat Tochachot* (a specific portion of the Torah called "Admonition Portion"). He says that these are real curses and troubles.

It is as we ourselves see that curses exist in reality, that there are feelings of dreadful, unbearable torments in this world. Yet, we should believe that we should attribute all these torments to Providence, that He does everything. Moses took these curses and attributed them to the Creator. This is the meaning of "and in all the great terror."

And when you believe in that, you also believe that "there is judgment and there is a judge." This is why the sayer would make *Aliya* on *Parashat Tochachot*, since only he could attribute the curses and the suffering to the Creator, since he believed that "there is judgment and there is a judge." And through all that, real blessings stem from these curses, since "God hath so made it, that men should fear before Him."

And this is the meaning of "the bandage is made out of the blow itself." That means that from the very place where the wicked fail, the righteous will walk. This is because when coming to a place where there is no support, the *Sitra Achra* has a hold in that place. Then the wicked fail in them. This wicked, who cannot go above reason, falls because he has no support. Then he remains between heaven and earth, since they are wicked, and can only do things within reason, by way of "evil eye, haughty of eyes."

But the righteous are considered "my heart is not haughty, nor mine eyes lofty," and they do walk in it. It follows that it turns into blessings. Thus, by attributing all the suffering to Providence and taking everything above reason, it creates within him the proper vessels to receive blessings.

## 234. WHO CEASES WORDS OF TORAH AND ENGAGES IN CONVERSATION

*Adar Aleph* 1940, on the way to Gaza

"Who ceases words of Torah and engages in conversation is fed coals of broom." This means that when one engages in Torah and does not stop, the Torah is considered for him a blazing flame that burns the evil inclination, and he can then continue with his work. However, if he stops in the midst of his study, even if he soon starts anew, the Torah for him is already like coals of broom. This means that it can no longer burn the evil inclination, and the taste of Torah is spoiled for him, and he must cease his work. Hence, when he returns to his study, he must take note that he will resolve to never again cease in the midst of his study. And through the decision for the future, the blazing flame of the Torah will reignite.

## 235. LOOKING IN THE BOOK AGAIN

After one sees some words of Torah in a book and memorizes them, since what enters the mind is already blemished. Hence, when looking in the book again, one can elicit the Light so as to receive illumination from what he is seeing now. And this is already considered new and unblemished.

## 236. MINE ADVERSARIES TAUNT ME ALL THE DAY

*Tishrei* 6, September 17, 1942

"Because zeal for Thy house hath eaten me up; mine adversaries taunt me... all the day" (Psalms 69). The form of cursing and swearing appears in several manners:

1. During the work, when he performs an act of *Mitzva*, the body tells him: "What will you get out of it, what benefit?" Hence, even when he prevails and does it coercively, this *Mitzva* is still considered a burden and a load. This brings up a question: If he really is keeping the King's commandment and serving the King, he should have been glad, as it is natural for one who is serving the King to be in gladness. But here it is to the contrary. It follows that here he feels a state of cursing and swearing, and this coercion proves that he does not believe that he is serving the King, and there is no greater cursing than that.
2. Or, he sees that he is not adhered to the Creator the whole day, as he does not feel a real thing, and it is impossible to be adhered to an empty thing. Hence, he shifts his mind from the Creator (whereas a real thing, where there is pleasure, is hard to forget. And if he wishes to shift his mind, he must make great efforts

to take it out of his mind). This is, "mine adversaries taunt me... all the day."

This thing applies in every person, but the difference is in the sensation. Yet, even if one does not feel it, it is because one has not the attention to notice the state as it truly is. It is similar to one who has a hole in his pocket, the money falls out, and he loses all the money. It makes no difference whether or not he knows that he has a hole. The only difference is that if he knows he has a hole, he can then fix it. But this makes no difference in the actual losing of the money. Hence, when he feels how the body, called "mine adversaries," curses the Creator, he says, "Because zeal for Thy house hath eaten me up," and he wishes to correct it.

## 237. FOR MAN SHALL NOT SEE ME AND LIVE

"For man shall not see Me and live" (Exodus 33:20). This means that if one sees the revelation of Godliness in a greater extent than he is ready to see, he may come into reception, regarded as oppositeness from the Life of Lives, and then he comes to death. Hence, one must advance on the path of faith.

## 238. HAPPY IS THE MAN WHO DOES NOT FORGET THEE AND THE SON OF MAN WHO EXERTS IN THEE

*Elul* 10

"Happy is the man who does not forget Thee, and the son of man who exerts in Thee" (a supplement for the *Rosh Hashanah* prayer). When one advances by way of whiteness, he should always remember that everything he has been granted is only because he assumed the discernment of blackness. And he should exert precisely in the "Thee," by way of, "and all believe that He is a God of faith," although he currently does not see any place where he has to work in faith, since everything is revealed before him. Nevertheless, he should believe above reason that there is more room to believe by way of faith.

And this is the meaning of "And Israel saw the great work... and they believed in the Lord." Thus, even though they had been awarded the discernment of "saw," which is seeing, they still had the strength to believe by way of faith.

And this requires great exertion; otherwise, one loses one's degree, like Libni and Shimei. This means that if it is not so, it means that one can listen to Torah and *Mitzvot* precisely at a time of whiteness; it is like a condition. However, one should listen unconditionally. Hence, at a time of whiteness, one should be careful of blemishing the blackness.

## 239. THE DIFFERENCE BETWEEN *MOCHIN* OF *SHAVUOT* AND THAT OF SHABBAT *MINCHAH*

There is a difference between *Shavuot*—considered the ascent of ZA to *Arich Anpin*, to *Behinat Dikna*—and Shabbat, during *Mincha*—which is an ascent to *Arich Anpin*, too. *Shavuot* is considered *Mochin de Hochma* from *YESHSUT*, meaning from *Bina* that returns to being *Hochma*. However, (Shabbat) is considered *Gar de Bina*, considered the actual *Hochma*. It is regarded as not having left the *Rosh*, and as being dressed in *Mocha Stimaa*, which is *Gar de Hochma* and not *Vak*.

And because she is *Gar*, she cannot... unless by way of from below upward, without any downward expansion. This is why she is regarded as female Light, since she has no expansion below. And this is why Shabbat is considered *Nukva*.

A good day, however, is considered *Zat de Bina*, regarded as *Vak*—it has expansion below. Hence, even after all the ascents in reality, the ladder of degrees still does not change.

And he said that the reason that the people of the world respect a good day more than Shabbat, although Shabbat is a higher degree, is that a good day is *Zat de Bina*, which is revealed below, unlike Shabbat, considered *Gar de Bina*, where there is no divulgence below. And of course the degree of Shabbat is much higher than a good day.

## 240. INQUIRE YOUR INQUIRERS WHEN THEY INQUIRE YOUR FACE

*Slichot* 1, from the honorable,
my father, my master, my teacher

"Inquire your inquirers when they inquire Your face, answer them from the heavens of Thy abode, and to do not shut Your ear to their pleading cries" (*Slichot* for the first day). It is... that the purpose of the creation of the world was to do good to His creations. But for the correction to be completed, there must be the sweetening of the quality of judgment in mercy.

Judgment is discerned as *Gadlut* (greatness). But to avoid coming into disparity of form by that, there must be a discernment that is a kind of compromise: the judgment says she would have received more, but she was still in danger of coming into disparity of form. However, when mingled with the quality of mercy, she does not receive the *Gadlut* of the Light, and can then come into equivalence of form. And the correction is done by turning the vessels of reception into reception in order to bestow.

Hence, when one comes to seek the Creator, he is still attached to reception, and one who has reception is considered deficient, and cursed, and a cursed does not adhere to the blessed. However, one who receives in order to bestow is called "blessed," since he does not lack anything or needs anything for himself. It follows that the only difficulty is for one to be in a state of blessed, as only by the virtue of Torah and *Mitzvot* can the vessels of reception be turned into vessels of bestowal. This is why we pray, "Inquire your inquirers."

There are two kinds of inquirers: some inquire only for Your face, who want only to bestow. Hence, what they inquire—to receive some salvation—is only for Your face. He said about that: "when they inquire your face." Those who inquire for Your face, "answer them from the heavens of Thy abode," meaning that the heavens of Thy abode will appear, since they will no longer blemish Above, as they are cleansed from reception. "Their pleading cries," that all their prayers and pleas are still for themselves, that they want to be close to the Creator, meaning that they are still not cleansed from reception.

This is so because there are two discernments in the work of God: there are those who want the Creator to be revealed in the world, that everyone will know that there is Godliness in the world. In that state, they are not in the middle, but merely want. In that state, it cannot be said that he has a discernment of reception, since he is not praying to be close to the Creator, only that the glory of Heaven will be revealed in the world.

And there are those who pray to be close to the Creator, and then he is in the middle. Then you can call it reception for oneself, since he wants to receive abundance in order to come closer to the Creator. This is called "pleas" and it is also called "cries." And those who are still in a state of pleas, that is, to be closer, they can do the crying, and to them "do not shut Your ear."

This is because only one who is deficient cries. But for another, it is not a cry, only a demand, as in "give my regards."[27] Hence, with the face, there is only a demand.

"From the heavens of Thy abode" means *Eynaim* (eyes), the Light of Wisdom, that they will receive the essence of the bounty, since their *Kelim* (vessels) are already in the form of reception in order to bestow. But those who are still in a state of pleading, "do not shut Your ear." Ear means *Bina*; they need to extend strength so they will have bestowal... over the Light of mercy.

## 241. CALL UPON HIM WHILE HE IS NEAR

"Call ye upon Him while He is near" (Isaiah 55:6). We must understand what "while He is near" means, since "the whole earth is full of His glory"! Thus, He is always near, so what does "while He is near" mean? It would seem that there is a time when He is not near.

The thing is that states are always evaluated with respect to the attaining individual. If one does not feel His nearness, then nothing will come out of it, as everything is measured according to one's sensation. One person may feel the world as filled with abundance, and the other will not feel the goodness of the world, so he cannot say that there is a good world. Instead, he states as he feels–that the world is filled with suffering.

And the prophet warns about that: "Call ye upon Him while He is near." He comes and says, "Know that the fact that you are calling upon the Creator means that He is near." It means that now you have an opportunity; if you pay attention, you will feel that the Creator is near you, and this is the sign of the Creator's nearness.

27 The actual phrasing in Hebrew is "demand my regards to..."

And the evidence of it is that we must know that man is not naturally qualified for adhesion with the Creator, since it is against man's nature. This is so because by creation, he has only the desire to receive; while adhesion is only to bestow. However, as the Creator calls upon man, it creates a second nature within him: he wants to revoke his own nature and cleave unto Him.

Hence, one should know that his speaking words of Torah and prayer, is only from the Creator. He should never think of saying that it is "my power and the might of my hand," since it is the complete opposite of his might. This is similar to one who is lost in a dense forest, without seeing an outlet that will lead him to an inhabited place, so he remains despaired and never thinks of returning to one's home. But when he sees a person from afar or hears a human voice, the desire and the craving to return to his origin will immediately awaken in him, and he will begin to shout and ask of someone to come and save him.

Similarly, one who has lost the good way and entered a bad place, and has already accustomed himself to live among beasts, from the perspective of the will to receive, it would never occur to him that he should return to a place of reason and Sanctity. Yet, when he hears the voice calling him, he awakens to repent.

But this is the voice of God, not his own voice. But if he has not yet completed his actions on the path of correction, he cannot feel and believe that this is the Creator's voice, and he thinks that it is his power and the might of his hand. This is what the prophet warns of, that one should overcome one's view and thought, and believe wholeheartedly that it is the voice of God.

Hence, when the Creator wishes to bring him out of the dense forest, He shows him a remote Light, and the person gathers the remains of his strength to walk on the path that the Light shows him, in order to attain it.

But if one does not ascribe the Light to the Creator, and does not say that the Creator is calling him, then the Light is lost from him, and he remains standing in the forest. Thus, he could have now shown his whole heart to the Creator, to come and save him from the evil place, from the will to receive, and bring him to a place of reason, called a place of the sons of Adam (people), as in *Adameh la Elyon* (I will be like the Most High), meaning the will to bestow, in adhesion. Instead, he does not take advantage of this opportunity and remains as before, again.

## 242. WHAT IS THE MATTER OF DELIGHTING THE POOR ON A GOOD DAY, IN THE WORK

*Sukkot* inter 3

In *The Zohar*: "The Creator's share is to delight the poor," etc.. In the *Sulam* (commentary), he interprets: since the Creator saw that the *Lo Lishma* (not for Her Name) does not bring him to *Lishma* (for Her Name), He rose up to destroy the world, meaning his abundance is stopped (*The Book of Zohar*, "Introduction of The Book of Zohar," item 6-7).

We could say that when one receives an illumination from Above, even while one has not been purified, if one takes this illumination in order to raise oneself from one's lowliness and approach bestowal, it is considered that the *Lo Lishma* brings him *Lishma*. This means that he is advancing on the path of Torah.

And this is called "One who is happy on holidays." A holiday is a good day. And certainly, there is no greater good day than when some illumination shines for a person from Above, which brings one closer to the Creator.

## 243. EXAMINING THE SHADE ON THE NIGHT OF *HOSHANA RABBAH*

*Adar Aleph*, 24, March 1, 1943

Concerning the shade. On the night of *Hoshana Rabbah* (the seventh day of the Feast of Tabernacles), it is a custom that each one examines himself to see if he has a shadow, and then he is certain that he will have abundance (*Shaar HaKavanot (Gate of Intentions)*, *Sukkot* Commentaries, 6-7). The shade implies clothing, the clothing in which the Light dresses.

There is no Light without clothing, since there is no Light without a *Kli* (vessel). And according to the measure of the clothes, the Lights increase and multiply. And when one loses the clothing, the Light that belongs to that clothing is proportionally absent from him.

This is the meaning of truth and faith. Truth is called "Light," and faith is called "*Kli*." This is the meaning of "the Creator and Divinity," and the meaning of "Let us make man in our image," and "Surely man walketh as a mere image." Man's walk depends on the *Tzelem* (image), meaning on faith. And this is why on *Hoshana Rabbah* one should see if one's faith is complete.

And why do we call the worlds Above *Tzelem*? After all, Above, there is no weight of faith? However, what appears to us as dryness is a great Light Above, except we call that name "Above" because it appears to us as a shade, and we name Above after the lower one.

*Bina* is called "faith," which is the Light of the *Awzen* (ear), meaning hearing. *Hochma* (wisdom) is called seeing, which is a Light that comes into the vessels of reception, considered eyes.

*The End*

# Appendix One
# Further Reading

To help you determine which book you would like to read next, we have divided the books into five categories—Beginners, Intermediate, Advanced, All Around, and Textbooks. The first three categories are divided by the level of prior knowledge readers are required to have. The Beginners Category requires no prior knowledge. The Intermediate Category requires reading one or two beginners' books first; and the Advanced level requires one or two books of each of the previous categories. The fourth category, All Around, includes books you can always enjoy, whether you are a complete novice or well versed in Kabbalah.

The fifth category—textbooks—includes translations of authentic source materials from earlier Kabbalists, such as the Ari, Rav Yehuda Ashlag (Baal HaSulam) and his son and successor, Rav Baruch Ashlag (the Rabash).

Additional translated material that has not yet been published can be found at *www.kabbalah.info*. All materials on this site, including e-versions of published books, can be downloaded free of charge.

## BEGINNERS

### *Kabbalah for Beginners*

*Kabbalah for Beginners* is a book for all those seeking answers to life's essential questions. We all want to know why we are here, why there is pain, and how we can make life more enjoyable. The four parts of this book provide us with reliable answers to these questions, as well as clear explanations of the gist of Kabbalah and its practical implementations.

Part One discusses the discovery of the wisdom of Kabbalah, and how it was developed, and finally concealed until our time. Part Two introduces the gist of the wisdom of Kabbalah, using ten easy drawings to help us understand the structure of the spiritual worlds, and how they relate to our world. Part Three reveals Kabbalistic concepts that are largely unknown to the public, and Part Four elaborates on practical means you and I can take, to make our lives better and more enjoyable for us and for our children.

### *Kabbalah Revealed*

This is a clearly written, reader-friendly guide to making sense of the surrounding world. Each of its six chapters focuses on a different aspect of the wisdom of Kabbalah, illuminating the teachings and explaining them using various examples from our day-to-day lives.

The first three chapters in *Kabbalah Revealed* explain why the world is in a state of crisis, how our growing desires promote progress as well as alienation, and why the biggest deterrent to achieving positive change is rooted in our own spirits. Chapters Four through Six offer a prescription for positive change. In these chapters, we learn how we can use our spirits to build a personally peaceful life in harmony with all of Creation.

### *Wondrous Wisdom*

This book offers an initial course on Kabbalah. Like all the books presented here, *Wondrous Wisdom* is based solely on authentic teachings passed down from Kabbalist teacher to student over thousands of years. At the heart of the book is a sequence of lessons revealing the nature of Kabbalah's wisdom and explaining how to attain it. For every person questioning "Who am I really?" and "Why am I on this planet?" this book is a must.

### *Awakening to Kabbalah*

A distinctive, personal, and awe-filled introduction to an ancient wisdom tradition. In this book, Rav Laitman offers a deeper understanding of the fundamental teachings of Kabbalah, and how you can use its wisdom to clarify your relationship with others and the world around you.

Using language both scientific and poetic, he probes the most profound questions of spirituality and existence. This provocative, unique guide will inspire and invigorate you to see beyond the world as it is and the limitations of your everyday life, become closer to the Creator, and reach new depths of the soul.

### *Kabbalah, Science, and the Meaning of Life*

Science explains the mechanisms that sustain life; Kabbalah explains why life exists. In *Kabbalah, Science, and the Meaning of Life*, Rav Laitman combines science and spirituality in a captivating dialogue that reveals life's meaning.

For thousands of years Kabbalists have been writing that the world is a single entity divided into separate beings. Today the cutting-edge science of quantum physics states a very similar idea: that at the most fundamental level of matter, we are all literally one.

Science proves that reality is affected by the observer who examines it; and so does Kabbalah. But Kabbalah makes an even bolder statement: even the Creator, the Maker of reality, is within the observer. In other words, God is inside of us; He doesn't exist anywhere else. When we pass away, so does He.

These earthshaking concepts and more are eloquently introduced so that even readers new to Kabbalah or science will easily understand them. Therefore, if you're just a little curious about why you are here, what life means, and what you can do to enjoy it more, this book is for you.

### *From Chaos to Harmony*

Many researchers and scientists agree that the ego is the reason behind the perilous state our world is in today. Laitman's groundbreaking book not only demonstrates that ego has been the basis for all suffering throughout human history, but also shows how we can turn our plight to pleasure.

The book contains a clear analysis of the human soul and its problems, and provides a "roadmap" of what we need to do to once again be happy. *From Chaos to Harmony* explains how we can rise to a new level of existence on personal, social, national, and international levels.

## INTERMEDIATE

### *The Kabbalah Experience*

The depth of the wisdom revealed in the questions and answers within this book will inspire readers to reflect and contemplate. This is not a book to race through, but rather one that should be read thoughtfully and carefully. With this approach, readers will begin to experience a growing sense of enlightenment while simply absorbing the answers to the questions every Kabbalah student asks along the way.

*The Kabbalah Experience* is a guide from the past to the future, revealing situations that all students of Kabbalah will experience at some point along their journeys. For those who cherish every moment in life, this book offers unparalleled insights into the timeless wisdom of Kabbalah.

### *The Path of Kabbalah*

This unique book combines beginners' material with more advanced concepts and teachings. If you have read a book or two of Laitman's, you will find this book very easy to relate to.

While touching upon basic concepts such as perception of reality and Freedom of Choice, *The Path of Kabbalah* goes deeper and expands beyond the scope of beginners' books. The structure of the worlds, for example, is explained in greater detail here than in the "pure" beginners' books. Also described is the spiritual root of mundane matters such as the Hebrew calendar and the holidays.

## ADVANCED

### *The Science of Kabbalah*

Kabbalist and scientist Rav Michael Laitman, PhD, designed this book to introduce readers to the special language and terms of the authentic wisdom of Kabbalah. Here, Rav Laitman reveals authentic Kabbalah in a manner both rational and mature. Readers are gradually led to understand the logical design of the Universe and the life that exists in it.

The Science of Kabbalah, a revolutionary work unmatched in its clarity, depth, and appeal to the intellect, will enable readers to approach the more technical works of Baal HaSulam (Rabbi Yehuda Ashlag), such as *The Study of the Ten Sefirot and The Book of Zohar.* Readers of this book will enjoy the satisfying answers to the riddles of life that only authentic Kabbalah provides. Travel through the pages and prepare for an astonishing journey into the Upper Worlds.

### *Introduction to the Book of Zohar*

This volume, along with *The Science of Kabbalah*, is a required preparation for those who wish to understand the hidden message of *The Book of Zohar*. Among the many helpful topics dealt with in this text is an introduction to the "language of roots and branches," without which the stories in *The Zohar* are mere fable and legend. *Introduction to the Book of Zohar* will provide readers with the necessary tools to understand authentic Kabbalah as it was originally meant to be, as a means to attain the Upper Worlds.

### *The Zohar: annotations to the Ashlag commentary*

*The Book of Zohar* (*The Book of Radiance*) is an ageless source of wisdom and the basis for all Kabbalistic literature. Since its appearance nearly 2,000 years ago, it has been the primary, and often only, source used by Kabbalists.

For centuries, Kabbalah was hidden from the public, which was deemed not yet ready to receive it. However, our generation has been designated by Kabbalists as the first generation that is ready to grasp the concepts in *The Zohar*. Now, we can put these principles into practice in our lives.

Written in a unique and metaphorical language, *The Book of Zohar* enriches our understanding of reality and widens our worldview. Although the text deals with one subject only–how to relate to the Creator–it approaches it from different angles. This allows each of us to find the particular phrase or word that will carry us into the depths of this profound and timeless wisdom.

## ALL AROUND

### *Attaining the Worlds Beyond*

From the introduction to Attaining the Worlds Beyond: "...Not feeling well on the Jewish New Year in September 1991, my teacher called me to his bedside and handed me his notebook, saying, "Take it and learn from it." The following morning, my teacher perished in my arms, leaving me and many of his other disciples without guidance in this world.

He used to say, "I want to teach you to turn to the Creator, rather than to me, because He is the only strength, the only Source of all that exists, the only One who can really help you, and He awaits your prayers for help. When you seek help in your search for freedom from the bondage of this world, help in elevating yourself above this world, help in finding the self, and help in determining your purpose in life, you must turn to the Creator, who sends you all those aspirations in order to compel you to turn to Him."

*Attaining the Worlds Beyond* holds within it the content of that notebook, as well as other inspiring texts. This book reaches out to all those seekers who want to find a logical, reliable way to understand the world's phenomena. This fascinating introduction to the wisdom of Kabbalah will enlighten the mind, invigorate the heart, and move readers to the depths of their souls.

### *Basic Concepts in Kabbalah*

This is a book to help readers cultivate an approach to the concepts of Kabbalah, to spiritual objects, and to spiritual terms. By reading and re-reading in this book, one develops internal observations, senses, and approaches that did not previously exist within. These newly acquired observations are like sensors that "feel" the space around us that is hidden from our ordinary senses.

Hence, *Basic Concepts in Kabbalah* is intended to foster the contemplation of spiritual terms. Once we are integrated with these terms, we can begin to see, with our inner vision, the unveiling of the spiritual structure that surrounds us, almost as if a mist has been lifted.

Again, this book is not aimed at the study of facts. Instead, it is a book for those who wish to awaken the deepest and subtlest sensations they can possess.

### *Together Forever*

On the surface, *Together Forever* is a children's story. But like all good children's stories, it transcends boundaries of age, culture, and upbringing.

In *Together Forever*, the author tells us that if we are patient and endure the trials we encounter along our life's path, we will become stronger, braver, and wiser. Instead of growing weaker, we will learn to create our own magic and our own wonders as only a magician can.

In this warm, tender tale, Michael Laitman shares with children and parents alike some of the gems and charms of the spiritual world. The wisdom of Kabbalah is filled with spellbinding stories. The Magician is yet another gift from this ageless source of wisdom, whose lessons make our lives richer, easier, and far more fulfilling.

## TEXTBOOKS

### *Shamati*

Rav Michael Laitman's words on the book: Among all the texts and notes that were used by my teacher, Rabbi Baruch Shalom Halevi Ashlag (the Rabash), there was one special notebook he always carried. This notebook contained the transcripts of his conversations with his father, Rabbi Yehuda Leib Halevi Ashlag (Baal HaSulam), author of the *Sulam* (Ladder) commentary on *The Book of Zohar*, *The Study of the Ten Sefirot* (a commentary on the texts of the Kabbalist, Ari), and of many other works on Kabbalah.

Not feeling well on the Jewish New Year in September 1991, the Rabash summoned me to his bedside and handed me a notebook, whose cover contained only one word, *Shamati* (I Heard). As he handed the notebook, he said, "Take it and learn from it." The following morning, my teacher perished in my arms, leaving me and many of his other disciples without guidance in this world.

Committed to Rabash's legacy to disseminate the wisdom of Kabbalah, I published the notebook just as it was written, thus retaining the text's transforming powers. Among all the books of Kabbalah, Shamati is a unique and compelling creation.

## *Kabbalah for the Student*

*Kabbalah for the Student* offers authentic texts by Rav Yehuda Ashlag, author of the *Sulam* (Ladder) commentary on *The Book of Zohar*, his son and successor, Rav Baruch Ashlag, as well as other great Kabbalists. It also offers illustrations that accurately depict the evolution of the Upper Worlds as Kabbalists experience them. The book also contains several explanatory essays that help us understand the texts within.

In *Kabbalah for the Student*, Rav Michael Laitman, PhD, Rav Baruch Ashlag's personal assistant and prime student, compiled all the texts a Kabbalah student would need in order to attain the spiritual worlds. In his daily lessons, Rav Laitman bases his teaching on these inspiring texts, thus helping novices and veterans alike to better understand the spiritual path we undertake on our fascinating journey to the Higher Realms.

# Appendix Two
# About Bnei Baruch

Bnei Baruch is a group of Kabbalists in Israel, sharing the wisdom of Kabbalah with the entire world. Study materials in over 20 languages are based on authentic Kabbalah texts that were passed down from generation to generation.

## HISTORY AND ORIGIN

In 1991, following the passing of his teacher, Rabbi Baruch Shalom HaLevi Ashlag (The Rabash), Rav Michael Laitman, Professor of Ontology and the Theory of Knowledge, PhD in Philosophy and Kabbalah, and MSc in Medical Bio-Cybernetics, established a Kabbalah study group called "Bnei Baruch." He called it Bnei Baruch ("Sons of Baruch") to commemorate the memory of his mentor, whose side he never left in the final twelve years of his life, from 1979 to 1991. Rav Laitman had been Ashlag's prime student and personal assistant, and is recognized as the successor to Rabash's teaching method.

The Rabash was the firstborn son and successor of Rabbi Yehuda Leib HaLevi Ashlag, the greatest Kabbalist of the 20th century. Rabbi Ashlag authored the most authoritative and comprehensive commentary on *The Book of Zohar*, titled *The Sulam Commentary (The Ladder Commentary)*. He was the first to reveal the complete method for spiritual ascent, and thus was known as Baal HaSulam ("Owner of the Ladder").

Today, Bnei Baruch bases its entire study method on the path paved by these two great spiritual leaders.

## THE STUDY METHOD

The unique study method developed by Baal HaSulam and his son, the Rabash, is taught and applied on a daily basis by Bnei Baruch. This method relies on authentic Kabbalah sources such as *The Book of Zohar,* by Rabbi Shimon Bar-Yochai, *The Tree of Life,* by the Holy Ari, and *The Study of the Ten Sefirot,* by Baal HaSulam.

While the study relies on authentic Kabbalah sources, it is carried out in simple language and uses a scientific, contemporary approach. Developing this approach has made Bnei Baruch an internationally respected organization, both in Israel and in the world at large.

The unique combination of an academic study method and personal experiences broadens the students' perspective and awards them a new perception of the reality they live in. Those on the spiritual path are thus given the necessary tools to research themselves and their surrounding reality.

## THE MESSAGE

Bnei Baruch is a diverse movement of many thousands of students worldwide. Students can choose their own paths and the personal intensity of their studies, according to their unique conditions and abilities. The essence of the message disseminated by Bnei Baruch is universal: "unity of the people, unity of nations and love of man."

For millennia, Kabbalists have been teaching that love of man should be the foundation of all human relations. This love prevailed in the days of Abraham, Moses, and the group of Kabbalists that they established. If we make room for these seasoned, yet contemporary values, we will discover that we possess the power to put differences aside and unite.

The wisdom of Kabbalah, hidden for millennia, has been waiting for the time when we would be sufficiently developed and ready to implement its message. Now, it is emerging as a solution that can unite diverse factions everywhere, better enabling us, as individuals and as a society, to meet today's challenges.

## ACTIVITIES

Bnei Baruch was established on the premise that "only by expansion of the wisdom of Kabbalah to the public can we be awarded complete redemption" (Baal HaSulam).

Therefore, Bnei Baruch offers a variety of ways for people to explore and discover the purpose of their lives, providing careful guidance for the beginners and the advanced student alike.

### *Kabbalah Today*

*Kabbalah Today* is a free monthly paper produced and disseminated by Bnei Baruch. It is apolitical, non-commercial, and written in a clear, contemporary style. Its purpose is to expose the vast body of knowledge hidden in the wisdom of Kabbalah at no cost and in a clear, engaging format and style for readers everywhere.

*Kabbalah Today* is distributed for free in every major U.S. city, as well as in Toronto, Canada, London, England, and Sydney, Australia. It is printed in English, Hebrew, and Russian, and is also available on the Internet, at *www.kabtoday.com*.

Additionally, a hard copy of the paper is sent to subscribers at delivery cost only.

### *Internet Website*

Bnei Baruch's homepage, *www.kabbalah.info*, presents the authentic wisdom of Kabbalah using essays, books, and original texts. It is the largest Kabbalah website on the net, and contains a unique, extensive library for readers to thoroughly explore the wisdom of Kabbalah. Additionally, there is a media archive, *www.kabbalahmedia.info*, containing more than 5,000 media items, downloadable books, and a vast reservoir of texts, video and audio files in many languages. All of this material is available for free download.

### Kabbalah Television

Bnei Baruch established a production company, ARI Films (*www.arifilms.tv*) specializing in the production of educational TV programs throughout the world, and in many languages.

In Israel, Bnei Baruch broadcasts are aired live through cable and satellite on Channel 98 Sunday through Friday. All broadcasts on these channels are free of charge. The programs are adapted specifically for beginners, and do not require prior knowledge of the material. This convenient learning process is complemented by programs featuring Rav Laitman's meetings with publicly known figures in Israel and throughout the world.

Additionally, ARI Films produces educational series and documentaries on DVDs, as well as other visual teaching aids.

### Kabbalah Books

Rav Laitman writes his books in a clear, contemporary style based on the key concepts of Baal HaSulam. These books serve as a vital link between today's readers and the original texts. All of Rav Laitman's books are available for sale, as well as for free download. Rav Laitman has thus far written thirty books, translated into ten languages.

### Kabbalah Lessons

As Kabbalists have been doing for centuries, Rav Laitman gives a daily lesson at the Bnei Baruch center in Israel between 3:15-6:00 a.m. Israel time. The lessons are simultaneously translated into six languages: English, Russian, Spanish, German, Italian, and Turkish. In the near future, broadcasts will also be translated into French, Greek, Polish, and Portuguese. As with everything else, the live broadcast is provided gratis to thousands of students worldwide.

### *Funding*

Bnei Baruch is a non-profit organization for teaching and sharing the wisdom of Kabbalah. To maintain its independence and purity of intentions, Bnei Baruch is not supported, funded, or otherwise tied to any government or political organization.

Since the bulk of its activity is provided free of charge, the prime source of funding for the group's activities is donations, tithing–contributed by students on a voluntary basis–and Rav Laitman's books, which are sold at cost.

# HOW TO CONTACT BNEI BARUCH

1057 Steeles Avenue West, Suite 532
Toronto, ON, M2R 3X1
Canada

Bnei Baruch USA,
2009 85th street, #51,
Brooklyn, NY 11214,
USA

E-mail: info@kabbalah.info
Web site: www.kabbalah.info

Toll free in USA and Canada:
1-866-LAITMAN
Fax: 1-905 886 9697